Post-apartheid South Africa

Post-apartheid South Africa

Economic and Social Inclusion

Vusi Gumede

Cambria African Studies Series
General Editor: Toyin Falola
Associate Editor: Moses Ochonu

CAMBRIA PRESS
Amherst, New York

Library of Congress Cataloging-in-Publication Data

Names: Gumede, Vusi, author.

Title: Post-apartheid South Africa : economic and social inclusion / Vusi Gumede.

Other titles: Cambria African studies series.

Description: Amherst, New York : Cambria Press, 2016. |
Series: Cambria African studies series

Identifiers: LCCN 2016021833 |

ISBN 9781604979299 (alk. paper)

Subjects: LCSH: South Africa--Politics and government--1994- |
South Africa--Economic conditions--1991- |
South Africa--Social conditions--1994-

Classification: LCC JQ1931 .G86 2016 |
DDC 320.968--dc23
LC record available at https://lccn.loc.gov/2016021833

Table of Contents

List of Tables

Acknowledgements

I thank Dr Phumzile Mlambo-Ngcuka for writing the foreword to this book. Thanks also to Mr Joel Netshitenzhe and Prof Thandika Mkandawire for doing blurbs for the book. As I was finalising this manuscript three colleagues provided invaluable assistance: Dr Samuel Oloruntoba, Dikeledi Mokoena, and Tshego Sehlodimela.

I must acknowledge my former students at the University of Johannesburg and Prof Adam Habib who brought me there. I acknowledge colleagues at the erstwhile Graduate School of Public and Development Management (now called the School of Government) at the University of the Witwatersrand. Many of the students I taught during 2009–2014 have shaped this manuscript through the heated debates in and outside class, as well as those who attended sessions I facilitated for the Public Administration Leadership and Management Academy (renamed the National School of Government) and our own students and colleagues at the Thabo Mbeki African Leadership Institute at the University of South Africa.

I have to thank the anonymous reviewers. Similarly, I have to thank the publisher, particularly the colleagues directly responsible for publishing this manuscript. It has been a pleasure working with the editor of Cambria

Press, David Armstrong. I have no words to express my gratitude to Prof Toyin Falola who commissioned this manuscript.

Thanks also to many people who play different roles that have enabled me to contribute to knowledge production.

Acronyms

AIDS: Acquired Immune Deficiency Syndrome
ANAs: Annual National Assessments
ANC: African National Congress
ANCYL: African National Congress Youth League
AsgiSA: Accelerated and Shared Growth Initiative of South Africa
AU: African Union
BEE: Black Economic Empowerment
BBBEE: Broad-Based Black Economic Empowerment
BUSA: Business Unity South Africa
CDE: Centre for Development Enterprise
CES: Centre d' Economie de la Sorbonne
CHE: Council on Higher Education
CLARA: Communal Land Rights Act
Codesa: Convention for Democracy in South Africa
Cosatu: Congress of South African Trade Unions
DBE: The Department of Basic Education
DED: Department of Economic Development
DoE: Department of Education
DoHE&T: Department of Higher Education and Training
DFI: Development Finance Institution

DPE:	Department of Public Enterprise
DPME:	Department of Performance Monitoring and Evaluation
DTI:	Department of Trade and Industry
DMS:	Development Merchant System
EFF:	Economic Freedom Fighters
EIP:	Enterprise Investment Programme
ESAP:	Economic Structural Adjustment Programme
ETQAs:	Education and Training Quality Assurance Authorities
FAO:	Food and Agricultural Organisation
FDI:	Foreign Direct Investment
FET:	Further Education and Training
FOSAD:	Forum of South African Directors-General
EPWP:	Expanded Public Works Programme
GAA:	Group Areas Act
GBE:	Government Business Enterprise
GDP:	Growth Domestic Product
GEAR:	Growth, Employment and Redistribution Framework
GHS:	General Household Survey
GNU:	Government of National Unity
HSRC:	Human Sciences Research Council
HIV:	Human Immunodeficiency Virus
HDI:	Human Development Index
HPI:	Human Poverty Index
HPI-1:	Human Poverty Index (for developing countries)
HPI-2:	Human Poverty Index (for developed countries)
IDC:	Industrial Development Corporation
IDP:	Integrated Development Plan
IDZ:	Industrial Development Zone
IDTT:	Inter-Developmental Task Team
IFI:	International Financial Institutions
IFP:	Inkatha Freedom Party
IJR:	Institute of Justice and Reconciliation
IMF:	International Monetary Fund
IPAP:	Industrial Policy Action Plan

IPR:	Intellectual Property Rights
IRP:	Integrated Resource Plan
ITAC:	International Trade Administration Commission
ITED:	International Trade and Economic Development
JIPSA:	Joint Initiative for Priority Skills
LRP:	Land Reform Programme
LRRP:	Zimbabwean Land Reform and Resettlement Programme
MAFISA:	Micro Agricultural Finance Institute of South Africa
MDGs:	Millennium Development Goals
M&E:	Monitoring and Evaluation
MEC:	Mineral-Energy-Complex
MERG:	Macro-Economic Research Group
MPC:	Monetary Policy Committee
MTEF:	Medium Term Expenditure Framework
MTSF:	Medium Term Strategic Framework
NA:	National Assembly
NAMAC:	National Small Business Advisory Council
NAP:	National Agricultural Policy
NCOP:	National Council of Provinces
NDP:	National Development Plan
NDR:	National Democratic Revolution
NDS:	National Democratic Society
Nedlac:	National Economic Development and Labour Council
NEET:	Not in Education, Employment or Training
NEF:	National Economic Empowerment Fund
NIEP:	National Institute of Economic Policy
NIPF:	National Industry Policy Framework
Nepad:	New Partnership for Africa's Development
NGM:	National Gender Machinery
NGOs:	Non-Governmental Organisations
NGP:	New Growth Path
NHI:	National Health Insurance
NIPP:	National Industrial Participation Programme
NEDP:	National Export Development Programme

NLA:	Natives Land Act
NLM:	National Liberation Movement
NP:	National Party
NPC:	National Planning Commission
NPM:	New Public Management
NQF:	National Qualifications Framework
NSF:	National Skills Fund
NSDS:	National Skills Development Strategy
NSDP:	National Spatial Development Perspective
NRCS:	National Regulatory for Compulsory Specifications
NYDA:	National Youth Development Agency
OBE:	Outcomes-Based Education
ODA:	Overseas Development Assistance
OECD:	Organisation for Economic Cooperation and Development
PAC:	Pan African Congress
PCAS:	Policy Coordination and Advisory Services
PF:	Peoples Front
PICC:	Presidential Infrastructure Coordinating Commission
PFMA:	Public Finance Management Act
PPPFA:	Preferential Procurement Policy Framework
PRC:	Presidential Review Committee
PSRs:	Poverty Strategy Papers
R2G:	Ready to Govern
RDLR:	Department of Rural Development and Land Reform
RDP:	Reconstruction and Development Programme
RNCS:	Revised National Curriculum Statement
SABC:	South African Broadcasting Corporation
SABS:	South African Bureau of Standards
SADC:	Southern African Development Community
SANDF:	Defence ForceSouth African National
SACP:	South African Communist Party
SAIRR:	South African Institute of Race Relations
Samaf:	South African Micro Finance Apex Fund

Sanac: South African National Aids Council
Sanco: South African National Civic Organisation
SANAS: South African National Accreditation Systems
SAPs: Structural Adjustment Programmes
SAPS: South African Policy Service
SAR: South African Railway
SARB: South African Reserve Bank
SAQA: South African Qualifications Authority
SARS: South African Revenue Service
Sawid: South African Women in Dialogue
SDA: Skills Development Act
SETAs: Sector Education and Training Authorities
Seda: Small Enterprise Development Agency
SEZ: Special Economic Zone
SGB: School Governing Body
SHI: Social Health Insurance
SME: Small and Medium Sized Enterprises
SMMEs: Small, Micro and Medium Enterprises
SMTs: School Management Teams
SoC: State Owned Companies
SOEs: State Owned Enterprises
SSA: Sub-Saharan Africa
Stats SA: Statistics South Africa
TB: Tuberculosis
TCC: Transnational Capitalist Class
TEO: The Enterprise Organisation
TGRs: Third Generation Reforms
TIA: Technology Innovation Agency
TNPA: Transnet National Ports Authority
TRC: Truth and Reconciliation Commission
TVET: Technical, Vocational Education and Training
UDF: United Democratic Front
UN: United Nations
UNISA: University of South Africa

WB:	World Bank
WHO:	World Health Organization
ZANU:	Zimbabwe African National Union

Foreword

It was a great pleasure to read Vusi Gumede's new book *Post-apartheid South Africa: Economic and Social Inclusion.* The book contains rare insights making it an important scholarly contribution that adds to the necessary production of radical knowledge. It is an incredible opportunity to traverse Vusi Gumede's mind; as an advocate of critical thinking, his evolution has been intriguing. Gumede's extensive awareness in macroeconomic tools makes him a crucial agent in the transformation of South African society. This book comes at a very crucial moment in our history as a young democracy. Many views have been expressed as to the experience of the democracy; however, Gumede provides his own take, not shying away from confronting issues and directly engaging with them—unambiguously showing policy oversights and explicitly stating ways to create the society envisaged by the liberation project.

The task of writing this foreword came as a challenge simply because the contents of this book confront existing foundations and views. It is an arduous task to give brief representation of radical scholarship that is important for Africa's renewal despite the safety and security provided by conventional stances. The book echoes the type of brave scholarship needed for Africa to shake off the developmental quagmire it finds itself in. The era of publishing uncomfortable proposals and views is nigh if we seek to fully grasp the context in which our interventions are to be implemented.

I worked with Vusi Gumede for a lengthy period in the South African government. His service in the public sector coupled with his robust knowledge of economics and public policy has created a suitable and well-rounded wordsmith with digestible articulations and recommendations for the South African policy landscape. Gumede's book provides well-informed and well-thought out interventions for steering public policy gaps and the troubled South African society into a gear of progress toward sustainable and inclusive development. The book invites us to think critically about the state of South African society, bringing to the surface the visibility of the fissures and cracks of the post-apartheid dispensation. It guides us on a reflective journey of where we are. It also reminds us of the real mission of the political struggle—Gumede recalls the 1943 Bill of Rights in the Africans' Claims and discusses the meaning of the 1955 Freedom Charter and the National Development Plan.

The book is a critical introspection of the social and economic trajectory that has been pursued by successive post-apartheid administrations since 1994. The author confronts hard but necessary truths for South Africa's future. The book brings us to the realization that our history of forced settlements, racial intrusion, and violation of minority groups over the majority continue to be salient barriers in the attempt to foster nation building. It also highlights the perpetual economic and social injustices that contribute to the challenges of social and economic inclusion. Moreover, the sacrosanct projects of the African National Congress such as the National Democratic Revolution are shred into pieces through interrogating their relevance in an evolved South African society. This radical offering by Prof Gumede is enough to raise blood pressures for those who religiously hold onto these stale documents.

It is commendable that Gumede's excellent work through this book is an analysis that is not myopic to the contextual challenges South

Africa is located within in terms of the global distribution of power and the legacy of apartheid colonialism. The author impeccably gives us a thorough conceptual understanding of South Africa and the constraints encountered. This allows us to grasp the limitation as well as opportunities for innovative solutions. The invitation for a reader to think critically is also met with suggested solutions through the author's extensive years of experience in the public sector, lecturing and advisory services in policy work. The reader is guaranteed a rich informative experience aimed at providing cutting edge solutions.

I recommend this book, especially to policy makers and all those concerned with the future of our country. I am confident that this book will also be a valuable text in lecture halls and in research. The readers are warned to brace themselves for a riveting thriller into the analysis of the post-apartheid development experience.

Dr Phumzile Mlambo-Ngcuka
Executive Director of UN Women, United Nations
Former Deputy Minister, Minister, and Deputy President in the Republic of South Africa

Preface

South Africa has undergone a significant, almost unpredictable, evolution since 1994. Ten years into democracy, cracks started to show especially to those in the policy making and analysis space. In 2006 we observed—in a discussion document that was examining socioeconomic trends since 1994—that although the government had been able to bring about some important improvements in the lives of many people, it had only just scratched the surface. As a way forward, among other things, we said that "there is [was] a need, at least more effectively, to articulate an overarching vision for the country attached to which should be the detailed programmes and partnerships already in place."[1] We also started noticing in the 2005–2006 period that there were areas that had not been given sufficient attention—or rather, the policies, legislation, and programmes pursued had not effectively addressed some critical areas of redress—for instance, economic inequality. Many new programmes and policy frameworks were conceptualised to ensure higher levels of economic growth, reducing unemployment, poverty, and tackling inequalities. We left government abruptly when former President Thabo Mbeki was recalled in 2008—I formally left in September 2009 but continued to serve in government structures occasionally until 2011, after a year as a special advisor to the Minister of Public Enterprises.

In 2010, I set out to write a book, from an insider's perspective, on the broader political economy of post-apartheid South Africa with a focus on whether or not South Africa was becoming a developmental state. From about 2005, we started discussing—in government—how South Africa could become a developmental state. In 2007, it was publicly declared that South Africa was to be a democratic developmental state. Arguably, we were quietly reverting to the 1992 *Ready to Govern Discussion Document.* It is in this context that this book uses a framework of a developmental state in examining social and economic inclusion in post-apartheid South Africa.

While I was writing this book, I was fortunate to receive a grant from the Council for the Development of Social Science Research in Africa (CODESRIA) to write another related book. In that book—*The Political Economy of Post-Apartheid South Africa*—I mainly elaborate on the various political economy issues that are worth discussing two decades since the dawn of political independence in South Africa. As I was writing *The Political Economy of Post-Apartheid South Africa*, it became clear what this book should address. I also revisited what I had thought to be a very comprehensive analysis of policies and legislation since 1994, but none of the South African presses I approached would publish it—I published milder versions of its chapters in journals and edited books. I also had an opportunity to ruminate on the mistakes we made while in office: I had worked as an advisor in the Ministry of Trade and Industry, as a policy analyst in the Presidency and as a special advisor in the Ministry of Public Enterprises. I had been part of policy thinking since 1999. I saw all the hard work of government in practice until 2011 and I observed it afterwards and I occasionally interviewed those at the helm of the Zuma administration. It occurred to me that an important book that delves deeper into the post-apartheid development experience was necessary.

In a 2015 publication[2] of a conference proceedings reflecting on the two decades of democracy in South Africa, Joel Netshitenzhe and I observed that:

> In the twenty years since South Africa made the transition from apartheid to democracy, much had been achieved to transform society, informed by the injunctions of the Constitution which formally guarantees equal opportunities without regard to race, gender and other social fault-lines. This period has seen some improvements in people's quality of life and tentative steps towards national unity and social cohesion. Yet, much work lies ahead in realising the aspirations of many South Africans who still experience the effects of unemployment, poverty and inequality. Much has to be done to build a capable developmental state...

Through this book, besides describing why inclusive development has been elusive, I have attempted to provide suggestions of necessary steps to ensure a socially and economically inclusive society. I analyse all theoretical frameworks, theories, and perspectives that have shaped the policies that have been pursued since 1994, dating as far back as the 1955 Freedom Charter. I also confront the national question. I examine the implications for South Africa of obtaining global distribution of power and the relationship between the state and capital within South Africa. Essentially, the fundamental challenge that constrains South Africa's ability to further achieve inclusive growth and development relates to policy. The argument I have been advancing is that South Africa has pursued and continues to pursue inappropriate policies in the context of redressing apartheid colonialism—apartheid colonialism is a preferred political characterisation in this book because it captures the centuries of a discriminatory system of colonialism and decades of systemic social and economic exclusion of the majority in South Africa; both colonialism and apartheid were formal systems of racial domination and white supremacy.

The various political economy and development interventions pursued since 1994 have been general rather than specific in tackling the ramifications of apartheid colonialism. The successive post-apartheid administrations appear to have been concerned primarily with growing the economy and pursuing a broad socioeconomic development agenda, instead of policies that directly affect those who endured the brunt of apartheid colonialism. It is, therefore, not surprising that it is in the area of economic hardship where the ramifications of apartheid colonialism are glaring, and that black people are most affected by poverty and other social ills. Arguably, the first twenty-one years of democracy have gone largely into state building instead of nation building. For post-apartheid South Africa, it is more meaningful and relevant to see a nation as a community that acknowledges and respects its repulsive political and economic history of deprivation, through systematic restitutionary, reconciliatory, and restructuring measures, and equitable sharing of resources—than the myth of a *rainbow nation.*

Just to be clear, policies are considered inappropriate or weak if they do not take account of particular contexts. The global environment, the domestic context, and other contexts have changed since 1994, but policy changes or shifts (i.e., reforms) and their sequencing have not been alive to new realities, especially since 2005. South Africa, arguably, has not confronted apartheid colonialism directly. It is perhaps understandable that in the first ten years of political independence it was difficult to confront complex, important issues such as the land and agrarian question. It is also understandable, perhaps, that restructuring the economy is difficult. However, Sampie Terreblanche, Hein Marias, Lawrence Hamilton, John Saul, and Patrick Bond, among others, suggest that the overall development experience of post-apartheid South Africa has to be understood within the context of "elite transition." In simple terms, the transition from apartheid colonialism to democracy involved compromises among the elite, and the compromises reached could be constraining development. This view, however, cannot take away from the possibility that policies could have improved more lives in post-apartheid South Africa and that there are policy mistakes that have nothing to do with the "elite transition." There was a policy space, particularly ten years after political independence, to turn things around. Recommendations were made about what needed to be done—take for instance what was said in the *Towards a Ten Year Review: Discussion Document*—and a "major intervention required should be directed at consolidating democracy with measures aimed at integrating all of society into a growing economy from which they can benefit."[3]

As hinted above, the book takes apartheid colonialism as its point of departure. Between 1811 and 1906, there were at least ten wars of resistance by Africans against white settlers in the most southern tip of the African continent. This excludes the many battles and wars that Africans fought against whites starting in 1510 when Africans fought and won against Portuguese colonialists in what is now known as Cape Town. Apartheid colonialism created racialised categories in order to enslave Africans. South Africa's population remains classified into: Blacks, Coloureds, Indians, and Whites. In this book, people are classified into two categories: African and non-African. Africans are those that have endured the historical experience of colonialism and other forms of enslavement.

The book uses the category of "African" to refer to South Africans or their earlier generations who have experienced the evils of apartheid colonialism. Although Coloureds and Indians also endured white domination, they were afforded some rights denied to those classified as Blacks. Robert Mangaliso Sobukwe, Founding President of the Pan-Africanist Congress, defined African "as anyone who lives in and pays his allegiance to Africa and who is prepared to subject himself to African majority rule."[4] Kwesi Kwaa Prah[5] argues that being African should not be confused with citizenship and that "if everyone is African, then nobody is an African."

I must say that by invoking a particular definition of "African" by no means do I imply that Africans must practice any form of apartheid. I must say also that the definition advanced does not mean that Africans would not exist if various forms of enslavements did not occur—it is particularly because of the various forms of enslavements that one has to be categorical, otherwise the question of who is an African would not exist. The definition I am advancing, however, implies that inasmuch as there exists an African diaspora in the West, Whites in particular are a European diaspora whether living or born in Africa.

In a nutshell, the book—anchored on African-centred paradigms—asserts subject place within the context of African history as Molefi Kete Asante and Ama Mazama would put it in relation to Afrocentricity. It asserts the identity that has been denied, as the late Achie Mafeje would say, in the context of Africanity. It is part of the process of creating an African self-understanding as the late Dani Nabudere said with regard to Africology. The African-centred paradigms referred to privilege African agency; that Africans should do things for themselves for they have done so before they were rudely interrupted by colonialism and because Africans have a proud history in knowledge production and so forth.

The book hopes to contribute to a conversation among Africans regarding what is to be done in South Africa in an effort to bring about the nation that so many sacrificed their lives for. I will not be surprised if Darly Glaser and other like-minded scholars and politicians sharing a similar view would consider my ideological stance as "racial-nationalistic excess" (see Glaser 2011). I am of the view that Africans should not be apologetic to freely express themselves, as non-Africans do express themselves. As indicated elsewhere, the challenge of development in South Africa is a challenge for Africans. As such, Africans need to engage with these relevant issues among themselves. And, as Glaser (2011, 89) argues, "whites should be educated about past iniquities and encouraged to see that the better-off among them (even those born post-apartheid) have incurred obligations to the country's black poor as a result of these." However, I think the issue is not as simplistic as just "education."

The overall characterisation that this book gives for post-apartheid South Africa is a corporatist state, referring to the state that is influenced, if not captured, by business interests. It is a state that is not (sufficiently) concerned with socioeconomic transformation. A corporatist state, different from the neo-liberal state, is fundamentally characterised by privileging capital over people—a neo-liberal state is generally understood as a state that pursues neo-liberal economic policies. It is almost a given that a corporatist state functions within neo-liberal principles, but it is not necessarily a neo-liberal regime. The notion of a corporatist state is useful, in my view, because it distinguishes the character of the post-apartheid state and disagrees with the notion of a neo-apartheid state as some have characterised post-apartheid South Africa.

I propose the following. First, economic policy has to address the challenges of unemployment and poverty, as well as reducing inequality. Second, social policy has to be robust. Third, labour market policies should be ameliorated. More importantly, social and economic policies have to work together for socioeconomic development. To achieve this, South Africa needs a new consensus on the ideal framework or approach to its socioeconomic development—the National Planning Commission's vision is a step in the right direction for ensuring that various stakeholders agree on South Africa's socioeconomic development model.

Given the abovementioned premise, discussed in detail in the chapters of the book, it follows that the fundamental task at hand is the reconfiguration of societal relations. Failing to address this, South Africa would continue to drift further away from becoming a democratic developmental state just as we have significantly drifted further away from becoming a nation.

Vusi Gumede, PhD
Tshwane, South Africa

NOTES

1. The Presidency 2006, *A Nation in the Making: A discussion document on macro-social trends in South Africa,* Government Communications and Information System (GCIS), Pretoria, 99.
2. Mapungubwe Institute for Strategic Reflection (2015), *20 Years of South African Democracy: So Where to Now.* Johannesburg: Real African Publishers, 6.
3. The Presidency. 2003. *Towards a Ten Year Review: synthesis report on implementation of government programmes, a discussion document of the Policy Coordination and Advisory Services, The Presidency,* Pretoria, 103.
4. See Pheko, M. 1994. *The Land is Ours: The Political Legacy of Mangaliso Sobukwe,* New York: Pheko and Associates.
5. Prah, K.K. 1999. African Renaissance or Warlordism. In Makgoba, M.W. (ed.) 1999.*African Renaissance: The New Struggle.* Johannesburg/Cape Town: Mafube/Tafelberg.

Post-apartheid South Africa

Chapter 1

Introduction

> We, the African people in the Union of South Africa, urgently demand the granting of full citizenship rights such as are enjoyed by all Europeans in South Africa.
>
> Bill of Rights, Africans' Claims in South Africa 1943

Introduction

The year 1994 was momentous for South Africa, and Africa in general. It dramatically marked the formal end of a repugnant system of oppression by the white minority over the African majority. South Africa was the sole country on the African continent that did not have political independence; the wave of political liberation of the 1960s and 1970s that swept across the African continent never reached South Africa. Africans in South Africa have had to endure about 350 years of white domination. In this book, Africans are those that have endured the historical experience of colonialism and other forms of enslavement.[1]

Between 1910 and 1994, the Boers[2] and British meted extreme forms of enslavement and oppression on blacks. The year 1948 marks the beginning of one of the most discriminatory systems ever conceived. When the

Boers took over the predatory 'State' of the Union of South Africa, they systematically designed and implemented a repulsive apartheid agenda which lasted until 1994. The totality of the historical experience of colonialism, imperialism, racism, apartheid and other forms of enslavement are denoted as apartheid colonialism in this book.

Various policy and strategy documents provide a clear sense of the kind of the post-apartheid South Africa that was envisaged: the 1943 Bill of Rights in the Africans' Claims in South Africa, the 1955 Freedom Charter, the 1962 Road to South African Freedom, the 1992 Ready to Govern Discussion Document, the 1994 Reconstruction and Development Programme, the 1998 Discussion Document on the State, Property and Social Transformation, the 1996 Constitution including documents of the National Liberation Movement (NLM) and speeches of its leadership, especially the political leadership of the African National Congress (ANC). In addressing the first Congress of the Popular Movement for the Liberation of Angola (MPLA) in Luanda in December 1977, Oliver Tambo made a point that, "the African National Congress visualises a South Africa in which the people shall govern, in which the wealth of the country shall be restored to the people...a society free of exploitation."[3]

Since the dawn of South Africa's political independence, a fundamental question arose as to whether South Africa was on course to being the country that was conceptualised and pursued for decades by the broader liberation movement: that is, a socially and economically inclusive society. A socially and economically inclusive society is one where all racial and ethnic groups are considered to be part of society with equitable access to opportunities and a just share in the fruits of the economy. Social and economic inclusion must involve redress in the form of opportunities, gender, geography, and other possible means especially in a deeply divided society where some races were systematically excluded from the mainstream. Neville Alexander (2013,41) contends that "the demise of apartheid...did not lead to the kind of society that many of us, including many in government, had imagined a post-apartheid South Africa would be."

On 24 May 1994, the first president of a democratic South Africa, Nelson Mandela, in his inaugural address, in accordance with the policy aspirations of the Freedom Charter, opened a Joint Sitting of Parliament with the following words:

> My Government's commitment to create a people-centred society of liberty binds us to the pursuit of the goals of freedom from want, freedom from hunger, freedom from deprivation, freedom from ignorance, freedom from suppression and freedom from fear. These freedoms are fundamental to guarantee human dignity. They will therefore constitute part of the centrepiece of what this Government will seek to achieve, the focal point on which our attention will be continuously focused (Nelson Mandela 1994).

The Freedom Charter has been sacrosanct in the ANC's understanding and the mission to build an inclusive society. The adoption of the Freedom Charter by the Congress of the People on 26 June 1955 was seen as a critical point in the political struggle for a free South Africa.

Background

The Freedom Charter, and its pursuit of social and economic development, has served as a philosophical prism through which the understanding of the "new society" has been articulated. On assumption of political power, the ruling ANC appeared to have a clear philosophical outlook for the kind of society it desired to build. The ANC introduced a number of various policies, strategies, and programmes in order to respond to the material challenges that faced South Africa. As indicated earlier, this society was meant to be socially and economically inclusive within democratic principles, respect for human rights, and other such standard desires of progressive societies.

According to Gumede (2015f, 4), "the first democratically elected government inherited an economy and society that was in a profound crisis." The majority of the population was disproportionately bearing the brunt of poverty, marginalisation, and underdevelopment. Whilst South Africa's economy had begun to adjust in the 1990s, the harsh reality of a significantly distorted income distribution and consequent structural distortions in the demand for goods and services eventually resulted in a significant economic crisis. Stephen Gelb (see for instance Gelb 2003; 2010) has written extensively from an economist's viewpoint about the economic crises that have continuously bedevilled South Africa, both before and after apartheid colonialism. In this book, the discussion of the economic issues will take on a political stance. It is in this context that I share the view by Seraaj Mohamed (2010) that the South African economy, even the post-apartheid one, has been in a crisis. Like many others, Mohamed (2010) attributes the economic crises of the post-apartheid South Africa to neoliberal policies which resulted in internationalisation, financialisation, and deindustrialisation in the economy. I have argued (see, for instance, Gumede 2013a; 2014a; 2015a) that the challenge faced by the South African economy has to do with delayed and, in some instances, inappropriate reforms. The book deals with these challenges in detail.

The apartheid social systems not only prejudiced and disadvantaged blacks, but also failed to meet the socioeconomic needs of the country as a whole. High levels of unemployment and poverty, highly unequal income distribution, and low levels of investment became deeply entrenched during the economic crisis of the 1990s. Contrary to the experiences of other comparable economies with similar endowments and/or equivalent initial conditions, South Africa was stagnating with further adverse effects on the economic participation and wellbeing of the majority. From 1994, legislation and policy interventions had to be implemented to redress the ramifications of apartheid colonialism on blacks in general and Africans in particular.

The ANC, since 1994, committed to a series of strategic undertakings that intended to combine growth and development, reconstruction and redistribution, popular participation, and respect for human rights. According to Gumede (2015f, 5), "it is against this backdrop that the ANC contested the first democratic elections—on 27 April 1994—based on a vision of 'A Better Life for All'." The outlines of, and the strategic path towards, this "better life" are elaborated in the 1992 Ready to Govern (R2G) strategy document and particularly in the 1994 Reconstruction and Development Programme—a policy framework underpinned by the vision for reconstruction and development of a new South Africa. South Africa's new Constitution enshrined the rights of all South Africans to equality and provided for specific measures to be taken to redress historical imbalances and the monumental historical injustice of apartheid colonialism.

A number of political economy or development interventions and initiatives have been explored by the ANC-led government: namely, the 1996 Growth, Employment and Redistribution (GEAR) framework, the 2005 Accelerated and Shared Growth Initiative of South Africa (AsgiSA), and the 2010 New Growth Path (NGP). Chapters 4 and 6 of this book discuss these economic frameworks and the Reconstruction and Development Programme (RDP) as well as other major policy directives of the successive post-apartheid administrations in detail. Whilst the various administrations serving post-apartheid South African have made concerted efforts to deal with the historical socioeconomic challenges, progress is broadly mixed and largely disappointing.

As South Africa transitions and evolves in the next twenty years of political independence, South African society must consolidate the gains made and take charge of the processes of reshaping and restructuring society in a manner that acknowledges the centrality of the racial, gender, and class relations, and how they find expression in post-apartheid South Africa as well as its role in the nation-building project. South Africa also needs to deal with policy constraints experienced since 1994 that have to do with limitations imposed by the global socioeconomic and political order.[4] Essentially, to better transform South African society, state-market relations should be reconfigured. These views and arguments are elaborated in the subsequent chapters, particularly in chapter 3.

NATION AND NATION BUILDING

Similar to various social-science subject matters, it has not been easy to develop a single theory that correctly explains and interprets nation building and social cohesion. The complexities and difficulties in undertaking this type of enterprise are informed by the different historical trajectories through which nations evolve. Differences in the experiences of societies in their formative and developmental stages also hinder the development of theories that apply to all societies and nations. Besides, the similarities that exist among related terms such as *nation*, *nationalism*, *nation building*, and *nation state* make the case for the development of a comprehensive theory of any one of these concepts particularly challenging. What one obtains, generally, are the theoretical constructs that try to explain these concepts in varying depths. It is, however, important that this book reflects on the notion of a nation, given the issues that it is addressing. Chapter 5 confronts the difficult issue of the *national question*.

Charles Tilly (1975, cf. Jaffrelot, 2003) notes that "nation remains one of the most puzzling and tendentious items in political lexicon." The study of nation building has traditionally been the preserve of historians. However, in the late 1980s and early 1990s, political scientists have taken up the challenge of understanding the salience of nation building as well as nationalism. The need to lay a theoretical foundation for a book of this nature is largely informed by the importance that the fundamental issues of nation building and nationalism, and the imperative of building a nation state continue to assume in the modern world.

As Benedict Anderson (2006, 4) argues, "many old nations once thought to be fully consolidated find themselves challenged within their borders

—the reality is quite plain: the end of the era of nationalism so long prophesised, is not remotely in sight. Indeed, nation-ness is the most universally legitimate value in political life of our time." Despite the ubiquitous nature of globalisation and the high hopes of the Internationalists for a global alliance of the working class, national consciousness and emotional attachment to defined boundaries remain high in both developed and developing countries.

Karl Deutsch (1969, as cf. Jaffrelot, 2003, 8) hoped that

> modernisation will lead to the disappearance of ethnic peculiarities and the assimilation of minority groups into the dominant group: the members of the peripheral groups, which participate in social mobilisation are supposed to accept the cultural modes of the dominant group, even if only to take part in the division of labour practiced in the urban areas.

However, such hopes seem to be fading away. In many societies in the contemporary world, sub-national groups continue to appeal to historical artefacts, linguistic similarities, and shared religious beliefs as a basis of autonomous identity. The cases of Scotland and the United Kingdom, Ukraine and Crimea, and others in different regions of the world are clear testimonies of the salience of subgroup consciousness.

In an attempt to theorise nation building and nationalism, Anderson (2006, 8) defines nation as "an imagined community, whose imaginary is both limited and sovereign." Anderson (2006, 8) argues that nations are imagined,

> because the members of even the smallest nation will never know most of their fellow-members, meet them, or even hear of them, yet in the minds of each lives the image of their communion... The nation is imagined as *limited* because even the largest of them, encompassing perhaps a billion living human beings, has finite, if elastic, boundaries, beyond which lie other nations... It is imagined as *sovereign* because the concept was born in an age in which Enlightenment and Revolution were destroying the legitimacy

> of the divinely-ordained, hierarchical dynastic realm... Finally, it is imagined as a *community,* because, regardless of the actual inequality and exploitation that may prevail in each, the nation is always conceived as a deep, horizontal comradeship.

The import of Anderson's explanation of a nation is that nationhood is artificial and socially constructed, especially by the elites who derive power and privileges from such constructions. This explanation is limited to the extent that it fails to recognise the link that exists between the concept of nations and nationalism. Whereas the nation may be an abstract construction, nationalism is a practical expression of the feeling of oneness that defines one group or race from the others. For instance, the active, consistent, and sometimes violent resistance of the colonised peoples of the various colonial governments in Africa and Asia in the last century or so were evidently expressive of the awareness of the differences that exist between the colonised and the coloniser.

Based on his historical account of nation building in Europe, Tilly (1990, cf Jaffrelot, 2003) argues that the making of nations is indeed "by wars," which helped rulers to develop fiscal administration. Jaffrelot (2003) contends that even though the theories of nation building do not explain nationalism, nationalism is a process of nation building and that the foundations of nationalism are rooted in identity politics and culture. The nation is the natural space for the expression of this identity and culture. It goes without saying, arguably, that part of the identity and culture defining a nation is language, among other key factors.

A missing link in the various theories that have been developed to explain nations or nation building is the importance of territory as a constant referent in identifying where one belongs. Although people of similar historical backgrounds and origins, such as the Jews, are found in different parts of the world, they tend to associate a geographical space as their origin. Thus, nations are not an abstraction as Anderson would have us believe. The people who make up a nation normally occupy a geographic space. It is within this space that the process of nation building takes place. Arguably, the conditions under which the occupiers of a territory came about and the character of the relations between the peoples that inhabit that geographic space matter for nation building and social cohesion. In instances where there are relations that exist between the host and the immigrant that are borne out of mutual understanding and respect, nation building becomes manageable. However, when such are borne out of imposition, forced settlement, and racial intrusion, nation building as well as state building become difficult as the society will be constantly subjected to centrifugal forces emanating from the subjugated community.

The salience of consciousness of belonging to a nation is even more pronounced in countries that experience settler colonialism such as South Africa. Although South Africa has developed a constitutional framework that seeks to incorporate the various nationalities into a nation state, the continuity of the old patterns of relations and privileges by one race over the other (i.e., the European settlers over the African hosts) have tendentiously undermined the efficacy of the constitutions in blurring the racial divides. Indeed, what has happened, and continues to happen in South Africa, is that despite the freedom that post-independence has yielded, emancipation in the form of access to economic justice and equity remains an illusion.

Despite attempts by the Truth and Reconciliation Commission (TRC) to achieve catharsis from the ills of the past, lack of honest and remorseful acknowledgement of the evils of the apartheid regime have continued to spur revolutionary pressures from the previously disadvantaged group. FW de Klerk, the last apartheid President of South Africa, was reported to have said on CNN in 2012 that the apartheid regime was only "morally repugnant in a qualified way."[5] Dave Steward, the Executive Director of the FW de Klerk Foundation, also mentioned in a 16 January 2015 article that despite the apartheid regime, South Africa is much better than other African countries which did not experience apartheid. Steward (2015, 3) says that:

> The fact is that 21 years ago, the ANC took over the governance of by far the most developed country in Africa. There are far more kilometres of railways and highways in any country in Africa; we (then) generated more electricity than the rest of the continent combined; we had developed sophisticated industries and world class business. Despite apartheid, the black population of South Africa was in many respects more advanced than any other people in Africa. How much of this would have existed without the contribution that white South Africans made to the development of the country?'

The aforementioned quotations reinforce the racist and ahistorical notion that African people are incapable of developing themselves without the intervention of the European settler. They omit the fact that these celebrated achievements by "whites" were realised with the resources found on the land—resources that were extracted with the forced labour of blacks, who were mostly treated as mere property.

Regardless of the constitutional provisions for nation building in South Africa, comments such as the ones made by key figures of the apartheid regime can only succeed in fanning the ember of anger, disgust, and revenge. Such statements complicate the process of nation building because they inflict more psychological damage to the people whose rights had been denied for centuries. Thus, the form of relations that exist between the various peoples that represent a geographical space matter for nation building. It is also in this context that chapter 5 concludes that South Africa is drifting further away from becoming a nation.

In the case of South Africa, the political elite, the intelligentsia, and the civil society have an important role in placing the historical and contemporary realities of the country in perspective through dialogue, debates, and firm commitment to mutual respect, equality, and restorative justice. Rather than resorting to war (as it was done in Europe) in fostering a nation state and building nationhood in post-apartheid South Africa, contemporary realities show that in the foreseeable future, consciousness along racial lines will continue to determine the relationship between the peoples that constitute South Africa.

The fundamental issue that South Africa must confront is the making of a South African nation. While the draconian laws and repulsive policies of the British Empire and National Party have been eradicated since the advent of democracy, South African post-apartheid society is still grappling with the deeply entrenched socioeconomic effects of systemic racism and abuse of blacks (and Africans in particular); fundamentally, it is yet to change in order to be considered a just and equitable society. Hence, I argue that as far as becoming a nation, South Africa seems to be drifting further away at the expense of Africans.

Scope of the Book

The book scrutinises the progress made and the prospects facing post-apartheid South Africa; it discusses the extent of social and economic inclusion since 1994. I also assess the manner in which successive post-apartheid administrations have performed in implementing their constitutional (and political) mandates and unpack selected social and economic policies of the "new" South Africa, including the approach used in the pursuit of transformation and institutional arrangements for policy making and implementation, and propose suggestions on elaborating on the transformation project in order to ensure complete liberation. In addition, I discuss various microeconomic interventions since 1994; I interrogate the changes that have taken place regarding the general wellbeing of South African society.

The book examines pertinent political economy issues within a broader framework of a "developmental state." The definition of a developmental state as used in this book "is a state that is active in pursuing its agenda, working with social partners, and has the capacity and is appropriately organised for its predetermined developmental objectives."[6] This definition is informed by research on the subject and influenced by Evans's[7] notion of "embedded autonomy"; Leftwich's[8] model of a developmental state; Cummings and Nørgaard's[9] four dimensions of state capacity; as well as definitions and features of developmental states by South African scholars such as Luiz,[10] Mhone,[11] Swilling et al,[12] and Edigheji.[13]

The notion of a developmental state is all encompassing in the sense that the vision of what the democratic post-apartheid South Africa would be like is effectively encapsulated in the developmental state framework. It is within this context that aspects of an unfinished business of social and economic inclusion are examined, especially two decades after the dawn of political independence in South Africa.

The idea of making South Africa a developmental state features in many important policy documents of the ANC and of the successive post-apartheid administrations, including the seminal Ready to Govern (R2G) discussion document—the R2G articulates the ANC's vision of the future and sets out policy guidelines for a democratic South Africa with more clarity than many of the policy and strategy documents of the ANC or the NLM broadly. I should, however, hasten to make a point that, from an Africanist point of view, the 1943 Africans' Claims in South Africa framework remains the most relevant piece of philosophical underpinnings for bettering the lives of blacks. It should be noted, though, that the National Development Plan, otherwise known as *Vision 2030* released by the National Planning Commission[14] in 2012, talks of a "capable state."

I discuss the shift (perhaps in emphasis) between the Africans' Claims and the Freedom Charter in chapter 4. I also problematise the various theoretical notions, such as the National Democratic Revolution[15] and Colonialism of a Special Type,[16] that have shaped the ANC's approach in socioeconomic development.

Chapter 2 examines what I have termed "development dilemmas"—there are other scholars who have used this formulation.[17] This chapter explores the set of problems that can be considered as "development dilemmas" because of the intractable nature of these challenges, accentuated by the socioeconomic nuances that characterise them. The chapter posits that weak race relations, economic inequality, and poverty are the three development dilemmas that stand out in the South African context. In addition, because of the challenges relating to health care, education, and the labour market, South Africa's human development has not significantly improved during the first twenty years of democracy. In order to address poverty and/or inequality, the structure of the economy has to change. The chapter proposes restructuring South Africa's economic landscape in order to sustainably address poverty and/or inequality. I am mindful that restructuring the economy and society is complex; however, concrete suggestions for restructuring are provided. I also recommend a vision for the economy and society and a robust socioeconomic development model that will make the big change needed in South Africa.

Chapter 3 presents theoretical reflections on state-market relations and discusses the post-colonial and a post-apartheid South African development experience. The land question and the issue of education are teased out as a case of incomplete liberation that southern Africa and South Africa in particular endure.

Chapter 4 discusses policy reforms at a macro level; it discusses the various macroeconomic interventions, social policy reforms, and the changes that have taken place regarding the general wellbeing of the South African society. As such, the 1994 Reconstruction and Development Programme (RDP) and the 1996 Growth, Employment and Redistribution (GEAR) are discussed in detail. GEAR was a macroeconomic policy framework intended to stabilise the economy and rescue an economy that was already falling apart. In 2005, when the government realised that the redistributive performance of the economy had not adequately met the needs of society, the government pursued another economic policy reform through the Accelerated and Shared Growth Initiative for South Africa (AsgiSA). AsgiSA was intended to accelerate the growth of South Africa's economy, as well as accelerate wealth redistribution.

The life of AsgiSA, however, was brief. In 2010, AsgiSA was replaced by the New Growth Path (NGP), which places emphasis on job creation through infrastructural development. The chapter deals with these issues in detail and engages with various scholars' views on these broader policy directives. As a precursor to chapter 5, chapter 4 debates the colonialism of a special type thesis, the theory of the national democratic revolution, and the Freedom Charter.

Chapter 5 deals with the *national question*, within the context of social and economic inclusion (and not from a sophisticated Fanonian perspective). Simplistically, a national question implies that there is an appropriate balance of power and influence among all population and/or ethnic groups in a nation state. It is argued that language, culture, and similar factors are critical in the imagination of a political community as complementary efforts in nation building—nation building (not state-building) can be viewed as the strengthening of unity, coherence, functionality, and pride in a nation state. Contrarily, nationalism refers to loyalty based on nationality—it could be an association premised on commonality of language, religion, or ethnicity and so on. Indeed, as indicated earlier, South Africa seems to be drifting further away from becoming a nation. I proffer that for post-apartheid South Africa, it will be more meaningful and relevant to see a nation as a community that acknowledges and respects its repulsive political and economic history of deprivation, through systematic, restitutionary, reconciliatory, and restructuring measures, and equitable sharing of resources.

Chapter 6 begins with a review of policy directions pursued by the successive post-apartheid administrations: the Nelson Mandela administration, the Thabo Mbeki administration, and the Jacob Zuma administration. It first discusses the evolution of South Africa's policy framework in its quest to transform society and then examines social and economic transformation. The chapter argues that whilst South Africa has achieved significant social and economic development in two decades of democracy, there are several areas of social and economic endeavour that have limited the country's achievement of the targets set in 1994. In essence, the economic policy has been unclear or non-existent resulting in an economy that has not risen to its potential Growth Domestic Product (GDP) growth rate, particularly in relation to comparable economies.[18] The necessary reforms in the economy have been weak because of poor policy development and a lack of vision for the economy. Regarding social development, the chapter argues that the lack of, or weak, social policy has constrained the advancement of wellbeing. Overall, from about 2006, because of the various weaknesses in post-apartheid administrations, the intricacies tied to state-market relations have made it difficult for the government to further advance wellbeing.

Chapter 7 concludes with policy options that can ensure that South Africa becomes an adequately inclusive society, socially and economically, within constraints accentuated by the global order. It argues that the post-apartheid development dilemmas call on South Africa to make concerted efforts to realise new commitments towards alternative development paths. The interminable crises of the global economy imply that South Africa cannot leave the wellbeing of its people squarely in the hands of the market. South Africa urgently requires a shift in policy perspective, as well as a new mix of policy options, that will give meaningful expression to balanced and equitable growth. South Africa needs to strengthen the backbone of the developmental state to achieve the much yearned for inclusive society. Paramount to such an endeavour is the reconfiguration of state-market relations.

NOTES

1. Refer to the preface for a detailed discussion of the ideological orientation of this book and the view of who is an 'African.'
2. Boer is synonymous to Afrikaner, the first settler race in the most southern tip of the African continent in the middle of the seventeenth century
3. See Tambo, A., *Oliver Tambo Speaks*, Cape Town: Kwela Books, 2014.
4. Lungisile Ntsebeza, a leading South African scholar on land reform, in a paper he delivered at Yale University in 2008 makes a point—in the context of why South Africa's land reform has been slow—that "a more substantial explanation, I would argue, cannot afford to ignore the global political and economic order that emerged after the collapse of Soviet Communism from the late 1980s and how this affected the balance of forces. The transition to democracy in South Africa in the early 1990s took place at a critical moment." Without discounting the powerful negative implications of the end of the Cold War, there are many countries on the African continent that find themselves in a similar situation as South Africa, including Zimbabwe, and those countries suffer from the skewed global order even though they gained independence prior to the collapse of "Soviet Communism."
5. http://www.news24.com/SouthAfrica/Politics/Outrage-of-FW-de-Klerk-comments-20120511. Outrage over FW de Klerk comment. Accessed February 2, 2015.
6. Gumede, 'Public Policy Making in a Post-Apartheid South Africa – A Preliminary Perspective', *Africanus: Journal of Development Studies,* 38 (2), 9.
7. Evans, *Embedded Autonomy: States and Industrial Transformation,* Princeton: Princeton University Press.
8. Leftwich, 'Bringing Politics Back In: Towards a Model of a Developmental State,' *Journal of Development Studies,* 31(3), 400–427.
9. Cummings and Nørgaard, 'Conceptualising State Capacity: Comparing Kazakhstan and Kyrgyzstan,' *Policy Studies,* 52(4), 685–708.
10. Luiz, 'South African State Capacity and the Post-apartheid Economic Reconstruction,' *International Journal of Social Economics,* 29(8), 594–614.
11. Ibid.

12. Swilling, Breda, Van Zyl, and Khan, 'Economic Policy-making in a Developmental State: Review of the South African Government's Poverty and Development Approaches, 1994–2004,' *Economic Policy and Poverty Alleviation Report Series,* Research Report 3.
13. Edigheji, *The Emerging South African Democratic Developmental State and the People's Contract,* Johannesburg: Centre for Policy Studies, 2007.
14. National Planning Commission, *The National Development Plan 2030.* Ministry of Planning. Pretoria: The Presidency, 2012.
15. The gist of the National Democratic Revolution (NDR) is the creation of a National Democratic Society (NDS); a society where all citizens have equal rights, access and responsibilities—a society free of poverty and underdevelopment. Bond (2011) summarises the aim of the NDR to be state transformation and redress of class inequality. As a theory, the NDR envisages two-stages: national democracy during the first stage and socialism in the second and last stage. The NDR was adopted in 1969 at an ANC Conference in Morogoro in Tanzania.
16. The South African Communist Party (1962) described Colonialism of a Special Type as a form of colonialism "in which the oppressing White nation occupied the same territory as the oppressed people themselves and lived side by side with them."
17. See, for instance, Freund, B. and Witt H. (eds) (2010). *Development Dilemmas in Post-Apartheid South Africa.* KwaZulu Natal: University of KwaZulu Natal Press, 2010 and Ramphele, M. *Laying Ghosts to Rest: Dilemmas of the transformation in South Africa.* Cape Town: NB Publishers, 2008.
18. It should be acknowledged though that the South African economy, in terms of Gross Domestic Product, has effectively tripled since 1994, now at about $400 billion, it has been overtaken by Nigeria as the biggest economy in Africa.

Chapter 2

Development Dilemmas

> Therefore, we, the people of South Africa, black and white together as equals, countrymen and brothers adopt this Freedom Charter; And we pledge ourselves to strive together, sparing neither strength nor courage, until the democratic changes here set out have been won.
>
> (Freedom Charter 1955)

Introduction

South Africa is faced with a number of intractable development challenges, similar to other African societies or developing economies in general. A number of the challenges confronting the country have to do, internally, with the ramifications and remnants of apartheid colonialism and, externally, with the capitalist imperialist system. The challenges in question have been noted by many, ranging from government to researchers. My premise is that the many problems (e.g., weak leadership and corruption) and challenges (e.g., poor service delivery) are symptomatic of bigger and deeper fundamental issues.

This chapter deals with a set of challenges that can be classified as "development dilemmas" because they are intractable. These are challenges that, even if government has the right policies and capacities, would still be an upheaval to resolve. This chapter focuses on the internal development dilemmas that constrain South Africa's ability to be a developmental state and/or factors that constrain inclusive development in South Africa. The main dilemmas discussed are: weak race relations, economic inequality, and poverty. Linked to these main development dilemmas are unemployment because of a poorly performing economy, and weak human development because of poor education and health care. The chapter also discusses public service delivery protests—these could be conceived of as part of development dilemmas relating poverty, inequality, and poor human development.

RACE, GENDER, AND CLASS

The very creation of a South African society was premised on various forms of discrimination, and from 1948 to 1994 these forms of discrimination were systematic and comprehensive. South Africa is a conundrum in many respects. Since the arrival of European settlers, first in early sixteenth century and ultimately in the middle of the seventeenth century, South Africa assumed the status of a class society with the creation of a bourgeois society in a racist regime. South Africa, therefore, has had to deal with the intersection of class, race, and gender. In all these areas, progress is disappointing as we shall see.

Discrimination, often covert, along the racial, gender, and class fault lines remains a major challenge in South Africa. Although, for instance, the number of management and professionals that are African had increased from 216,772 in 1995 to 359,438 in 2005,[1] it has become evident that entrenched inequalities continue to characterise South Africa's economy despite a broad range of state interventions aimed at overcoming these challenges. Economic disparities, racial and gender inequalities in the distribution of and access to wealth, income, skills, and employment persist and, as a consequence, the South African economy continues to perform below its full potential. Entrenched racial and gender inequalities as well as ethnically defined wealth disparities continue to threaten South Africa's social fabric, particularly as economic growth appears to be exacerbating these inequalities and inequities. Persisting inequalities render South Africans vulnerable and threaten South Africa's social and political sustainability both in the medium and especially in the long term. As indicated in chapter 1, Lawrence Hamilton (2014) predicts a revolution, dismissing Adam Habib (2013), who, metaphorically, proclaims "South Africa's suspended revolution." Hamilton (2014, 128) concludes that South Africa is a case of "revolution still pending."

According to the 2011 Census—the latest census available at the point of finalising this book—South Africa's population stands at 51.77 million. Blacks are in the majority, making up 79.2 percent of the population; coloured and white people respectively represent 8.9 percent of the total; and the Indian/Asian population 2.5 percent. The "other" category population group comprises 0.5 percent of the total. In addition, of the total population in 2011, 26,581,769 (51.3 percent) were female and 25,188,791 (48.7 percent) were male. Understanding these demographics is essential to understanding the root of South Africa's development dilemmas as they reveal themselves along racial, class, and gender lines as well as geography/spatial lines. In other words, those in the majority, blacks and the female population, historically and disproportionately bear the brunt of South Africa's socioeconomic challenges.

Though much has been done in a bid to transform race, gender, and class relations in South Africa, weighted outcomes reveal disappointing progress. According to human development measures discussed subseqently in this chapter, Africans are most affected by poverty and have a lower level of human development. Of note is that whites and Indians have better human development indices than the average for the richest 20 percent of all South Africans, which suggests that there are additional factors other than household income that determine inter-racial differences in human development (and this is captured in much lower life expectancy rates for African population groups). Race, it would seem, if not without a doubt, remains a key marker of one's level of human development and life in South Africa.

The 2011 Census results show that whilst South African households earned more than twice the average annual income of R103,204 as of October 2011, the African majority still earned significantly less than their coloured, Indian, and white counterparts. African-headed households were found to have an average annual income of R60,613 in 2011, whilst white households earned on average about six times more at R365,134 per annum. The average coloured household made approximately R112,000 a year, and Indian households just over R250,000 (Statistics South Africa 2012). This skewed distribution function is reminiscent of the apartheid era and is evident in other areas such as education and land ownership.

The various Employment Equity Reports also affirm the persistent racial and gender inequalities in South Africa's labour market. Whilst there has been slow improvement of figures in the employment of Africans at top and senior management levels, white males and females are more likely to be recruited or promoted. Top and senior management positions in the private sector are still dominated by white males, while Africans, in particular African females, appear stuck in the lower rungs of unskilled and semi-skilled jobs (see the 2011/2012 Employment Equity Report for instance). This is instructive given that capital (i.e., the private sector) is traditionally white in South Africa—the capitalisation of the Johannesburg Securities Exchange is but one indicator of the predominance of whites in the ownership of the means of production (to use a Marxist formulation). The "bargain reform" that Roger Southall (2010) talks about—sometimes referred to as "elite transition" or "elite compromise"—meant that the private sector was given a *tabular rasa* to operate as it deemed fit. In addition, Southall (2010, 5) sees "reform bargain" as a mechanism that "facilitated South Africa's success [which] was underpinned by the new government's commitment to providing the opportunity for large scale business to internationalise..." It is therefore not surprising that even after two decades since political independence whites are predominantly represented at the top management echelons of companies just as they are in many facets of South African professional and economic spheres.

The persistence of racial inequalities is supported by a report published by the Organisation for Economic Cooperation and Development (OECD) in 2010 that argues that levels of poverty and inequality in South Africa continue to bear a persistent racial character. The OECD (2010) concludes that rising inequality within the labour market—higher unemployment and significant wage inequalities—is the backbone of the increased levels of aggregate inequality. I will demonstrate later on that economic inequality remains a race (i.e., between population groups) rather than a class (i.e., within particular population groups) question. Therefore, many of those who seem to privilege class over race in South Africa are probably being politically correct or naïve or brazenly hiding the truth because it suits them.

It is not surprising that race relations are deteriorating in South Africa. In fact, as I will discuss later, public opinion suggests that race relations and the gap between the rich and poor is worsening as evidenced from the data. Of course many black South Africans experience racism and white supremacy tendencies—there are frequent public outbursts on social networks by racists and white supremacists calling Africans all sorts of derogatory names. At issue, arguably, is that the remnants of a racist system of white domination remain pronounced. It is therefore not surprising that Lawrence Hamilton (2014), in his recent book, sets out to answer the profound and pertinent question: are South Africans free? As indicated earlier, I beg to differ with Hamilton (2014) that all South Africans are not free. Although the theorisation about "freedom" contained in his book should be congratulated because it is necessary to better theorise about freedom and justice in particular, it is indisputable that the historical injustice and subsequent deprivations are mainly a consequence of centuries of dispossession and oppression by the white minority over Africans—it is Africans that require true freedom.

With regard to race relations, public opinion on race relations improved between 2002 and 2004 and it remained at the same level until about 2007 (Ministry of Monitoring and Evaluation 2014). A large percentage (about 60 percent) of South Africans during 2004–2007 felt that race relations were improving. However, since 2008, the share of those who believed that race relations were improving has declined significantly, and in 2012 dropped to levels not seen since 2001. Only 40 percent believed that race relations were improving in 2001, and in 2012 race relations where perceived to be improving by 40 percent of those interviewed, implying that a larger share believes that race relations are deteriorating—in 2013, only 36 percent said race relations were improving (Ministry of Monitoring and Evaluation 2014). If media reports are anything to go by, it is unsurprising that race relations are deteriorating. As we shall see subsequently, it also makes sense that race relations are deteriorating given a high income inequality between whites and Africans.

The dismal employment equity (EE) figures are a general reflection of persistent racism that is ingrained in the workplace in South Africa, despite the enactment of the Employment Equity Act in 1998. Race continues to be a significant determinant of the probability of acquiring a degree and employment, for instance. Though much has been done by government, a lot more needs to be done to address the challenges imposed by a dynamic and fast-changing labour market.

It is glaringly evident from the abovementioned figures that the government's objective to achieve the vision of an adaptive economy characterised by growth, employment, and equity by 2014 was a pipe dream. South Africa's economy continues to reflect similar attributes of the apartheid colonial economy. The apartheid patterns of relations are systematically and purposefully entrenched. The majority of South Africans continue to be restricted from meaningful participation in the economy. Access to assets, economic opportunities, and skills continues to be racially determined. As in apartheid colonialism wherein accumulation and the creation of wealth were confined to a racial minority, the process of economic empowerment today seemingly mirrors apartheid colonial patterns. The result is an economic structure that today still reflects much of the character and contents of colonial apartheid, hence the call to de-racialise the economy. The legacy of apartheid colonialism lingers on and its ugly head rears prominently lately.

An analysis of the shortcomings of South Africa's economic empowerment strategy is revealing. It would seem that whilst gains were made within the public sector, the overall approach towards black economic empowerment lacked a clear policy focus and an overarching strategic framework (Presidency 2013). Whilst, on many occasions, there has been confusion on defining who is black, the absence of a strong and coherent voice of African business has compounded matters. South Africa's black business community has struggled to mobilise coordinated leadership in what is an essential process for the long-term security of black economic empowerment (Presidency 2013). Neville Alexander (2013,134) argues that the black economic empowerment programme/policy "is a policy that benefits mainly the rising black middle class and in effect deepens the inherited class inequalities."

Even in small and medium businesses, the divisions and weaknesses of the long-standing black business organisations have had a negative impact on the government's interventions. Broad-based economic empowerment (BBEE) has also experienced serious challenges characterised by the low levels of initial capital endowment by the black business community, which on their own are characteristic functions of apartheid colonialism (Presidency 2013). Needless to say, constraints in finance and credit compounded by dependency have been highly problematic, exacerbated by corporate structures that have been equally as problematic on their own. Africans are generally finding it difficult to succeed in the private sector because the private sector remains white and discriminatory. It should, however, be mentioned that most Africans are not serious about business—they are mesmerised by material possessions instead of productive economic activities.

Whilst financing consortia or "special purpose vehicles" are employed to compensate for the shortage of finance, the generation of empowerment deals faced many structural challenges of their own (Presidency 2013). Whilst high profile empowerment deals brought forth "new generations" of African South African business leaders, economic empowerment is yet to see substantive increases in the number of Africans owning, controlling, and managing significant and important parts of the economy.

While much has been done towards de-racialising the economy, the extent to which previously disadvantaged groups participate meaningfully in the economy has to be accelerated. This is a necessary requirement for building a stable, integrated, and prosperous society. It is also critical that other structural forms of discrimination—namely gender-based discrimination and discrimination based on disability—are dealt with simultaneously with the process of de-racialisation (Presidency 2013). Discrimination is accentuated when race intersects with gender and/or disability. To deal with all these issues effectively, policy clarity is paramount.

Poverty, Inequality, and Human Development

According to Gumede (2015f, 116), "two important development issues that continue to haunt post-apartheid South Africa are poverty and inequality. These two issues are linked to the structure of the South African economy. On one hand, the economy or the labour market is not creating jobs that could dent structural poverty. On the other hand, the structure of the economy reproduces inequality by benefiting those with certain skills or patrimonial linkages while excluding the rest of society."

It is when we examine poverty and inequality in post-apartheid South Africa that the legacy of apartheid colonialism is more evident. Apartheid colonialism relegated Africans to low skilled and unskilled sectors.

It systematically ensured that Africans received inferior education. It entrenched a particular structure on the economy. These and other injustices would take a long time to redress. It is unsurprising that whites continue to benefit more from the South African economy—when it grows they benefit and they can diversify or invest offshore should it deteriorate.

Because of the challenges relating to health care, education, and the labour market, South Africa's human development has not had a significant improvement since about the year 2000. Human development refers to the general wellbeing of society or the quality of life for a particular society. The Human Development Index (HDI) measures, on one hand, human development as a composite indicator consisting of life expectancy, literacy, and per capita income. The Human Poverty Index (HPI), on the other hand, is an attempt to bring together in a composite index the different features of deprivation in the quality of life to arrive at an aggregate judgment on the extent of poverty in a community. The HPI combines measures of life expectancy, child nutrition status, and access to improved water sources and income.

Human development, as quantified by the HDI, in South Africa is actually doing relatively well when compared to similar countries despite an unchanged HDI of about 0.61 since 2009. Table 1 presents HDIs of selected countries, including South Africa. Norway has the highest HDI globally and United States is number three. Some other countries can be said to be comparable to South Africa (i.e. India, Brazil, Malaysia, Mauritius, China, and Botswana).

South Africa's HDI is higher than India's but below other comparable countries. It would seem that the Indian HDI has been catching up with that of South Africa. Interestingly, Botswana's HDI overtook that of South Africa in 2005. It is also worth highlighting that Brazil had a comparable HDI to South Africa in 1990, but it greatly exceeds South Africa's today. In 1990, Mauritius—of the two so-called developmental states in Africa, alongside Botswana— had an HDI comparable or rather almost equal to that of South Africa but the Mauritius HDI has now surpassed South Africa's. However, South Africa's HDI has marginally increased in the past couple of years.

Looking at specific indicators of human development, such as literacy and enrolments,[2] the recent progress is somewhat mixed. Table 2 gives various human development related indicators.[3] The calculations on poverty and literacy substantiate other analyses that suggest that South Africa is meeting targets related to poverty and literacy. Regarding poverty, the share of those living below the poverty line[4] has declined, though marginally from 46 percent in 2008 to 45 percent in 2010.

In terms of geographical locations, poverty has remained the same for North West but increased, relatively significantly, for the Northern Cape during 2008 and 2010—one hypothesis is that such an increase in the share of those below the poverty line in Northern Cape during 2008 and 2010 can be attributed to the effects of the global economic recession. It is in this context that it is strange to argue that South Africa is resilient to global economic crises. It is actually absurd when one thinks about the very high levels of the financialisation and internationalisation of the South African economy. Also, people who are effectively on the poverty line can easily fall below the poverty line due to an external shock such as a global economic crisis. As argued elsewhere, one needs to also bear in mind that the South African economy had been on its way into a recession even before the recent global economic recession.

Literacy rates improved effectively across all the provinces, including for the African populations, although marginally. Literacy is measured for those fifteen years and older. Interestingly, there is a marginal decline in literacy rates for the white population group and an increase in the share of the white population group that is below the poverty line.

Another important indicator of human development, or human poverty, is access to clean water sources. The percentage of those that lack access to clean water declined from 7 percent (in 2008) to 5 percent (in 2010). Water is important for other indicators, especially those that relate to health and/or mortality. The improvement of access to water, therefore, should be noted.

Of major concern, among other issues, is education, which remains a major challenge as will be discussed in detail in chapter 7. Gross enrolments have deteriorated rather significantly in a short period. For females, as an example, there is a decline from 77 percent to 67 percent and for Africans the decline is from 79 percent to 69 percent (2008–2010). The same trend can be discerned in the provinces.

Overall, gross enrolments have deteriorated. The deterioration in education statistics can also be seen in the education index in table 3—the education index measures a country's relative achievement in both adult literacy and combined primary, secondary, and tertiary gross enrolment. Table 4 also shows other indices of human development—the indices that make up the Human Development Index and the Human Poverty Index. The life expectancy index, one of the main variables for human development, has improved between 2008 and 2010. The life expectancy index measures the relative achievement of a country in life expectancy at birth. In the aggregate, it was 0.41 in 2008 and it was 0.46 in 2010. However, the index did not change for females (at 0.44). The province with a notable improvement is KwaZulu Natal (0.34–0.43). In simple terms, this implies that people are increasingly living slightly longer.

The deprivation index shows overall improvement; for the country as a whole, the index declined from 7.91 to 6.14 which is an improvement because the deprivation index is a measure of the level of deprivations. The human and poverty indices themselves show improvements, as table 5 depicts. It is insightful to compare human poverty indices measured for developing countries (HPI-1) and those for developed countries (HPI-2). HPI-1 consists of child nutrition status, access to clean water sources, and life expectancy. HPI-2 consists of indicators of access to employment as well as social inclusion, over and above life expectancy, and per capita income. I calculated both HPI-1 and HPI-2 for South Africa, and they both show improvements across the board. If South Africa were a developed country, levels of human poverty would still be decreasing.

The HDI has marginally improved. It went from 0.58 in 2008 to 0.59 in 2010. KwaZulu Natal, as table 4 indicates, has the most notable HDI improvement (0.49 in 2008 and 0.54 in 2010) while Gauteng has experienced a marginal decline from 0.68 in 2008 to 0.64 in 2010.

Another important issue that the human development calculations show is inequality in outcomes as a result of inequality of opportunity in South Africa. South Africa has one of the highest economic inequality measures in the world—it is reported to have a Gini Coefficient of 0.69 (Bhorat and Van der Westhuisen 2010). From a human development and human poverty perspective, there are significant differences in indices for the whites and Africans. For instance, the latest estimates show Africans as having an HDI of 0.54 while that for whites is 0.73. The interracial differences are also obvious in other measures that constitute the HDI. For instance, the GDP index of Africans is 0.38 while that of whites is 0.71—and whites have an almost zero deprivation index while Africans stand at 6.81 as shown in table 4.

Regarding income poverty, table 5 shows very high levels of poverty, especially for higher income poverty lines. Although income poverty has declined, particularly between 2005 and 2009, the percentage share of those living below the various poverty lines remains very high. For instance, in 2009, the income poverty line of R551.78 per person per month showed a staggering 46 percent of people living below the poverty line as table 5 indicates.

Therefore, the main point is that poverty remains very high in South Africa—and the 2009 and later figures may have increased as a result of the recent global economic recession and the general poor state of the economy and the labour market. Another key measure of poverty in South Africa is access to basic services. Basic services include water, sanitation, refuse removal, and electricity. Based on the Constitution, the country's policies and legislation recognise the need to prioritise access to basic services by the poor. However, in practice this has not proven to be the case. It goes without saying that the groups that suffer this lack of access are Africans, and mostly female generally. For example, according to the Socio-Economic Rights Institute (2013) in fourteen of the poorest South African municipalities (all rural and all in former homeland areas), over 50 percent of the population (each with an average of approximately 100,000 residents) have no sanitation provision. Water access and electricity connection are also a major challenge.

In addition, within the richer municipalities, those people based in the informal settlements suffer as a result of inadequate access to services while those in the more affluent areas enjoy the benefits of clean and safe water sources and up-to-standard sanitation, electricity connection, and a healthier living environment. One might argue that due to the general migration of men from rural areas into (peri)urban areas in search of economic opportunities, it is mostly African women who remain in the rural areas to take care of their families that suffer the most lack of access.

Looking at the 2013 Human Development Report, it would seem that South Africa's HDI has been increasing, albeit marginally, in the past few years. It should be noted that estimates in the 2013 Human Development Report are based on a new methodology and new data compared to previous reports. As table 6 shows, in 2010 South Africa's HDI was 0.604, and has steadily increased to 0.629 in 2012.

Similarly, as table 6 shows, per capita incomes have been increasing along with life expectancy although the increase in life expectancy has effectively been negligible. Other useful numbers in the 2013 Human Development Report relate to schooling: data implies that South Africans have, on average, five fewer years of school than expected. Since 1995, according to the 2013 Human Development Report, the expected years of schooling in South Africa is 13.1 years. The mean years of schooling has remained at 8.5 years since 2010. Overall, arguably, a firm foundation exists that can allow South Africa to achieve the noble ideals set out in the various policy and strategy documents of the government and the ruling ANC. As the book argues, policy clarity is critical if the challenges such as those relating to education are to be sufficiently addressed. Policy must be informed by a thorough understanding of the challenges at hand, which are ramifications of apartheid colonialism.

ECONOMIC INEQUALITY

Economic inequality has remained very high in South Africa. Arguably, given systemic and entrenched racist policies and legislation of the past, economic inequality—and many other types of inequalities—would have been much higher (if estimations were done). All estimates of income inequality in South Africa, using standard measures of economic inequality, place inequality above 0.60. It should be acknowledged that there is no single generally accepted or best measure of inequality, although the Gini Coefficient[5] is the widely used measure. In economics, there is an understanding, if not acceptance, that inequality measures perform differently under different kinds of income transfers. The Gini Coefficient, on one hand, is much less sensitive to income transfers between households if they lie near the middle of the income distribution compared to the tail end. The Atkinson Index, on the other hand, is strongly correlated with the extent of poverty and is, therefore, more "bottom-sensitive" than other measures. The Robin Hood Index is insensitive with respect to income transfers between households on the same side of the mean income.

As Frye, Farred, and Nojekwa (2011, 260) put it, "poverty and inequality in South Africa have a very clear racial bias as a result of the colonial and apartheid policies or racial discrimination and deliberate impoverishment." Similarly, Bhorat and Van der Westhuizen (2012, 14) have argued that "in the South African context, the strong inequality between racial groups as a result of apartheid has always been a significant driver of aggregate inequality." In essence, inequality in South Africa remains a racial phenomenon. In addition, racial inequality in South Africa is, first and foremost, a political question—more than it is an economic question.

Bernard Magubane (1979, 3) viewed "racial inequality...as an aspect of imperialism and colonialism."

From an economic perspective, income inequality is a function of the labour market in South Africa—the wage differentials in the labour market account for the high income inequality in South Africa (cf Leibbrandt et al 2010). Bhorat and Van der Westhuizen (2012) argue that income inequality in South Africa has to do with the structure of the economy. It might be in this context that Frye et al (2011) characterise South Africa's inequality as *structural inequality*. The restructuring of the South African economy, by implication, would redress income inequality. In chapter 7, I present concluding remarks on how the South African economy could be restructured.

A number of economists have concluded that economic inequality has increased during the first twenty years of democracy because intra-inequality, within the African group, has increased. Jeremy Seekings and Nicoli Natrass (2006) wrote a whole book on this, and since then numerous publications have been written effectively substantiating the argument that "race had given way to class" (Seekings and Natrass 2006, 377) and/or the "the basis of disadvantage shifted from race to class" (Seekings and Natrass 2006, 4). Bhorat and Van der Westhuizen (2012, 14), on the contrary, argue that "in the South African context, the strong inequality between racial groups as a result of apartheid has always been a significant driver of aggregate inequality." In fact, Bhorat and Van der Westhuizen (2012, 13) demonstrate that "it is very clear that African inequality remained virtually unchanged over the period with the 1995 and 2005 Lorenz curves almost indistinguishable. In contrast, the Lorenz curves for white individuals graphically confirm increasing inequality within this cohort over the period."

From historical experiences of exploitation and systematic exclusion of Africans, I consider the work of Bhorat and Van der Westhuizen (2012) more credible and convincing than those who argue that the increase in inequality during the first twenty years of democracy is a class question.

Another way of examining racial inequality is to look at asset ownership patterns. Although data is not readily available, indications are that whites remain with many more assets than Africans—land being the obvious case in point. For instance, white-owned commercial farmland in South Africa still comprises about 80 million hectares (Gumede 2014a). Another interesting illustration of asset inequality is that whites still own more cars than blacks. According to the South African Institute of Race Relations (SAIRR) (2013), in 2012, there were 2.4 million Africans owning cars compared to 2.6 million whites owning cars (in a country where Africans constitute 80 percent of the population and whites only 9 percent). The 2013 SAIRR report also indicates that, in 2012, 92 percent of whites whereas 84 percent of Africans owned a mobile phone.

Table 7, produced using Gelb (2004), Leibbrandt et al (2009), Bhorat et al (2012), and my own calculations using Statistics South Africa's data, actually demonstrates that all population groups have experienced some increase in (in-group) inequality—it is not convincing that the African population accounts for the significant increase in income inequality that post-apartheid South Africa is reported to be experiencing. In fact, income inequality for the African population appears to be relatively steady from 2005 to 2011 (for the latest available data). In a ten year period, from 1995 and 2005, as table 7 shows, there was a relatively significant increase in income inequality within the African population group (0.49 in 1995 to 0.56 in 2005); however, income inequality within the African population group has remained similar to the 2005 level at least until 2011.

Although discussion abounds concerning income inequality, there are no thorough studies that quantify income inequality beyond 2011. This could be due to a lack of relevant data that can be used to estimate the latest Gini coefficients. This is not to dispute widely held claims that income inequality has increased in South Africa. However, the assertion that the Gini coefficient has increased because income inequality within the African population group has increased is debatable. If anything, the period 2009–2011, as illustrated in table 8, suggests that a significant increase in income inequality occurred within the white population group. This, I argue, has to do with the structure of the economy which, in general, favours the white population group with a possibility of favouring some whites over others.

The South African economy has been enduring a decline—effectively a recession—since about 2008. For whites who have invested well, the recession has had little impact—in fact, they continue to reap the fruits of a skewed economy. Whites do not lose jobs just because the economy is shrinking. Also, it can be argued that whites have many possibilities for economic activity, such as pursuing business which could earn them more income than normal employment.

The labour market provides a plausible explanation for higher income inequality in South Africa, given the shift from apartheid to democracy: many Africans became gainfully employed, and the labour market created employment opportunities that increased wage differentials for the African population group.

It is also important to understand, as Richard Wilkinson and Kate Picket (2010) argue, that it is the perception of inequality that matters more than what numbers may suggest—this point is even more pertinent given that there are many measures of inequality and they all have methodological and fundamental shortcomings emanating from South Africa's ugly political history of white domination and racism. In fact, Richard Wilkinson and Kate Picket—in their insightful book—remind readers that inequality in itself, not the character of it per se, is bad for any society. It is also important to acknowledge that, as Joseph Stiglitz (2012) demonstrates in the case of United States, inequality slows economic growth and can result to economic instability, and that it is dangerous for political stability. In fact, it is critical to understand that Joseph Stiglitz attributes the increase in inequality to the top 1 percent of American society. In the case of South Africa, many studies confirm that whites continue to earn far more than Africans, for instance.

PUBLIC PROTESTS

Public protests have been on the increase, and are increasingly becoming violent. Adam Habib (2013, 13) indicates that "strikes and service delivery protests – numbering 12,654 and 11,033 in 2010 and 2013 respectively – continue to multiply." As indicated earlier, Southall (2010) views the increase in public protests as indicative of the ANC losing its ability to "shape and control society." Alexandra (2010, 25), however, argues that "since 2004, South Africa has experienced a movement of local protests amounting to a rebellion of the poor. This has been widespread and intense, reaching insurrectionary proportions in some cases." Gillian Hart (2013, 87) has characterised the "proliferating expressions of popular discontent [as] movements beyond movements."

The former Secretary General of Cosatu, Zwelinzima Vavi, described the increasing rate of service delivery protests as a "ring of fire closing in on major cities that could result in a Tunisia style revolution" (Mkokeli 2011). Njabulo Ndebele (2012,6), the former Vice Chancellor of the University of Cape Town and the Chairman of the Nelson Mandela Foundation, contended that "widespread service delivery protests may soon take on an organisational character that will start off as discrete formations and then coalesce into a full-blown movement."

Some attribute the increase in public protests to corruption and/or patronage politics. Ndletyana, Makhalemele, and Mathekga (2013, 16) argue that "patronage politics is not only a serious problem, it is also persistent. Consequently, community protests have not only been a frequent sight in our communities, but have also been violent." Others see the protests largely as typifying the communities' unhappiness as a result of poor service delivery—see for instance, Habib (2013), Hart (2013), and Alexandra (2010). One other view (cf. Brown 2015) sees public protests as epitomising new politics where citizens are insurgents. However, my view is that public service delivery protests in South Africa epitomise policy failure. The delay in policy reforms coincide with an increase in public protests. The weaknesses in policy thinking, emanating from

2008, coincide with a further increase in public protests. Social policy, in particular, required strengthening but was largely ignored. Economic policy was inappropriately reformed: AsgiSA was effected in 2006 but it was prematurely terminated in favour of the New Growth Path in 2010.

Indeed, as the data suggests, there was a dramatic surge in protests shortly after President Jacob Zuma first took office in 2009. Data from the Municipal IQ indicates that since 2008 more than 2 million protesters have taken to the streets every year, with most protests occurring in the Western Cape and almost half of all protests occurring in informal settlements. Both the Western Cape and Gauteng provinces effectively account for half of the protests nationwide, supporting the view that service delivery protests are largely an urban phenomenon (Karamoko and Jain 2010; 2011).

The *Business Day* reported that "2009 and 2010 together account for about two-thirds of all protests since 2004." The number of protests was ten times higher in 2009 than in 2004 and much higher in 2010. Data offered by Municipal IQ (2012), a local government and intelligence service in South Africa, also recorded that "35.76 percent of the service delivery protests documented between February 2007 and May 2011 took place between December 2008 and November 2009, a twelve-month period." The frequency of public protests rises during economic hardship, including so-called xenophobic attacks. It is not surprising that the months during the economic recession were characterised by higher levels of public protest activity than any other months in the previous years. Given that the global financial crisis and the subsequent global economic recession independently contributed to rising unemployment and reduced savings, it is likely that this period increased the frequency of service delivery protests as well (Karamoko and Jain, 2010; 2011).

Interestingly, public protests are high during winter months compared with summer months. Karamoko and Jain (2010; 2011) have advanced some of the possible reasons for this difference: electricity shortages, environment damages, and severe hardship that winter brings.

There are other issues about public protests that are worth highlighting. I have observed that those partaking in public protests, including xenophobic attacks, are relatively young. The lack of a comprehensive youth development policy and non-existent labour market policy are to blame for this; hence my view that public protests epitomise policy failure. Although Jeremy Seekings and Nicoli Nattrass (2005) raised a red flag on this issue, not much has been done to address it. Their argument was that "no significant policy shifts occurred [from apartheid to post-apartheid government] to stem the rise in unemployment" (Seekings and Nattrass 2005, 4).

Also, service delivery protests have taken a violent nature, with many being very disruptive and leading to intimidation and loss of life. Whilst South Africa has seen peaceful protests wherein protesters have mobilised marches handing over memoranda detailing lists of grievances, there are, however, many more instances where ward councillors get attacked in their homes, and instances of severe damage to state property. The hardships faced by citizens, which I predict would intensify, propels anger that results in violent protests.

Figure 1 suggests that 2009 was marred by a stark increase in service delivery protests relative to previous years. A significant number of the protests that took place were also violent (Municipal IQ 2014). It would seem that public protests have been on the rise since 2009 culminating in 2014. According to a research report by Karamoko and Jain (2011), approximately 55.64 percent of protests in 2010 were violent indicating an alarming rise from 38.13 percent in 2008. It appears that public protests have, over time, not only increased but also become more violent. As indicated earlier, Alexandra (2010, 25) sees public protests as "a rebellion of the poor."

People see patronage and/or corruption; they observe the intolerable economic inequality within the context of severe economic hardship. People are also compelled to respond violently because the security apparatus is unleashing violence on civilians—violence begets violence.

The killing of Andries Tatane and the spectre of tragic violence that the police meted on the Marikana miners are just a few of the high profile shameful cases of violence by the post-apartheid security-establishment, which through the South African Policy Service (SAPS), terrorises and kills innocent people regularly.[6] The legacy of apartheid colonialism rears its ugly head again: violence was a particular cornerstone of the apartheid regime. Africans were killed as though their lives were worthless. The post-apartheid government has not dealt with this painful past. Therefore, institutions that are supposed to protect civilians and safeguard this fledgling democracy actually terrorise ordinary people. The SAPS is leading the charge with trigger-happy cops.

There have also been instances of rising levels of xenophobia wherein foreign nationals are perceived to be benefitting from service delivery opportunities ahead of local people and have thus been attacked (Karamoko and Jain 2010; 2011). In these instances, foreigners have had their shops burned, looted, or vandalized during service delivery protests. Between 2000 and March 2008, sixty-seven people were reported to have died in what were identified as xenophobic attacks. In May 2008, a series of riots left sixty-two people dead (Hart 2013). In 2015, as I was finalising this book, attacks on foreign nationals took a very disturbing turn when gruesome attacks on foreigners in the KwaZulu Natal province sent shockwaves all over the world. It is worth noting though that South Africans, too, become victims of these attacks.

Since the attacks are believed to be motivated by xenophobia and generally affect Africans from the continent, they are often characterised as Afrophobia. Protesters accuse foreigners of taking the available work and businesses; many foreigners have been accused of willingly accepting lower wages during periods of chronic unemployment and severe economic hardship. Foreign nationals have also been accused of unfairly benefitting from the government's housing scheme by bribing government officials; there is a perception that some foreigners are involved in criminal activities such as drug trafficking and perpetuating prostitution. As a result, some municipalities have resorted to the forced removals of foreigners. The occurrence of such attacks appears to be a consequence of competition for scarce resources.

Since 2006, policy failures have manifested these ugly instances of violence. Of course, criminal elements also take advantage of such situations. The issue of xenophobic attacks deserves special attention. A concomitant result of the damage caused by the colonial apartheid system, South Africa has become a largely violent society. However, among the key issues is that post-apartheid South Africa needs to work harder to de-racialise its colonial apartheid economy, lest South Africa remain susceptible to xenophobic attacks. If these attacks are not adequately addressed, we may see the violence shifting focus from foreigners to tribal/civil wars. It is not inconceivable that black South Africans could turn against each other along ethnic lines, if transformation remains weak. It is also not farfetched to suggest that black South Africans could turn on white South Africans if the economy remains racialised with no visible reductions in other inequalities.

As argued in Gumede (2015b),[7] political inequality is one major issue that needs attention. Political patronage is fuelling political inequality in South Africa, among other challenges. Sidney Verba (2001, 2)[8] defines political inequality as referring to "the extent to which citizens have an equal voice over governmental decisions." Although racial inequality is still very pronounced, it is expected to be an issue for some time into the future. Among Africans there appears to be those that amass wealth overnight through political connections while many communities face severe socioeconomic hardship. One cannot discount the possible negative impacts of this on service delivery protests and/or xenophobic attacks.

The 2013 South African Reconciliation Barometer report by the Institute of Justice and Reconciliation (IJR) on the perceptions of South Africans regarding issues related to progress since 1994 presents interesting results. Table 8 illustrates selected aspects.

As table 8 indicates, there are many respondents to the survey who felt that many aspects of 'freedom' have worsened since 1994. Relative to those that feel that there are improvements, there are more who feel that employment opportunities and the gap between the rich and poor has worsened. In particular, 36.7 percent feel that the gap between the rich and poor has worsened (compared to 30.30 percent of those that feel that the gap has improved)—we should bear in mind that Richard Wilkinson and Kate Picket (2010) argue that it is the perception of inequality that matters most, and this has a greater influence than what numbers may suggest. Overall, 42.10 percent feel that employment opportunities have worsened (relative to 31.10 percent who feel that employment opportunities have improved). These perceptions speak volumes: the sense that any of the aspects of 'freedom' has worsened since 1994 is an indictment on the pursuit of justice and freedom. Notwithstanding, it is encouraging that there are those—not a negligible percent—that feel that there are improvements in the various areas since the advent of democracy in South Africa.

Fragmented Civic Society

Another related issue of importance is *civic participation*. The ruling party enjoys significant authority over policy outcomes. Policy changes over the years have largely relied on the political will of the ruling party as well as the courts, both of which have significant authority to determine policy outcomes. The judiciary has the advantage of constitutional supremacy and the ability to nullify or inform policy decisions of government or to force the government to review policy positions deemed contrary to the letter and law of South Africa's constitution.

Though the ruling political elite enjoy hegemony over the policy process, there is sufficient evidence that confirms that civic groups do play a significant role in shaping policy outcomes with a number of cases capturing how civic organizations can force the state or oblige it to amend public policy. This has largely been a result of court interdicts instituted by the courts in favour of civic conglomerates, wherein human rights lobby groups have successfully used the courts as an instrument of policy change, particularly in favour of minority groups.[9]

Noticeable in this regard has been the use of discursive spaces and the use of new narratives to influence policy outcomes, namely through social media such as Facebook, email, Twitter, MySpace accounts, and so forth to launch national campaigns, as well as the technical jargon relating to human rights and social justice, and imagery of victims to communicate people's stories and to present human faces. However, it is also important to note the limitations of civic society organisations, particularly the causes it has failed to see through such as food and electricity prices, housing provision, rising unemployment, and salary/wage increments.

The historic proximity of civic movements such as the Congress of South African Trade Unions (Cosatu) and the South African National Civic Organisation (Sanco) to the ruling party (i.e., ANC), both formally and informally, has limited its ability to change policy outcomes. The South African Communist Party (SACP) appears to have fallen into a similar trap. Rather than mobilising support through public action, for instance, Sanco has often opted to maintain a silent posture on critical questions facing its constituency. Civil society has been unable to partner constructively with other, more adversarial, social movements such as the Landless People's Movement to effect change. Since the advent of democracy, civil society has been largely unorganised and/or fragmented, which exacerbated the situation; ironically, civil society has often been unable to organise itself due to its heterogeneity. On one hand, it is perceived that government created this by alienating civil society. On the other, it is claimed that civil society organisations lack capacity to effectively engage government for social change.

Other Socio-Economic Dilemmas

With regards to poverty, South Africa has significantly reduced the number of people experiencing the worst levels of income poverty and other dimensions of poverty. Additionally, the country has achieved the Millennium Development Goals (MDGs) target of reducing the number of people living on less than $1.25 a day. The government's comprehensive social protection programme contributed to this success. The programme includes income support in the form of social grants, access to free education and primary health care for the poor, and provision of free basic services, such as water and electricity for the indigent people. That said, South Africa still has a large number of people in poverty—as indicated earlier in whichever measure used, at least 40 percent of South Africans live below some predetermined minimum living level.

On youth employment, the African youth in South Africa carry the biggest brunt of poverty, unemployment, and a lack of social security. The labour of youth is readily casualised, informalised, and externalised by the "invisible hand" of South Africa's labour market. The growing trend of youth unemployment and poverty is worrying, especially bearing in mind that the youth constitutes the majority of the populace, and that social security is a precondition for sustainable development and peace in societies in general. In countries emerging from colonial disharmony and conflict, access to employment for youth has proven integral to reconstruction and development processes.

Regarding education, South Africa has been successful in facilitating access to primary education; the country reached this target before its target of 2015. What is encouraging to note is that the number of girls attending primary, secondary, and tertiary education institutions has increased. Achievements in the attainment of education are not only good for girls who were previously deprived of an opportunity to attend school, but will also assist in reaching targets relating to other goals such as the empowerment of women as stipulated in the MDGs. The country also continues to invest in education because it believes that education is a catalyst to poverty eradication. It should, however, be emphasised that the attainment of numerical targets is not sufficient. The debate on the quality of education has been unyielding: the emerging consensus is that it is of poor quality and the curriculum is not well structured. It is noteworthy, however, that part of the challenge is that teachers are not well trained, which is a legacy of the Bantu education system.

On matters relating to health, South Africa has made progress in improving health care infrastructure and access to primary health care for all South Africans. However, increased access to health care—as is the case with education—has not yet translated into better health outcomes. Maternal and children mortality rates remain too high. Doctors, nurses, and teachers have also taken to the streets, protesting for better salaries and benefits. Hospitals have experienced mortalities while medical staff picket in the vicinity. Other hospitals, for the first time in their operational history, were closed due to strikes. The call for improved health care makes the case for national health insurance—which will ensure equal access to quality health care for all South Africans—even more convincing and imperative.

South Africa is viewed as a primarily corrupt state. The increasing nature of white collar corruption, both in the private and public sectors, raises serious concerns about South Africa's ability to achieve its developmental goals. South Africa is already ranked 55 out of 180 countries in Transparent International's 2009 Corruption Perception Index. Unless the state deals more decisively with corruption, the prospects of constructing a South African developmental state will diminish and remain yet another pipe dream.

Notwithstanding many positive developments, herewith, the challenges of socioeconomic development in South Africa remain immense. For instance, youth unemployment, structural poverty, corruption and white collar crime, gender-based violence, and other forms of violent crimes, racism and increasing racial polarisation, increasing urban poverty and food insecurity, among others, all remain challenges that threaten South

Africa's social fabric. These are surmountable challenges that require an agile and capable developmental state, as I have argued in the case of policy making in Africa (Gumede 2011c). The post-apartheid South African development experience appears to be following footsteps of the post-colonial African development experience. Within two decades of political independence, glaring cracks and intractable development dilemmas became accentuated. This is a result of political independence not being accompanied by robust reconfiguration of post-independent societies. South Africa should not fall into the same trap.

Conclusion

Race relations and racial inflections in the experience of poverty and delivery of basic services, gender discrimination, and economic inequality are the main aspects of development dilemmas that stand out in the South African context. All these issues are among the biggest intractable development challenges confronting democratic South Africa, and they are not easy to fix. As far as the South African economic structure and the legacy of colonialism are concerned, both poverty and inequality are structural and systemic. A comparative view of the levels of human development between Africans and non-Africans are notable: the inequalities engineered over three centuries will require radical transformation to dismantle.

To address poverty and inequality, the structure of the economy has to change. Restructuring the economic landscape in order to sustainably address poverty and inequality is complex. It is clear that the South African government, through policy prioritisation, recognises that certain groups (particularly Africans, females, the youth, the aged, and people with disabilities) need concerted attention. However, in practice, these very groups continue to define the overarching South African *development dilemma* as they remain the most disadvantaged in terms of human development and access to opportunities and services. Policy clarity is the most adequate solution. Race relations, on the other hand, require a different response: policy changes can only scratch the surface. To improve race relations, South African society needs reconfiguring, which is tricky. Cultural revolutions might assist. However, maintaining a suitable balance is complex, hence the possibility that the development dilemmas discussed could remain immutable. A clear and succinct vision for the society is needed instead of a longwinded and voluminous National Development Plan. South Africa needs a distinct vision for the economy and a well-defined socioeconomic development model.

The next chapter deals with this conceptual conundrum of the post-apartheid development experience.

Table 1. Human Development in South Africa and Selected Countries.

	1980	1990	2000	2005	2009	2010	2011
South Africa	0.564	0.615	0.616	0.599	0.61	0.615	0.619
India	0.344	0.41	0.461	0.504	0.535	0.542	0.547
Brazil	0.549	0.6	0.665	0.692	0.708	0.715	0.718
Botswana	0.446	0.594	0.585	0.601	0.626	0.631	0.633
Mauritius	0.546	0.618	0.672	0.703	0.722	0.726	0.728
Malaysia	0.559	0.631	0.705	0.738	0.752	0.758	0.761
China	0.404	0.49	0.588	0.633	0.674	0.682	0.687
United States	0.837	0.87	0.897	0.902	0.906	0.908	0.91
Norway	0.796	0.844	0.913	0.938	0.941	0.941	0.943

Source: Based on 2011 Human Development Report data

Table 2. Human Development Indicators.

	% below poverty line		Adult literacy		Lack of access to water		Gross enrolment	
	2008	2010	2008	2010	2008	2010	2008	2010
Gender								
Male	43	41	91.78	92.28	6.51	5.29	76.04	68.75
Female	49	48	89.18	89.07	7.27	5.72	77.42	67.33
Race								
African	55	53	88.58	89.11	8.67	6.72	79.32	69.33
Coloured	26	23	93.30	92.71	0.52	0.5	63.45	57.04
Asian/Indian	9	8	92.90	94.45	0	0.00	61.59	64.20
White	1	2	100.00	99.50	0	0.55	63.59	66.02
Province								
Western Cape	23	25	95.54	95.25	0.17	0.19	58.51	56.95
Eastern Cape	63	62	86.87	88.18	24.89	23.18	83.73	72.52
Northern Cape	33	38	88.07	89.46	0.37	0.89	69.91	65.37
Free State	45	44	93.47	94.06	0.52	0.04	78.39	69.90
KwaZulu Natal	62	56	85.48	85.84	13.86	9.8	78.29	65.04
North West	42	42	87.44	89.91	1.18	0.48	72.99	68.44
Gauteng	28	27	96.44	96.79	0	0.00	70.06	69.09
Mpumalanga	42	41	90.50	90.43	0.37	0.21	80.12	66.18
Limpopo	63	62	85.06	85	4.43	2.31	87.23	74.74
Total	46	45	90.40	90.56	6.91	5.52	76.72	68.05

Source: Calculated using the National Income Dynamics Study data[10]

Table 3. Indices for Human Development.

	Life expectancy index		Education index		GDP index		Deprivation index	
	2008	2010	2008	2010	2008	2010	2008	2010
Gender								
Male	0.38	0.46	0.87	0.84	0.48	0.49	7.33	6.39
Female	0.44	0.44	0.85	0.82	0.46	0.46	8.56	5.90
Race								
African	0.34	0.43	0.85	0.83	0.37	0.38	8.94	6.81
Coloured	0.62	0.43	0.83	0.81	0.47	0.50	4.10	4.27
Asian/Indian	0.86	0.73	0.82	0.84	0.65	0.65	0.00	0.00
White	0.82	0.68	0.88	0.88	0.72	0.71	4.12	0.28
Province								
Western Cape	0.57	0.54	0.83	0.82	0.52	0.52	1.40	2.38
Eastern Cape	0.42	0.38	0.86	0.83	0.35	0.40	15.96	12.65
Northern Cape	0.47	0.57	0.82	0.81	0.45	0.47	9.67	8.80
Free State	0.23	0.37	0.88	0.86	0.45	0.48	5.04	1.83
KZN	0.20	0.39	0.83	0.79	0.43	0.45	9.86	8.54
North West	0.44	0.43	0.83	0.83	0.45	0.45	7.73	6.21
Gauteng	0.63	0.50	0.88	0.88	0.55	0.53	5.45	3.27
Mpumalanga	0.34	0.35	0.87	0.82	0.50	0.48	5.80	2.34
Limpopo	0.47	0.48	0.86	0.82	0.37	0.38	8.95	6.65
Total	**0.41**	**0.46**	**0.86**	**0.83**	**0.47**	**0.47**	**7.91**	**6.14**

Source: Calculated using the National Income Dynamics Study data

Table 4. Human Development and Human Poverty.

	2008	2010	2008	2010	2008	2010
Total	0.58	0.59	27.11	21.42	46.95	42.35
Gender						
Male	0.58	0.60	25.88	20.80	47.25	42.11
Female	0.58	0.57	28.14	22.12	47.70	44.43
Race						
African	0.52	0.54	31.25	24.20	53.26	47.72
Coloured	0.64	0.58	10.51	16.58	31.42	34.64
Asian/Indian	0.78	0.74	4.92	3.85	19.12	9.66
White	0.80	0.73	10.13	8.12	12.43	12.61
Province						
Western Cape	0.64	0.63	14.40	10.52	28.84	34.54
Eastern Cape	0.54	0.54	23.35	29.36	54.51	52.52
Northern Cape	0.58	0.62	27.23	12.96	41.69	31.79
Free State	0.52	0.57	37.27	26.90	52.43	48.95
KZN	0.49	0.54	48.11	28.68	62.67	49.33
North West	0.57	0.57	25.59	16.03	44.24	48.90
Gauteng	0.68	0.64	10.28	28.89	34.39	32.19
Mpumalanga	0.57	0.55	40.43	29.00	45.54	53.56
Limpopo	0.57	0.56	19.44	23.18	48.25	46.71
Total	**0.58**	**0.59**	**27.11**	**21.42**	**46.95**	**42.35**

Source: Calculated using the National Income Dynamics Study data

Table 5. Income Poverty in South Africa, 2005–2009.

	Percentage of population living below various poverty lines (in 2009 constant Rand from GHS)	
	2005	2009
Expenditure Poverty Line [R551.78 per person per month]	70	65
Income Poverty Line [R551.78 per person per month]	59	46
Expenditure Poverty Line [R298.17 per person per month]	54	49
Income Poverty Line [R298.17 per person per month]	40	27
Expenditure Poverty Line [R149.08 per person per month]	31	25
Income Poverty Line [R149.08 per person per month]	23	12

Source: Based on Development Indicators data[11]

Table 6. Human Development in South Africa, 1980–2012.

	Life expectancy	Expected years of schooling	Mean years of schooling	GNI per capita (2005 PPP$)	HDI
1980	56.9	11.1	4.8	8,399	0.57
1985	59.8	11.1	4.8	7,892	0.581
1990	61.5	11.4	6.5	7,671	0.621
1995	59.9	13.1	8.2	7,350	0.65
2000	54.8	13.1	8.2	7,462	0.622
2005	51.1	13.1	8.2	8,420	0.604
2010	52.2	13.1	8.5	9,307	0.621
2011	52.8	13.1	8.5	9,463	0.625
2012	53.4	13.1	8.5	9,594	0.629

Source: Based on Human Development Reports data

Table 7. Gini Coefficient by Population Group.[12]

	1975	1995	2005	2009	2011
African	0.47	0.49	0.56	0.54	0.55
White	0.36	0.39	0.45	0.39	0.42
Indian	0.51	0.45	0.53	0.49	0.45
Coloured	0.45	0.49	0.58	0.52	0.53

Sources: Gumede (2015b, 97)

Table 8. Perception of South Africa's Progress Since 1994.

Economic circumstances	
Worsened	24.00%
Improved	39.50%
Race relations	
Worsened	17.40%
Improved	44.00%
Employment opportunities	
Worsened	42.10%
Improved	31.10%
Hope for your future	
Worsened	25.40%
Improved	39.10%
Gap between rich & poor	
Worsened	36.70%
Improved	30.30%
Personal Safety	
Worsened	26.00%
Improved	37.80%

Source: 2013 South African Reconciliation Barometer

Figure 1. Average Number of Public Protests, 2004–2014.

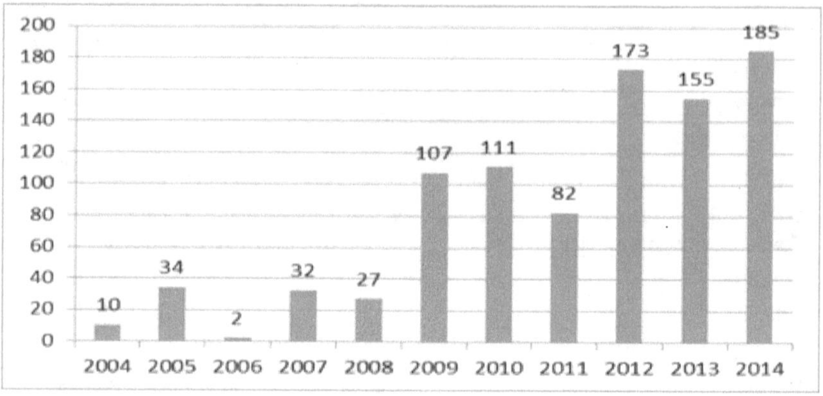

Source: Municipal IQ Hotspots Monitor, 2014.

Notes

1. Institute of Justice and Reconciliation's Transformation Audit (2010).
2. Literacy refers to the ability to read and write while the Gross Enrolment Ratio is calculated as total enrolment in a specific level of education, regardless of age, expressed as a percentage of the eligible official school age (i.e. 7–18 years) population.
3. Calculations or estimations are based on the National Income Dynamics Study (NIDS) datasets for 2008 and 2010.
4. South Africa still does not have an official poverty line. I used R515 per person per month in real 2008 rands. The NPC has recently proposed a poverty line of R418 per capita in 2009 prices (NPC 2012).
5. The Gini Coefficient ranges between 0.0 and 1 – perfect income inequality would have Gini coefficient of 1 and perfect equality would be 0. Another economic measure of inequality is the Lorenz Curve which is a graphical representation of the relationship between the cumulative percentage of income and the cumulative percentage of (ordered) population.
6. During the finalisation of this, four people had just been killed by the police during a public service delivery protest in Mothotlung near Brits, North West.
7. Gumede, V. 2015. Inequality in Democratic South Africa, in Mangcu, X., ed., 2015, *The Colour of Our Future: Does Race Matter in Post-apartheid South Africa*, Johannesburg: Wits Press.
8. Verba, S. 2001. Thoughts about Political Equality: What Is It? Why Do We Want It? Paper prepared for the Inequality Summer Institute, Harvard University.
9. Judgments include: obliging the state to the provision of anti-retro viral treatment to the poor, legalising same-sex marriages. and full abortion rights, etc.
10. The National Income Dynamics Study (NIDS) is a longitudinal survey and or panel study whose data is collected at 2-year intervals: 2008 was the inception year and 2010 was the second data collection phase. I use this data in particular because, when I was in the Presidency, I led the project that resulted to the NIDS and I have high confidence in it. The NIDS can be accessed freely at the South African Labour and Development Research Unit (SALDRU) at the University of Cape Town.

11. The Ministry of Monitoring and Evaluation in The Presidency regularly releases data, which is publicly available. The dataset is called Development Indicators.
12. Gini coefficients for 2009 and 2011 were calculated using Statistics South Africa's 2009 Living Conditions Survey and 2011 Income and Expenditure Survey.

Chapter 3

The Post-apartheid Development Experience

> The immediate and imperative interests of all sections of the South African people demand the carrying out of a national democratic revolution which will overthrow the colonialist state of White supremacy and establish an independent state of National Democracy in South Africa. The main content of this revolution is the national liberation of the African people.
>
> (The Road to South African Freedom 1962)

Introduction

There is a significant number of multiple factors and confluences that conspire in complicating a theory or hypothesis that could explain why socioeconomic development has not been as expected in South Africa. There is a myriad of factors, with far-reaching implications and ramifications, which characterise post-apartheid South African society. There are some people that take a rather simplistic stance regarding the development challenges facing post-apartheid South Africa. It has become commonplace to attribute challenges confronting South Africa to, for instance, corruption, poor leadership, and a lack of capacity.

The fundamental developmental challenge facing South Africa is more complex than meets the eye. Some of relatively recent books that have wrestled, to a significant extent, with this complexity include those by Ivor Chipkin (2007), Sampie Terreblanche (2012), and more recently Adam Habib (2013), Gillian Hart (2013), Lawrence Hamilton (2014), and John Saul and Patrick Bond (2014). Then there are those that appear rather simplistic in relation to what the fundamental challenge facing South Africa is. For instance, Jeffrey Herbst and Greg Mills (2015) suggest that the fundamental issue about South Africa relates to creating an enabling environment for economic growth. As we shall see in this chapter, and as already captured in the previous chapters, the challenge facing South Africa is a lot more complex and the solution is not just the creation of an enabling environment for economic growth. Granted, the economy is very important and ensuring that it grows is important—and more critical is that there is equitable sharing of the economy. The fundamental challenge has to do with apartheid colonialism and its ramifications—and the global distribution of power as well as state-capital relations, which also play a role in limiting the extent to which South Africa can advance or ensure inclusive development in particular. Herbst and Mills (2015, 39) do acknowledge that "the burden of the past continues to weigh on South Africa."

BACKGROUND

An apt starting point should be the acknowledgement that South Africa is a damaged bourgeois society—the average South African is a confused, angry, and violent citizen. South Africa is a troubled country—the liberation project is incomplete and the nation remains in a state of flux and is unsettled. South Africa is also a bipolar nation: there are moments of inexplicable euphoria and periods of severe depression. The miasma characterising South Africa further compounds what it means to be a

South African. South Africans appear unclear about their geographic and ideological affiliation. For instance, it is not uncommon for a South African to talk about 'going to Africa' when travelling to another African country. Also, Africans appear to underperform in many endeavours—this, it would seem, has to do with a sense of entitlement and general disregard of quality and high performance.

Africans in South Africa need to find themselves while whites must confront their deep-seated prejudices.[1] However, the late Neville Alexander had a differing view. Alexander (2013, 131) said of South Africa, "ours [as] a nation of dynamic cultural tributaries and streams that both flow into an ever-forming and ever-changing mainstream and are at the same time influenced by its fluidity." In my view, Steven Bantu Biko[2] remains the most appropriate source and inspiration for addressing the question of (South) Africanness. It is no wonder why the Boers killed him. Of the most direct injunctions Biko (1996, 23) made was that "white liberals must leave blacks to take care of their own business while they concern themselves with the real evil in our society—white racism—their presence among us is irksome and of nuisance value. It removes the focus of attention from essentials..." It seems to me that Africans must confront their demons while whites, separately, address their racism or white privilege and white supremacy before we can begin a proper process of reconciliation and nation building. We should not take for granted the damage that apartheid colonialism caused on both blacks and whites—of course more on Africans.

Another salient characteristic of the post-apartheid South Africa relates to the configuration of state-market relations. The South African society, under the leadership of a seemingly emasculated state, is under siege from the private sector. Like in most parts of the world, the government itself appears to be captured by capital. Africa as a whole suffers from a similar predicament. For South Africa, there is a significant overlap between the apartheid state market relations and the post-apartheid state market relations. The market or capital is privileged, over the people or against development. In essence, both the apartheid regime and the post-apartheid government allowed the private sector to operate as it desired. Roger Southall (2010) terms this the "reform bargain." Arguably, this "reform bargain" or what others have called "elite transition" and "elite compromise" maintained white privilege. It might very well be that the post-apartheid government could not be allowed to temper with whites. The global order, and so-called superpowers, must have ensured that South Africa's democracy is born and remains in chains, as Noami Klein (2007) would put it.

The challenge of development is indeed a historical one, and for South Africa it has to do with the manner in which the "South African nation" was created. Thabo Mbeki, former president of South Africa, addressing a seminar in Canada in 1978, contended that "the landing of the employees of the Dutch East India Company at the Cape of Good Hope, in 1652, represented in embryo the emergence of class society in our country. And that class society was bourgeois society in its infancy. The settlers of 1652 were brought to South Africa by the dictates of that brutal period of the birth of the capitalist class which has been characterised as the stage of the primitive accumulation of capital."

Sabelo Ndlovu-Gatsheni (2013,151) further argues that "the complex imperial and colonial encounters (read disarticulations) involving the Afrikaners, the British and the wars of conquest and resistance of the late nineteenth century and the early twentieth centuries also formed the broader discursive terrain within which the idea of South Africa developed as a contested concept with a racial tinge." Ivor Chipkin (2007,189) concludes that "in the absence of any traditional unifying principles, the identity of South Africans is elusive." Interestingly, Gillian Hart (2013, 6) makes a point that at the point of opening up political space, in 1990, the "South African nation was deeply in question...it had to be conjured up into existence from the rubble of a deeply divided society."

It might very well be that the existence of what we know as a South African nation is actually a myth. The argument that Biko (1996, 22) made still has relevance today:

> the myth of integration must be cracked and killed because it makes people believe that something is being done when in actual fact the artificial integrated circles are a soporific on the blacks and provide a vague satisfaction for the guilt-stricken whites.

Bantu Biko was correct: the various initiatives to strengthen "social cohesion"[3] become water under the bridge. Having a government that appears to be uncaring and irreverent about human development worsens matters. Social cohesion and nation building requires that there is unity, coherence, functionality, and pride (Gumede 2008a). It increasingly appears that all these important aspects are withering away.[4] Chapter 5 deals with these issues (i.e., the national question) in detail.

The gist of the South African challenge therefore has to do with apartheid colonialism and its profound legacy that lingers on. As indicated above, the formation of what we now know as South Africa is part of the bigger problem. A key outcome of the sophisticated brutal system of white domination and discriminatory policies of the apartheid government have led to what can be called a "culture" of violence and a disregard for the value of human life as well as disrespect for oneself. Arguably, this—the experience of apartheid colonialism—should be a starting point towards correcting the psychosocial, economic, cultural, spiritual, social, and political challenges confronting South Africa. Achille Mbembe (2001) points that colonial regimes in Africa never hesitated to use "brute force" and categorises the various forms of their violence into foundational violence, legitimating violence, and maintenance violence.[5]

Policies, particularly socioeconomic transformation policies, have to respond to this profound historical experience and its legacy in the form of racism, ethnicity, tribalism, sexism, inequality, and poverty among others. Therefore, a paramount programme for transformation should include thought liberation—liberating the mind, changing the mindset, and correcting the value system. Scholars of decolonial thought, as will be discussed later in this chapter, talk of decolonisation as a distinct liberation project from the ending of colonialism. Others, such as John Saul, argue that the South African development challenge can be attributed to incomplete liberation (Saul 2012).

Before delving into the South African development experience, the chapter starts with a brief review of the Africa-wide post-colonial development experience. I draw extensively on the works of Claude Ake, Frantz Fanon, Bade Onimode, Thandika Mkandawire, Adebayo Adedeji, Samir Amin, Patricia McFadden, Ibbo Mandaza, and Sabelo Ndlovu-Gatsheni in my review of the post-colonial African development experience. I then advance a theory about the post-apartheid South African development experience. The theory presented centres on the state-market relations configured on the eve of South Africa's political independence. In essence, drawing on the works of Sampie Terreblanche, Hein Marias, and Patrick Bond, among others, the development experience of post-apartheid South Africa had to do with the "elite transition."

The compromises derived from the political negotiations resulted in a settlement that gave advantages to capital over people. Sampie Terreblanche (2012) contends that the deal that favoured the private sector was sealed in the 1980s already. Adam Habib (2013, 20–202) argues that South Africa faces what he calls an "accountability deficit" and demonstrates that "the balance of power in favour of the business community explains the failure of the social pact of the 1990s." Gillian Hart (2013, 6) suggests that a better framework for understanding post-apartheid South Africa is through better appreciating "simultaneous practices and processes of *de-nationalisation* and *re-nationalisation.*"[6] As indicated, Roger Southall (2010, 5) sees "reform bargain" as a mechanism that "facilitated South Africa's success [which] was underpinned by the new government's commitment to providing the opportunity for large scale business to internationalise." The overriding theme appears to be the configuration of state-market relations as an Achilles heel for post-apartheid socioeconomic development.

Post-colonial African Development Experience

Africans have continued to suffer from large-scale underdevelopment and marginalisation, as succinctly captured by Walter Rodney (1973). The various development strategies that were put in place since the dawn of Africa's political independence have unsuccessfully developed the continent and Africans. The nationalist leaders that fought for independence from the colonial masters can be said to have been driven by a passion to develop the various countries on the continent, but their efforts have effectively come to naught. In the first decade of independence various African countries recorded levels of growth that were comparable to other parts of the developing world (Adedeji 2002). However, this achievement did not last long as the combination of domestic and international forces, and the political economy conditioning these countries effectively emasculated the process of development on the continent.

At a domestic level, the political environment became authoritarian as a majority of post-independence leaders, hiding under the banner of nationalism and national unity, became intolerant of opposition. As Mkandawire (2005) argues, these leaders felt that fast-track rapid development made a one-party state an immediate imperative. The intra-class conflict that ensued among the political elite led to social disorder, violence, and civil wars in different parts of Africa (Ndlovu-Gatsheni 2013). Such social disorders also provided convenient excuses for the military to stage various coups and counter coups in many African countries (Gowan 2001). In essence, the leaders that steered Africa into political liberation maintained the authoritarian nature and violent character of the colonial state into the post-colonial period. The colonial state was entirely anti-democratic as it relied exclusively on force to achieve its sole objective of exploitation and expropriation of natural resources in the interests of colonial head offices in London, Paris, Portugal, Belgium, and Berlin.

While the naïve and totalistic conception of nationalism created a process that stifled the development process in Africa, several contradictory and inherent factors were also responsible for the peripheral position of the continent in the global capitalist system. First, in the list of these factors, is the nature of the political economy that was bequeathed to the continent by the departing colonialists. As Claude Ake (1980) argues, the structural disarticulation that the colonial administrations created for post-independence Africa emanates from an extractive and exploitative economic system that was practiced on the continent. These diabolical colonial administrations were basically interested in mineral exploitation and this logic of exploitation informed the type of infrastructure that they established in the form of roads, rail system, and ports. Besides, Claude Ake further argues that the introduction of wage labour, which was occasioned by taxation, led to rural-urban migration. This singular act grossly dislocated the prospect of an agrarian revolution which should ordinarily precede industrial revolution (Ake 1980). There were many distortions that colonisers introduced to Africa's natural economy, as Archie Mafeje (2003) argues with regard to land ownership.

The exogenous factors that have shaped development in post-colonial Africa can be divided into different phases: global politics of the Cold War, the oil crisis of the 1970s, the collapse of the Soviet Union, and the triumph of market capitalism over socialism in an era of neo-liberal hegemony (see Spero and Hart 2010). However, the totality of the failure of development strategies in Africa can be traced to the incomplete decolonisation of the political economy, knowledge production, mental constructs (especially of the leaders), culture, and language on the continent (Ndlovu-Gatsheni 2013). Corruption, which has led to the pauperisation of the citizens, has also been a significant factor. Dependence on aid and foreign assistance has also obfuscated development on the continent.

During the Cold War, Africa was used as a pawn in the chess game of power between the West and the East. The ideological battle on communism and capitalism between these two blocs found eloquent expression in Africa as development efforts were either supported or opposed on account of which ideological lineage the country tilted towards. The politics of the Cold War had destructive effects on the African political economy as both the West and the East propped up leaders that were sympathetic with their ideologies—often with disastrous consequences. Radical and progressive leaders in Africa were either toppled by military coups or assassinated by agents of capitalist proponents who feared that such leaders might consolidate anti-capitalist ideologies. Examples of such victims of power play between the East and West are Patrice Lumumba of Congo, Amilcar Cabral of Carpe Verde, Kwameh Nkrumah of Ghana, Thomas Sankara of Burkina Faso, and Murtala Mohammed of Nigeria.

The oil crisis of the 1970s was a double-edged sword for the development trajectory of Africa. While it brought much needed revenues to oil-exporting countries like Nigeria, it led to serious macroeconomic problems for non-oil exporting countries. For the latter, the flush of unexpected revenues provided an unfortunate basis for massive corruption, waste, and mismanagement and loss of focus on the development of priority sectors. In Nigeria, for example, the sudden oil wealth led to the neglect of agriculture, which had contributed significantly to its economic growth from independence to the early 1970s. Contestation over oil wealth not only led to a gruelling 30-month civil war, but also created a perverse incentive for the centralisation of the economy as the central government under the military government became extremely powerful in determining the basis of allocation of revenues among other tiers of government (Olukoshi 2004).

The energy crisis of the 1970s and the slump in international commodity markets led to serious macroeconomic difficulties for many African countries. It was in a bid to solve these problems that African countries found themselves entrapped in a debt burden with private financial institutions in the West such as the Paris Club, the London Club, and several others under the supervision of the neoliberal International Monetary Fund (IMF). Even though most of these debts have been correctly classified as odious debts (see Adams 1991; Onimode 1988), the IMF made debt repayment as conditions for further loans required to stabilise African economies.

Based on the 1981 Berg Report entitled *Accelerated Development in Sub-Saharan Africa* prepared for the World Bank, the state in Africa was seen as the major obstacle to economic development. The Report coincided with the ascendance of neo-liberal economic doctrine as the philosophical touchstone for economic development both in the North and the South (Harvey 2007). The need to remove the distortions created by the state led to the World Bank and IMF recommendations that in order to overcome its development challenges, Africa needed to reduce the role of the state in economic management. As discussed by Gumede (2015d), it was argued that the role of the state should be limited to creating a conducive environment in the form of security of investment, provision and protection for property rights as well as provision of law and order for business to thrive. Economic policies such as the liberalisation of finance, trade, investment, deregulation, and privatisation were recommended as necessary requirements for facilitating economic growth and development (World Bank 1981).

These policies were not just recommended but were made preconditions for accessing loans and development assistance from the World Bank and associated institutions as well as developed countries. The package of reform associated with this policy was implemented under the structural adjustment programmes (SAPs) in Africa. As several African scholars have argued, the SAPs did not just fail to bring about socioeconomic development in Africa, they effectively emasculated and destroyed the state's capacity to plan and implement development strategies on the continent—SAPs also facilitated further asymmetric insertion of African countries into the global capitalist system (Olukoshi 1995; Soludo and Mkandawire 1989; Mkandawire 2001a; Shivji 2009).

Post-colonial African countries have devised several development strategies to extricate the continent and its people from the shackles of underdevelopment and marginalisation. As indicated in Adedeji (2002) and Shivji (2009), some of these strategies include:

- The Lagos Plan of Action for Economic Development in Africa.
- African Priority Programme for Economic Recovery.
- The African Alternative Framework to Structural Adjustment Programme.
- The African Charter for Popular Participation and Development.

As Adedeji (2002) recounts and Shivji (2009) reiterates, these strategies recognised and emphasised the need for self-reliance, industrialisation, regional and continental integration, active involvement of the state in enhancing peoples' welfare, and fostering participatory governance. However, as Adedeji (2002, 3) laments, "every attempt that has been made by Africans to forge their future and to craft their own indigenous development strategies and policies has been pooh-poohed by the international financial institutions with the support, or at least, the connivance of the donor community." In the place of these endogenously crafted development strategies are exogenously designed ones, which, according to Adebayo Adedeji (2002, 4), are informed by the Development Merchant System (DMS):

> Under which foreign crafted economic reform policies have been turned into a new kind of special goods, which are largely and quickly financed by the operations of the DMS, regardless of the negative impact of such policies on the African economies and polities.

The basis of financing the reform policies by the DMS provides the latitude and unrestrained freedom that they have to define, describe, direct, and prescribe the forms, content, and substance of the reform packages, usually in tandem with the DMS's idea of what development should be about. By so dictating the development strategies for Africans, the continent was denied the opportunity to execute endogenously designed development strategies. The culpability of African leaders in surrendering the development process to the logic of global capital cannot be denied. Post-independence African leaders have surreptitiously, and possibly also inadvertently, formed alliances with global capital in what Robinson (2004) calls the Transnational Capitalist Class (TCC). African liberation leaders' sense of dependence and naïve expectation of partnership with the global capitalist class is succinctly captured by Adebayo Adedeji (2002, 11), in the context of the New Partnership for Africa's Development (Nepad):

> There is always a child-like naivety among African leaders and policy makers that rhetoric and reality are the same and that claiming ownership is tantamount to having ownership. It is the Africans who are claiming that they are forging a partnership. The other side will no doubt continue to see it as a donor-recipient relationship.

Arguably, it is this "child-like naivety" that informed the New Partnership for African Development which is the latest of the development strategies on which Africa hopes to achieve its developmental objectives in the twenty-first century. While Nepad received support from the international community, it is full of contradictions as it based on the assumption of autonomous development while also relying on the West to provide huge amounts in development assistance. As Olukoshi (2002) argues, Nepad was accepted by the international community because it is more or less a replication of the much discredited and failed structural adjustment programme of the 1980s.

The development process in Africa cannot make sense until there is a conscious effort to decolonise the process itself, among many other aspects of Africa that need complete liberation. The decolonisation process must involve a deconstruction of the African leaders' mentality, a despatialisation of the arbitrary and artificial boundaries that the colonialists bequeathed on Africa and an intellectual redirection of the orientation of the citizens from waiting to act by holding the government accountable at all levels, as argued by Thabo Mbeki.[7]

It is in the light of the conundrum of development processes in Africa that the developmental state agenda in South Africa must be located. The political climate in post-apartheid South Africa shares several resemblances with other African countries gained after independence in the 1960s and 1970s. Although the NLM has been clear about its redistributive programme, the policies pursued in the post-apartheid dispensation could only deliver a different outcome. Twenty years after political majority rule in South Africa, the developmental state agenda remains rhetoric. For South Africa, and Africa as a whole, the process of development must be anchored on the logic of decolonisation both in theory and praxis.

State-Market Relations in South Africa

It would seem that the desire and the commitment of South Africa's leadership to achieve a developmental state must be located within the context of the global matrix of power,[8] under which South Africa is framed and under which it functions as a post-colonial state. This requires a historical excursion into the processes that led to the end of the repugnant racist apartheid regime and the events that continue to shape the evolution and the character of the state under a majority democratic rule.

South Africa has gone through various tragic experiences of "plunder, exploitation and enclave or bifurcated development" (Pillay 2010, 33). The evolution of the post-apartheid South African state, however, cannot be divorced from the colonial apartheid state. The state-market relations that South Africa has today could be seen as a continuation of the colonial apartheid state-market relations. Terreblanche (2012, 40) argues that "in the history of South Africa since 1652 a great variety of capitalist corporations have succeeded in 'identifying' themselves so triumphantly with successive political authorities (or with successive states) that they took over the states and (mis)used them to promote the narrow *class interests* of the capitalist/corporatists class to the detriment of society at large." In other words, the post-apartheid state, like the apartheid state, surrendered wittingly or unwittingly to the market.

The emergence of South Africa as a country is a complex one, as indicated earlier. This complexity is defined by the multiple identities of the peoples whose claim is not only belonging but whose ownership remains mired in controversy. As Sabelo Ndlovu-Gatsheni (2013, 151) argues, the idea of South Africa emerged as a figurative expression and has a long pedigree dating back to the 1830s. In this regard, Marks and Trapido (1987) argued that:

> In the 1870s at the beginning of mineral revolution, South Africa was a geographical expression. Pre-capitalist and capitalist modes of production existed side by side, as did state forms of varying sizes with their own ruling groups and systems of exploitation. There were two British colonies, two ostensibly politically independent republics and numerous still autonomous independent African politics. All these were multi-ethnic and multi-lingual, although not all languages and ethnicities were equal. Colonialists of British and European descent lived side by side in the colonies with large numbers of indigenous peoples, and in Natal with indentured labourers from the Indian sub-continent; African kingdoms were equally heterogeneous entities, composed of peoples of different origins (cited in Ndlovu-Gatsheni 2013, 151).

The next section presents a historical and theoretical perspective that provides a framework for understanding what has been conceived of as South Africa and illuminates the reasons why the liberation project appears unable to deliver a developmental state in South Africa.

South Africa in the Global Matrix of Power

The idea of a South Africa was also influenced by the contradictions in the power plays which manifest "betwixt clashes and syntheses between imperial and colonial imperatives, annexations, negotiations, reconciliations and unions that were invariably shaped by diverging and converging nationalisms of the English, Afrikaners and Africans" (Ndlovu-Gatsheni 2013, 151). The economic history of South Africa owed much to mineral extractions which started in the 1870s. The growth of manufacturing and the retreat of agriculture are directly linked to the dependence of the economy on mining and mineral exploitation. As Seeraj Mohamed (2010) argues, "historically, economic development in South Africa has been centred around extractive activities in mining and mineral sectors." According to Mohamed, the state and the mining industry have been working together to support the growth of manufacturing which has a strong link to what Fine and Rustomjee (1996) describe as the Mineral-Energy-Complex, a form of political compromise between large English mining interests and the large Afrikaner business and political establishment. Mohamed further stated the obvious but important point that the economic history of South Africa has been characterised by the "politics of oppression of black South Africans and the strict control over black workers" (Mohamed 2010, 44).

Paradoxically, just as the political economy of South Africa was a compromise between the global capital (which was represented by the Mineral-Energy-Complex) owned by the minority white and Afrikaner population during apartheid, the post-apartheid political economy is also a compromise between the African majority ruling ANC and the white minority who hold greater power in finance capital. In other words, even though the economy has undergone some restructuring with the transition to democracy, nothing much has changed as the economy is still subject to the control, manipulation, and exploitation of the global capitalist system (Saul 2012). Even RW Johnson (2015, 15) acknowledges that "the key to understanding South Africa's development lies in its integration into a world capitalist political economy."

The power play between the state and the market was evident during the difficult negotiations period between the apartheid government and the National Liberation Movement. While the ANC was desirous of a constitution that would ensure that the majority African population can form a government, the white minority represented by the National Party was concerned about the safety and continuity of the massive investment that they had in the country. In the Janus-faced configuration of power that ensued, the latter had the upper hand. Adam Habib (2013, 28) argues that "despite the illusions of activists and union-aligned academics, the corporate sector had decidedly more economic leverage than the union movement."

Sampie Terreblanche (2002) has been even more graphic in his narration of the events that transpired during the informal negotiations that preceded the assumption of office by the ANC in 1994. Terreblanche (2002, 96) relays that:

> The main characteristic of every phase of the All African Convention-led search for a new accumulation strategy was that the supreme goal of economic policy should be to attain a high economic growth rate and that all objectives should be subordinated to this. By convincing ANC leaders to accept the All African Convention's approach, the corporate sector in effect persuaded or forced the ANC to move away from its traditional priority, namely to uplift the impoverished black majority socially and economically.

The compromise made at this critical conjunction, which to a certain extent was in deferment to the global neo-liberal orthodoxy (made worse by the collapse of the Soviet Union), feeds into the structure of the economy in post-apartheid era. The elite compromise that the ANC leaders made with the corporate sector led to the effective abandonment of a key political-economic ideology on which the ANC rose to power, that is the National Democratic Revolution (NDR). Ivor Chipkin (2007) and Gillian Hart (2013), among others, discuss the NDR in detail in their respective books. I also discuss the NDR in chapters 4 and 5. Some have argued that the adoption of the neo-liberal orthodoxy by the ANC leaders has almost completely undermined the authority of the state and hindered the implementation of the developmental state model. As Terreblanche (2002, 97) further argues,

> by agreeing in the 'Statement' (*IMF inspired Statement on Economic Policy*), to contain expenditure, not to increase taxes, to maintain fiscal balance, and to lower the government deficit in order to prevent the danger of macroeconomic populism and attract FDI, the ANC committed itself –before the election of 1994 – to a macroeconomic and fiscal policy that clearly excluded a comprehensive redistribution policy for addressing the predicament of the poorest half of the population ...as soon as the ANC's leaders agreed to the Statement, they were trapped in the formidable web of the domestic corporate sector and the international financial establishment, represented by the IMF and the World Bank

It has been argued that the adoption of the 1996 Growth, Employment and Redistribution (GEAR) strategy was a clear testimony to the unrestrained insertion of the South African economy into the global capitalist system. Terreblanche (2002, 73) argues that despite the failure of GEAR to deliver on its promises, the hegemonic power of the corporate sector over the South African economy continues apace with the adoption of other neo-liberal inspired policies such as privatisation, relaxation of exchange controls, independence of the Central Bank, inflation targeting, and the permission given by the government to big corporations to move their listings to the United Kingdom and the United States of America.

Seeraj Mohamed makes an important point that the offshore listings that the government of South Africa permitted the corporate sector to effect have allowed the captains of industry who live and work as businessmen in both the global North and South Africa to change their power relationship with the new South African state. This permissiveness also gives them control over their assets in South Africa as well as on the movement of their capital (Mohamed 2010, 46). The corporate sector in South Africa has aligned with the global capitalist power brokers to exert pressures on the state to relinquish control over economic policy to the former—Gillian Hart (2013), as indicated earlier, characterises this as de-nationalisation.

The acquiescence of the ANC to such pressures came as a surprise to many. However, it was largely borne out of fear that the country may lose credibility with potential investors thereby affecting the credit rating of the country. Interestingly, Ralph Mathekga (2013) concludes that the neo-liberal economic policy of GEAR actually ensured international legitimacy of the ANC-led government. Indeed, the fear of global capital is not misplaced. This is because the corporate sector, in alliance with international financial institutions and neo-liberal inclined governments in the United States of America and Britain, has the means—in the form of propaganda—and the control over movement of capital to wreak havoc within a short period of time. As George Soros (1998) mentioned with respect to the Asian economic crisis of 1997–1998, it was the sudden withdrawal of the speculative investment by Western-based investors in countries such as Thailand, Hong Kong, and Indonesia that accentuated the crisis in those countries.

In twenty years of implementing neo-liberal economic policies, inequality and poverty remain very high. The promise of distributive growth, job creation, inflow of foreign investment, private savings, among other lofty objectives, have not materialised. In Terreblanche's (2002, 117) words:

> If the GEAR strategy is judged in terms of targets it set for itself, it has failed. The government reached three of its targets in the period until 2000 – the budget deficit was reduced to less than 3 percent of GDP; the inflation rate was reduced to an annual average of less than 6 percent; and imports tariffs were reduced to less than 7.6 percent of the value of imports. ....None of the other targets were reached, not even remotely. The economy grew by

> only 2.7 percent a year instead of 4.2 percent. Employment shrank instead of growing by 3 percent. Real government investment grew at 1.8 percent instead of 7.1 percent; and real private sector investment grew by only 1.2 percent instead of the projected 11.7 percent...In 2000 FDI amounted to less than R8 billion a year (or less than 1 percent of GDP) instead of some R30 billion (or 4 percent of GDP). Gross private savings averaged 15 percent a year, instead of 21.7 percent.

Despite the staggering failure of these neo-liberal policies, the hegemonic control of the global capitalist system looms large over the post-apartheid South African state. Notwithstanding the glaring and potentially dangerous level of poverty and inequality—what Adam Habib (2013) calls South Africa's *suspended revolution*—"the State has become hesitant about implementing progressive economic policies that could address unemployment and poverty for fear that these policies would drive down share prices and create a negative view of South African policies in international financial markets and business media" (Mohamed 2010, 47).

In Gillian Hart's estimation, "neoliberalism, understood as a class project and manifestation of global economic forces as well as rationality of rule, has become the dominant frame for many critical understandings of post-apartheid South Africa" (Hart 2013, 6) Although Hart argues that such framing is inadequate to explain the conundrum that currently characterises the development project in South Africa, the framing reflects the political economy and social constructions of the country. Arguably, however, Hart's idea of de-nationalisation feeds into the increasing connectivity of domestic capital with global capital, which undermines the realisation of the goal of developmental state in post-apartheid South Africa. She defines de-nationalisation as the "alliances through which corporate capital defined the terms of reconnection with the global economy as well as to the forces unleashed in the process" (Hart 2013, 6). The latitude that the ANC government gave the corporate sector to define the terms of reconnection with the global economy has worsened the socioeconomic problems in South Africa. Hart's (2013, 6–7) analysis of this situation:

> Directs attention to the heavily concentrated character of South African corporate capital; the highly advantageous terms on which these conglomerates engineered their re-engagement with the global economy after the fall of apartheid through their relations with strategically highly placed forces in the ANC; how the conglomerates have restructured and de-nationalised their operations; massive and escalating capital flight; the formation of a small but powerful black capitalist class allied with white corporate capital; understanding of the "economy" fostered through these alliances, their ongoing influence over ANC government policy; and multiple ways these forces continue to play into and intensify brutal inequalities and the degradation of livelihoods of a large proportion of the black South African population.

As mentioned earlier, the seeming powerlessness of the state in making the corporate sector serve the interest of the society is testament to the hegemonic control of global capital over the state, not only in South Africa but over Africa as a whole. This hegemonic control manifests itself as interference of the agents of the Transnational Capitalist Class (TCC) in policy making, knowledge production, and consumption patterns. Specifically, the passion and the pace in which the World Bank and the IMF continue to dispense the diagnosis of socioeconomic problems in Africa deserves further elaboration. The World Bank and the IMF have both acknowledged that the SAPs imposed on Africa in the 1980s were wrong footed (World Bank 2006; Stiglitz 2002). The IMF has also recently shifted ground on its fixation with the sanctity of capital account liberalisation as it agrees there is need for some capital control (IMF 2013).

Beyond such a Pontius Pilate-like claim of innocence, the global financial crisis of 2008–2009 has further called into question the primacy of the market as the best agent for allocation of resources. High levels of public debt, unemployment, inequality, and social crisis at the core of global capital in Europe and United States of America have provoked a massive rethink among scholars and policy makers on the sustainability of the market-based approach to development (Greenspan 2013; Stiglitz 2010).

Interestingly, in an interview with the *Financial Times* of London on 26 October 2013, Alan Greenspan, the former Chair of the US Federal Reserve Bank notes that the neo-liberal economic inspired model "failed at a time when it was needed most...and the failure was uniform, the Fed model failed, the IMF model failed...the whole structure risk evaluation, what they call the Harry Markovitz approach failed and today there are no easy answers or straightforward heroes or villains...in a shifting landscape we all need to keep challenging our assumptions and prejudices" (Greenspan 2013).

Yet, the reality of the limitation of the market-based approach to addressing contemporary challenges of poverty and inequality has not dissuaded the agents of global capital in recommending various reform programmes, whose cumulative effect is the further devaluation of labour as a factor of production. The IMF continues to recommend reforms that are geared towards labour flexibility (a euphemism for relaxed labour rights), investment friendliness, inflation targeting, capital mobility, and independence of the Reserve Bank (Terreblanche 2002). And there are those who appear to have somersaulted: Joseph Stiglitz, for instance, after feeding inappropriate neo-liberal dogma to many countries during his tenure at the World Bank, now argues that neo-liberal economics are not appropriate.

The relevance of the above narrative for the developmental state project in South Africa is this: the dream of a developmental state will end as mere political slogans and rhetoric unless the state has the autonomy to make informed policies that are geared towards uplifting the common man. Unfortunately, the ANC has no time to engage with such important issues as winds of discontent continue to blow across the land. As several scholars have warned, unless the twin issues of poverty and inequality are resolved through the instrumentality of a strong and activist state, the ANC may discover that its long-held credential of a social movement might no longer resonate with the electorate (see De Jager and Meintjes 2013; Habib 2013; Southall 2010).

Cases abound of the use of violence by the corporate sector (with tacit support of the state) to silence and further dehumanise people. Should there be any doubt as to the state's hesitation to defend the workers' interest and promote their welfare, the actions of state actors after the Marikana massacre, for instance, is confirmation of such. Prevarication, dithering, and the lack of determination to bring to justice the security agents who shoot defenceless civilians has become the defining character of the post-apartheid state.

Despite the imperative of social transformation in South Africa, the asymmetric power relations between the Global North and the Global South (which has been historically tilted in favour of the former) in order to seek a solution from this conundrum should be acknowledged. This asymmetry has both racial and ideological undertones. Its nuances are of particular relevance to the South African situation where minority whites have held hegemonic control over the economic, political, and social lives of the majority African population for over three centuries. Given the enormous privilege and power that the dominance confers, there is no doubt that the beneficiaries will do everything possible to retain such benefits. The complicated transition from white minority rule to majority rule by Africans has not fundamentally altered this imbalance of power and the forces that reinforce the hegemony of capital—the empire of capital as John Saul would put it—which is under the control of a tiny section of the population. The political independence of 1994 was a mere translation of change of government from white hands to African hands.

In what Ndlovu-Gatsheni (2013, 65) calls the "Myths of Decolonisation and Illusions of Freedom," post-apartheid South African leaders have been unable escape the tyranny of the global matrix of power in terms of leverage to adopt home grown development strategies that will correct many years of injustice on issues of economic opportunities, land redistribution, and improvement in living conditions of the people. Although the various leaders are distinctly aware of the need for bold steps towards correcting these anomalies, and have made attempts through initiatives such as the economic empowerment programmes, these have not translated into true freedom for the people.

According to Ndlovu-Gatsheni (2013, 67), "the post-1994 South African situation speaks volumes about how the liberation movement was disciplined into an emancipatory force that finally celebrated the achievement of liberal democracy instead of decolonisation and freedom." This liberal democracy, as Claude Ake (2000) argues, is not the type of democracy that can bring about development of the people; it is the democracy whose *leit motif* is the protection of the property of the bourgeoisie class and monopoly capital—a democracy of the market, investment friendliness, and capital. But it is not for the people or the working class.

To build a developmental state under a liberal democracy is like attempting to build a bridge across the ocean! As much as a liberal democracy is based on the logic of the market and individualism, concern for income redistribution and empowerment of the masses will remain mere concerns as infighting and competition over resources will be the norm rather than the exception. The undue importance that foreign capital receives within the context of a liberal/market democracy ensures that public policies and state actors are always subordinated to the logic of capital. These contradictions have played out in the infighting, broken alliances, policy somersaults, and ideological convolution within the ruling ANC (see Hart 2013).

Land Dispossession as a Case in Point

The patterns of power relations and privilege in South Africa have been shaped, produced, and reproduced by historic accumulations of a regime dependent on the dispossession of the majority of people, particularly their right to use and control their own land. For almost 350 years,

Africans in South Africa have been subjected to discriminatory and unjust land laws. The year 2013 marked 100 years since the passing of the Natives' Land Act. Land dispossession has been used as a means to subjugate and oppress Africans in order to accumulate masses of land to be incorporated into the colonial Empire. Land dispossession has also been used to reduce Africans into labour reserves that ensured dispossession of the majority into wage-workers. At the heart of land dispossession lay an ideological superstructure, which maintained a brutal combination of racial, gender-based, and class subjugation, and provided justification for, and reinforced, the extreme racial inequalities that persist in South Africa even today.

Through the prism of race-based superiority, whites deemed themselves inherently superior to African men than women, as did the ruling elite over the working class and peasantry. The system of apartheid colonialism evolved accordingly, and imposed extensive laws on the African, in order to establish control over every facet of their lives. In the course of colonial expansion, millions of people were uprooted from their homes, often with untold brutality, and always without compensation. Many were forcibly dispossessed and moved from their lands into reserves. Conquest and land seizure were accomplished through weapons, warfare, and dubious "treaties," which colonists claimed were signed by chiefs or leaders of communities. Whilst African communities fought to defend and regain their land, the superior weaponry and collaboration by other local communities enabled their defeat.

As the settlers won the wars against poorly armed African forces, the core of South Africa's system of land dispossession warranted the need for a cheapened supply of African labour to ensure the continued exploitation of, and profit from, the country's great mineral wealth, which was generated through the production of gold, diamonds, uranium, copper, manganese, platinum, and vanadium. From a theoretical viewpoint, the history of land dispossession in colonial apartheid capitalism was based on exploitative production relations. The explosion of the mineral revolution, in the 1870s, with the discovery of diamonds and gold gave more impetus to the colonial regime to consolidate and entrench its rule through land dispossession. The British and Afrikaner landowners and industrialists set in motion a process that would consolidate their wealth, while excluding Africans (see Hendricks, Ntsebeza and Helliker 2013).

The law played a key role in legitimising systematic land dispossession and segregating South Africa. By the formation of the Union of South Africa, land dispossession had largely been accomplished and segregation was beginning to take root; the white minority state consolidated its stronghold by promulgating laws to dislodge Africans who had survived land dispossession by entering into sharecropping and tenancy in white-owned farms. The Natives' Land Act (NLA) passed in 1913 played a particularly pivotal role in denying Africans access to land by confining Africans into reserves–only 7 percent of arable land was allocated to Africans!

In addition, the NLA governed the right of an African to be in a prescribed area, and set conditions under which he or she could remain there. Life for the African was exacerbated by the chronic shortage of housing in urban areas. Many Africans were categorised into "non-productive," "unemployed," or "idle," and were outlawed and expelled from residing in urban areas. And if such individuals had no homes or families in the outskirts, resettlement camps were imposed as alternatives. Consequentially, communities were uprooted, disorientated, and alienated from each other.

When the National Party won the general election in 1948 on a platform of separate development, land dispossession and segregation was taken even further. Forced removals also took place under influx control laws in order to reduce the number of Africans living in white urban areas. The Group Areas Act, the Native Resettlement Act, and the Prevention of Illegal Squatting Act, among other laws, were introduced and sparked forced removals of Africans from where they lived and had built homes. Reserves were extended to become bantustans or homelands under the apartheid regime through the Group Areas Act (GAA), which was passed in 1950. The GAA enforced the segregation of the different races to specific geographical areas. The GAA resulted in the destruction and forced removal of African communities such as District Six in Cape Town, Sophiatown in Johannesburg, and Cato Manor in Natal when these areas were proclaimed as "white."

Legislation such as the Native Trust and Land Act, Natives (Urban Areas) Act, Trading and Occupation of Land Restriction Act, and the Pegging Act were passed with a specific focus targeting Africans and Indians. Historian W.J. du Plessis (2011) notes that:

> By the time of the advent of the new South Africa, about 17000 statutory measures had been issued to segregate and control land division, with 14 different land control systems in South Africa.

This demonstrates the importance of land dispossession in creating a racially and spatially divided South Africa. These laws had a negative impact on the economic, social, political, and general well-being and status of South Africans. This is because land dispossession in South Africa produced negative consequences such as a consignment of the majority to the most unproductive land, inequitable distribution of land ownership largely in favour of a minority racial group, dislocation of the social and economic systems of the indigenous people in relation to land use, and *tenantisation* through labour tenancy, sharecropping, and other slave-like forms of erstwhile owners. In its wake, it has left millions of Africans desperately poor and without any means for survival (Gumede 2014a). Its legacy lingers on!

Inferior Education as a Case in Point

It is widely held that the first European schools in South Africa were established by the Dutch Reformed Church in the Cape Colony at the turn of the seventeenth century. The main motivation for their establishment was biblical instruction which was key to church confirmation. This was later followed by British mission schools which sprouted after the arrival of British missionaries in the Cape Colony.[9]

In the 1900s the education system was characterised by a strong British influence following the victory of whites in the South African war. This primarily saw the installation of the English language and cultural values across the country, increased provincial autonomy in education, and the use of government funds mainly to educate whites. Afrikaans resistance to British influence persisted; however, when the National Party ascended into power in 1948, the government introduced repugnant polices that would further entrench racial fragmentation in the education system.

As to the ideological and structural impact of colonialism on education in South Africa, it is important to think of the negative impact of apartheid colonialism in the context of the African continent. There is general consensus among many Africanist scholars that the end of colonialism as a political system of rule on the African continent was only superficial. Equally insidious was the structural, systemic, discursive, and epistemological patterns of domination and exploitation that underpinned the colonialisation project which remains alive today (Ndlovu-Gatsheni 2013, 3).

Throughout the colonial period in South Africa, the Dutch and British colonial powers used the key institution of education to uphold and entrench patterns of domination and exploitation. This was done in South Africa—similar to other (former) African colonies—through the systemic marginalisation of African traditions, languages, knowledge, and identity while promoting Euro-American epistemology.

For centuries, the education system was not only segregated according to racial lines to the advantage and benefit of whites in terms of school infrastructure, resources, facilities, quality of education and all-around wholesome educational experience—therefore reflecting the broader socio-political status quo—it also deprived many Africans of equal access to educational opportunities as admission was selective. It also subjected the African child to an inferior system designed to further reinforce thinking patterns that uphold oppressive power relations.

It would be a mistake to assume that the educational marginalisation of Africans only began with the advent of apartheid. Long before the Nationalist Party (NP) assumed power in 1948, a system of segregation and unequal education already thrived in the country. On one hand, white schooling was free, compulsory, and growing, whereas African education was severely neglected. This neglect was manifested in financial under-provision and coupled with it an urban influx that led to insufficient schooling facilities, teachers, and educational materials— thereby leading to student absenteeism or non-enrolment.[10]

In the 1950s, the Boers introduced one of apartheid's most abhorrent policies: the Bantu Education Act of 1953. The NP government viewed education as an extension of the overall apartheid system and therefore it served the interests of white supremacy. The two key architects of the Bantu Education Act were Werner M. Eiselen and Hendrik F. Verwoerd.

The ideological framework for Bantu education can be traced back to a manifesto crafted in 1939 by Afrikaner nationalists; it was informed by a racist and paternalistic view that the education of Africans was a special responsibility of a superior white race. The manifesto declared that "Christian National Education," which advocated separate schools for different population groups, would be a guiding framework (Overcoming Apartheid Building Democracy 2013). Bantu education, as it related to Africans especially, was to create native education and teaching geared to the development of a separate, self-supporting, and self-maintaining native community based on a "Christian National" basis.

As such, government would formulate a system to separate all races creating a form of educational hierarchy with whites at the top followed by Asian people, then Coloureds, and lastly Africans. Essentially, "Bantu education was designed to teach Africans to be 'hewers of wood and drawers of water' for a white-run economy and society, regardless of an individual's abilities and aspirations" (Overcoming Apartheid Building

Democracy 2013). The now infamous quote by apartheid architect, Hendrik Verwoerd[11] captures the thinking behind the Act most succinctly:

> There is no place for [the Bantu] in the European community above the level of certain forms of labour ... What is the use of teaching the Bantu child mathematics when it cannot use it in practice? That is quite absurd. Education must train people in accordance with their opportunities in life, according to the sphere in which they live'. (Hendrik Verwoerd cited in Brian Lapping, 1987)

The adoption and implementation of the Bantu Education Act created untold damage to the African. The Act forced all state-aided mission schools (which the majority of Africans attended) to register with the state and removed control of African education from the churches and provincial authorities. The Bantu Education Department was created to control African education and keep it separate and inferior. Coloured schools also had to be registered with the government and in 1963 the Coloured Person's Education Act placed control of Coloured education under the Department of Coloured Affairs. Similarly, the 1965 Indian Education Act was passed to separate and control Indian education, which was placed under the Department of Indian Affairs.[12]

Furthermore, due to the homelands' policy, no new high schools were built in Soweto between 1962 and 1971 as students were supposed to move to their relevant homelands to attend the newly built schools. However, giving in to pressure from business in 1972, the government had to improve the Bantu education system to meet business needs for a better trained African workforce and more new schools were built in Soweto. In addition, in terms of higher education, the Extension of University Education Act 45 of 1959 put an end to African students attending white universities (mainly the universities of Cape Town and the Witwatersrand). The Act established separate tribal colleges for African university students; these so-called "bush" universities include Fort Hare, Vista, Venda, and the Western Cape.[13]

The inequalities remain astounding. The Institute of Race Relations (2011) asserts, for instance, that the odds of a pupil passing matric increase significantly when they attend a former "Model C" (white) school compared to those who attend other types of schools. The matric pass rate in former Model C schools always exceeds the national average —in 2009, for instance, the matric pass rate in former Model C schools was 94 percent compared to an overall pass rate of 60 percent. Also in infrastructural terms, the legacy of Bantu education remains an eyesore in democratic South Africa in the form of dilapidated school buildings, overcrowded classrooms, inadequate instruction, poor teacher training, and a lack of textbooks characterising the education of the majority of African children. Again, the remnants of the discriminatory education policies live on!

The Making of a South African Developmental State

In order to understand the framework of the developmental state, it is important to highlight the emergence of the "developmental state" in development discourse. The emergence of the notion of "developmental state" in development discourse follows the rapid rise of the East Asian Tigers (i.e. Taiwan, South Korea, Singapore, and Hong Kong) as an economic and consequent political force in the 1990s; Louis Amsden and Chalmers Johnson stand out as the two scholars who have written extensively about this or have significantly influenced the discourse about developmental states. Peter Evans has also written extensively, especially in the context of "new" developmental states (countries such as Brazil and India). Vivek Chibber, Patrick Heller, Adrian Leftwich, Amiya Bagchi, Ziya Onis, and Manuel Castells have also written significantly on the notion of developmental states. Thandika Mkandawire has written extensively about developmental states in Africa while Guy Mhone and Omano Edigeji have written about the notion of developmental states with a specific focus on South Africa. Issa Shivji is also worth mentioning, given his extensive works on matters of development on the African continent, so is Samir Amin.

Much of what is known to constitute a "developmental state" is, as a consequence, modelled on the Asian Tigers whose developmental states were characterised by state intervention in the economy in the pursuit of socioeconomic development. In this regard, as Mhone[14] puts it, the developmental state is a state that steers economic development as well as industrialisation in the interest of the public good. The "developmental state" concept is said to be an institutional model that adopts a statist approach to account for the high levels of growth of the recently industrialised nations. It affirms the state as central and beneficial in economic development, and in ways that are distinct from Soviet-type communist states. The Keynesian social-democratic states, for instance, have aspects of developmental states because the state is expected to intervene in the market economy in order to accelerate social equality and fairness.[15]

The developmental state emerges in stark contrast to neo-classical (or neo-liberal) economics that have long argued that "state interference" tampers with economic growth as it disrupts market equilibrium with devastating consequences. Institutional economics have since recognised the limitations of orthodox economics, whose failure(s) to explain market "anomalies" is largely attributable to its failure to recognise the importance of non-market related institutions (i.e. political and cultural institutions) in shaping the very same institutions required to achieve market equilibrium. The developmental state is also in recognition of power relations that shape development.

There is no single, agreed-upon definition of a developmental state—there is, however, a wide consensus on the characteristics of a developmental state. A developmental state can be viewed as a state that actively intervenes in the economy with the aim of advancing wellbeing together with a growing economy. As indicated in chapter 1, the definition of a developmental state used in this book is that "a developmental state is a state that is active in pursuing its agenda, working with social partners, and has the capacity and is appropriately organised for its predetermined developmental objectives" (Gumede 2008a, 9). As Dikeni (2012, 37) puts it, developmental state as a term primarily concerns itself with "the ways and means of how a state governs, intervenes in the lives of its citizens, and organises and mobilises resources for itself in order to transform and effect economic and social change in society for development purposes."

It must be noted, however, that the fact that the idea of a developmental state has currency does not presuppose a consensuses by scholars and policy-makers on the features or even the model South Africa has been following and/or should follow. Alan Hirsch (2013, 308), echoing Ralph Mathekga (2013, 206) who says that the "democratic South Africa is relatively an infant," argues that "it is too early to say that a democratic developmental state is impossible in South Africa [because] our political system is so young and immature..." Dikeni (2012, 37) makes a related point that, theoretically and conceptually thinking, the term [developmental state] cannot be seen and/or be used as a concept, nor can we attribute the meaning of a "theoretical model of development to the term... [the term] represents a grouping together of a series of some loosely-related phenomena of 'state' and 'development' under the rubric of a developmental state." Thandika Mkandawire (2001a) could disagree because, in his view, developmental states are "social constructs" that states and societies bring about, implying that there is value in the notion of a developmental state, even as a term.

It is suggested that it is not only possible but also necessary to empirically and conceptually gauge the extent to which South Africa can be characterised as a developmental state, especially two decades since the dawn of democracy. For instance, Marias (2010, 346) argues that to arrive at a view of whether South Africa is a developmental state or not, one should examine "features deemed essential" for South Africa to be a developmental state or assess whether South Africa "is already conducting itself in a manner of a developmental state." Essentially, therefore, there ought to be attempts, using sound analytical tools, to assess whether a country is progressively becoming a developmental state or not. That would help engage the various views on the notion of a developmental state in South Africa. For instance, Turok (2008, 4) concluded that "South Africa could not presently be characterised as a developmental state but that it has taken several significant steps in this direction."

As demonstrated by the different perspectives presented, there is no single narrative that accounts for the developmental state. It seems to me, however, that the differences are mainly attributable to differences in emphasis. In other words, one can recognise a developmental state simply by seeing it. In essence, developmental states are characterised by a number of features or multiple dimensions: namely, ideological (i.e., role of the state versus market), institutional (i.e., state autonomy and capacity), cultural (collectivism versus individualism), and socioeconomic attributes (i.e. economic growth, industrialisation, etc).

South Africa as a Developmental State?

In addition to the conditions that Marias (2010) states as an assessment of whether a country is a developmental state or not (as discussed in chapter 1), Mhone (2004) has suggested that one needs to look at whether the state is developmental in its thinking and action, and whether it is organised in a way that makes "developmentalism" feasible. Mhone defined developmentalism as a "proactive role of the state in pursuing and defining a developmental vision to be attained in the long-term, in coordinating economic activities and steering them toward desired outcomes, mobilizing and synergising class and social forces in support of the developmental agenda" (Mhone 2004). This is similar to Mkandawire's (2001a) differentiation between two components of a developmental state: the ideological and the structural.

Another point around the meaning or characteristics of developmental states is that they are traditionally associated with economic development.

Bagchi (2000), for instance, defines a developmental state as "a state that puts economic development as the top priority of governmental policy and is able to design effective instruments to promote such a goal." Economic development is largely associated with industrialisation and/or industrial policy. This perspective seems to feature prominently in definitions of developmental states by leading scholars in this field (see for instance Johnson 1982; 1999; Amsden 1989; Evans 1995; 2007).

A different perspective, which emphasises broader development, is presented by other leading scholars. However, it appears that all scholars highlight similar characteristics for developmental states. For instance, although Leftwich's (1995) definition of a developmental state seems to be focusing on broader development, his model contains characteristics similar to Evan's (1995) notion of "embedded autonomy."

The starting point, arguably, in a democratic South Africa, was institutional reforms alongside necessary legislative foundations. This process is continuing, focusing more on building effective governance and service delivery institutions. This would be reflected in South Africa as the constitution, as the cornerstone of South African law; in the general enforcement of the rule of law; relatively healthy democratic institutions; a bureaucracy that functions; and strategic alliances between the state and civil society, notably the alliance partners, (namely, Cosatu and SACP), and to a lesser degree, community based organisations (CBOs).

The second major step, it could be argued, is getting the economy right. In 1994, when the first democratic government was voted into office, the economy was in an appalling state; double-digit inflation, high debt levels, negative growth, budget and trade deficits, and so on. Moving from the premise that a growing economy will increase the pace of service delivery, the expansion of human capabilities, and the cohesion of the peoples of South Africa, it would seem that the government engaged in an intricate economic restructuring project. This is still underway, as the legacy of apartheid colonialism remains evident. Hirsch (2005) provides the logic—which contradicts most of what is discussed, especially from

Sampie Terreblanche—of why the post-apartheid government pursued neo-liberal economic policies. Hirsch (2005) made the point that it was critical to stabilise the economy, and he contended that the GEAR policy achieved its objectives although it missed some of the targets.

The third major step was a direct and explicit strategy focusing on eradicating poverty and strengthening social cohesion. Alongside further restructuring of the economy, this will probably occupy government and its partners for many years to come. Bagchi's (2000) point around social capital for a developmental state is very pertinent for this. Similarly, Evans' (2007) recommendations for twenty-first century developmental states, in relation to the new kind of "embedded autonomy" would be critical. Lastly, the various dimensions of state capacity that Cummings and Nørgaard (2004) describe would have to be in place to fully accomplish a fully fledged developmental state for South Africa.

It is important to acknowledge various processes in government—most of which started during the second term of the Thabo Mbeki administration[16]—aimed at strengthening capacities and meant to restructure/reorganise the state. The manner in which the democratic South African government sequenced the country's transformation agenda has aspects of a developmental state approach. Literature on developmental states highlights institutions, economic growth, and broader development involving various sectors in society.

As Onis (1991) argued that East Asian developmental states were shaped by their historical circumstances, the ANC has openly declared its aspiration to "build a developmental state that is shaped by the history and socio-economic dynamics of South African society" (ANC 2007, 5). The ANC's ideology (i.e., the NDR) features prominently in many government documents and political discourses. Mkandawire (2001a) alludes to ideology as one aspect of a developmental state. The second aspect, the structure, is clear in the detail of what the ANC deems a developmental state to be. The 2007 *Strategy and Tactics* says that the developmental state would have the capacity to intervene in the economy, implement social programmes that address unemployment, poverty and underdevelopment and also have the capacity to mobilise the people (ANC 2007). With some exceptions, the ANC appeared to adopt Leftwich's (1995) model of developmental states and combined Evans' (1995) "embedded autonomy" recommendation, while trying to ensure the "ideology-structure nexus" of Mkandawire (2001a).

From Leftwich's model, the following components seem to feature in the South African case, at least during 1998 and 2008: determined developmental elite; relative autonomy; the effective management of non-state economic interests; and legitimacy and performance. With regard to "ideology-structure nexus," the attributes that the ANC lists as the main attributes of the (envisaged) South African developmental state include issues such as the proposed strategic orientation (which emphasises people-centred and people-driven development) and capacity to lead the definition of an overarching developmental agenda and the mobilisation of people around it.

The ANC appears to also draw from Cummings and Nørgaard's (2004) dimensions of state capacity. It highlights organisational capacity (i.e., organisation of the state) and technical capacity (i.e., implementation capacity). It seems to have also tried to apply notions of "state-structure nexus" and "institutional coherence," which Robinson and White (1998) perceive as important institutional attributes of a democratic developmental state. The conclusion, drawn from literature, appears to be that South Africa is an emerging developmental state—it is "emerging" because whilst it has some of the attributes of a developmental state, it falls short in a number of cases that would qualify it as a developmental state.

Edigheji (2005) suggests that a democratic developmental state is a state that principally embodies the following principles: electoral democracy and popular participation in the development and governance processes, economic growth, state-driven socioeconomic development, and "embedded autonomy." Most of these are apparent in South Africa, but only to some extent, or arguably during 1999 to 2009. Edigheji further emphasises prevailing institutional arrangements as an important variable to the success of a democratic developmental state; the South African policy-making institutional mechanisms though appearing rigorous, seem less comprehensive especially in relation to the effective involvement of other stakeholders.

With regard to perspectives of leading scholars on developmental states (of East Asia), South Africa seems to have been trying to prioritise economic development. For instance, there have been various attempts to get the industrial policy off the ground; it could be argued that the "industrial elites" were once under the guidance of the state. The guidance of "industrial elites" has taken various forms, including Presidential Working Groups on business matters. There are elements in the South African state in the manner in which it determines the developmental agenda and mobilises society that partly resembles, to some extent, Japan, as described by Johnson (1982), Korea, as described by Amsden (1989), and Taiwan as described by Evans (1995).

Also drawing from Robinson and White (1998), some salient characteristics—such as "institutional coherence"—of a democratic developmental state seem visible in the South African state—again, to some extent, and perhaps they were more visible during 1999 to 2009. Also, Evans's (1995) concept of "embedded autonomy" which is central to the effectiveness of a developmental state seems to play itself out in the South African context. Evans's (1995) point is that state institutions have to be *autonomous* in so far as that facilitates the identification and promotion of strategic developmental objectives, while *embedded* in a sense that the state would be able to establish and sustain working partnerships with key social groups that would add much needed impetus to the achievement of development goals. In the South African context, this appears to be a case in point through the role of the state and its partners.

Linked to this is the state's commitment to "meritocratic" recruitment: the appointment of skilled bureaucrats that would ensure the important political "neutrality" that would in turn facilitate sound networks and delivery on developmental goals. This is one of the matters that is debatable, whether top civil servants are appointed on merit and whether they are insulated from political maneuvers. The Policy Coordination and Advisory Services (the Policy Unit) in the Presidency, for instance, recruited on the basis of merit. Ndletyana et al. (2013), however, find that due to patronage politics, meritocracy is not (or no longer is) respected.

Another issue for contestation is whether there is sufficient technical capacity, especially for planning and implementation. In comparison with other countries said to be developmental states, the erstwhile South Africa's Policy Unit had fewer technocrats. Also, some questioned the influence the National Treasury had in the South African policy making landscape. These are not only issues for debate but also empirical questions. Would, for instance, a larger policy unit have a better impact or would a less influential treasury be effective? Another relevant philosophical question perhaps is the extent to which the current institutional arrangements were based on a conscious and considered plan. Since the establishment of the new ministries, the number of technocrats has doubled in the policy, planning and monitoring, and evaluation functions in the Presidency. However, socioeconomic development is not significantly improving.

With regard to social policies, the World Bank[17] defines social policy as "a series of public policies designed to promote social development..." Mkandawire (2001b, 12) sees "social policy as an instrument for ensuring a sense of citizenship is an important instrument for conflict management, which is in turn a prerequisite for sustained economic development." It could be argued that the making of social policy in South Africa has taken into account various perspectives on social policy. Some of the areas that remain contested terrains include social pensions, as to whether they create a dependency or some perverse incentives. South Africa has adopted an approach largely similar to that of South American countries, except that social pensions or similar programmes are not (yet) conditional in South Africa.

Organisation and Capacity

The World Bank (1997, 6) describes state capacity as "the ability to undertake and promote collective actions efficiently."[18] This is broader than administrative or technical capacities of civil servants. It entails, also, institutional mechanisms that give politicians and civil servants the flexibility, rules, and restraints to enable them to act in the collective interest (World Bank 1997). This resonates with Cummings and Nørgaard's (2004) conceptualisation of state capacity along four dimensions: ideational, political, technical, and implementational. Cummings and Nørgaard (2004) define ideational state capacity as the degree to which the state—its actors, role, and policies—is legitimated and embedded in state institutions. Political state capacity refers to the effectiveness of state institutions in terms of governance structures, and technical and implementational state capacities refer to administrative capacities.

To some extent there is merit in the argument that the emerging South African developmental state requires additional capacity, especially in policy thinking. There is no a priori reason why a differently organised South African state should be more effective. The question relates more to whether the systems, such as monitoring, evaluation, and performance assessments, are effective in detecting inefficiency and deploying appropriate responses. For instance, Chibber (2002, 952) argues that for any state to be effective, "bureaucratic rationality must also be structured in an appropriate apportionment of *power* among state policy agencies." In short, Weberian bureaucracy is not enough just like the bureaucracy based on Confucius's perspectives was not enough; "interagency relations" are critical. Bureaucratic rationality, if the institutional setting is not supportive, can easily lead to processes that are not developmental or effective, as Chibber (2002) found in the case of India.

Overall, the analysis seems to suggest that South Africa as an emerging developmental state has undertaken public policies in a relatively sound manner. However, it could be argued that, lately, South Africa has been an ineffective state owing to its technical and implementational state capacity. This does not imply that the state should be organised differently per se, although coordination could be further ameliorated. It simply means that the capacity that is said to be lacking, such as long-term planning expertise, has to be created.[19] In fact, I argued that there were "various planning instruments and tools mainly focused on medium-term planning, not long-term developmental planning" (Gumede 2007). The long-term planning capacity, through the Ministry of Planning and the National Planning Commission, has since dealt with that shortfall.

PUBLIC PARTICIPATION

As indicated in Gumede (2008a, 14), "significant elements to the policy making and implementation process in South Africa are the efforts to involve non-state actors—what public policy literature broadly refers to as quasi-autonomous non-governmental organisations..." As highlighted earlier, the South African policy-making processes (used to) provide relatively ample room for public participation in its different forms. This approach is in accordance with the democratic nature of the South African government, giving voice and respect to the governed from different sectors, and from all walks of life. In a quest to achieve impartiality and independence of public views, the government has established, as mandated by the Constitution, several chapter nine institutions in order to strengthen constitutional democracy.

At the presidential level, former president Thabo Mbeki established several working groups (constituted by members outside government as well as selected Cabinet ministers and senior advisors from the Policy Unit) for different sectors. There were a number of such Presidential Working Groups: on youth development, women empowerment, business, higher education, commercial agriculture, and working groups with religious leaders and organised labour.[20] During the Mbeki administration, biannual meetings were scheduled with these groups to exchange policy and programme perspectives around topical issues affecting these groups and those they represent. It appears that in the Jacob Zuma administration the working groups were not given prominence, at least during his first term of office.

There are many examples of "outcomes" of the working group system. Perhaps the most significant one was the Growth and Development Summit of 2003. There are other important outcomes: commitments by business to increase domestic investments; commitments by vice-chancellors to increase throughputs and for universities to serve communities where they are located; the partnership between government and religious leaders to reduce poverty and improve social cohesion; poverty eradication projects for women leadership; attempts at a joint civil society; business and government response to the economic crisis, and so on.

Broader forums, supposedly more inclusive and participative, were also initiated during the Mbeki administration—the most common of which is called *Izimbizo*, meaning gatherings. One of important advantages of *Izimbizo* is that the government gains a better understanding of the realities of each locality, and various households—the government learns of different pressing issues that different localities face. In a nutshell, *Izimbizo* is about taking government to the people. The president and cabinet members as well as provincial and local government leadership spend a couple of days in a particular locality interacting with people from different walks of life.

The other important "institution" that ought to be playing an important role in the policy making landscape is the system of ward committees. Ward committees are expected to work with municipalities dealing with a range of matters, especially in ensuring that the needs of the communities are taken into account during policy-making processes. Outside the state umbrella, there are a number of institutions, bodies, and agencies that play active roles in policy-making processes. For instance, the National Economic Development and Labour Council (Nedlac) is one body through which the government comes together with organized business, labour, and community groups at a national level to discuss and reach consensus on issues of social and economic policies. Organised business is represented by Business Unity South Africa (BUSA), organised labour by the main labour federations in South Africa, and organised community made up by the South African Youth Council, National Women's Coalition, South African National Civics Organization, Disabled People South Africa, Financial Sector Coalition, and the National Co-operatives Association of South Africa.

Nedlac[21] works very closely with departments of labour, trade and industry, finance (National Treasury), public works and others with the aim of making socioeconomic decision making more inclusive and to promote the goals of economic growth, equity, and social inclusion. Regarding the women's sector, the South African government has opened its doors to engagement with the South African Women in Dialogue (Sawid) and the so-called National Gender Machinery,[22] which deals with policy issues related to poverty eradication and development in general. Sawid is an independent and impartial South African women's platform for dialogue committed to hearing the voice of every woman and to improving the status of women by engaging the national government to shape community, provincial, and national agendas in a manner that responds appropriately to the needs of South African women from all walks of life. In the health sector, the government has also established the South African National Aids Council (Sanac) to provide a platform for collaboration and interaction between government and key stakeholders such as the Treatment Action Campaign and the National Association of People living with HIV and AIDS. This platform allows for discussions on policy and programme responses to health challenges facing the country, with a specific focus on HIV and AIDS.

It can be argued that there is an important link between public participation and human development, not that public participation leads to improved human development per se. According to Buccus et al. (2007), public participation was "receiving increasing attention in South Africa, especially at local government level." There appears to be consensus that the democratic government has made significant efforts to include the public in policy making and implementation as well as monitoring and evaluation. *Izimbizo*, Nedlac, the ward committees, and other systems/processes have been attempts to involve civil society in policy making, implementation and monitoring, and evaluation.

The question of the efficacy of the abovementioned systems and processes has not been resolved. With regards to *Izimbizo*, for example, it is hard to tell whether they have been effective, especially in relation to monitoring and evaluation at a community level. In ensuring the success of community-based consultative processes, local government is tasked with ensuring that the views as expressed by the public during an *Imbizo* are taken into consideration and followed up to ensure that they are addressed. This does not seem to be happening or rather it appears that this does not happen sufficiently. It is reported that the decline in numbers of those attending *Izimbizo* is an indication that community members do not see the benefits thereof. Also, the increase in the number of protests is seen as an indication that participatory democracy has not been fully implemented. The same could be argued with regards to ward committees. Some argue that part of the problem in ward committees is weak capacity, while others say it is corruption. Lastly, other structures such as the working groups, Nedlac, and others have been criticised for some sort of elitism: that only leaders of organised formations take part on such structures and not the relevant people.

A more recent programme similar to *Izimbizo* is the *Siyahlola Presidential Monitoring Programme*. "Siyahlola" is an isiZulu term that loosely means "we are inspecting." The programme was formally launched by President Jacob Zuma in July 2012 and is an on-site monitoring of government performance in services delivery to the communities. The idea is that these visits give the president an opportunity to assess first-hand any progress with various service delivery initiatives in the community. It would seem that the *Siyahlola* programme was not meant to replace *Izimbizo*, but rather for the two initiatives to complement each other. It appears that, in the Jacob Zuma administration, *Izimbizo* and

Siyahlola involve effectively similar goals and activities. A difference is that *Siyahlola* involves surprise visits to specific localities or points of public provisioning. Another difference is that *Siyahlola* is orientated towards monitoring specific outcome areas such as health, education, and others whereas *Izimbizo* is an open community meeting with the president and his cabinet.

With regards to knowledge-sharing networks, it appears that the government does not have a structured relationship with think tanks and academics/scholars around policy making and implementation. Most government departments and the different spheres of government seem to relate with researchers or research institutions as and when there are specific research or policy issues requiring capacity outside the public sector.

Outside Parliament as an institution, parliamentarians do play a role in policy making. However, this seems to be happening largely at a political level. For instance, all parliamentarians on the side of the ruling party get involved in most policy discussions in various platforms of the ruling party—traditionally, since 1994 or so, there are policy discussions in the ruling party which inform policy thinking in government in South Africa. Overall, however, many are of the view that parliamentarians, researchers/academic scholars, traditional leaders, and others that can inform policy are not systematically involved in the policy-making processes and implementation as well as in monitoring and evaluation.

Lastly, the Constitution of South Africa impresses upon local government to involve communities and community organisations in local government. The legal/policy framework for such is the White Paper on Local Government and the Municipal Systems Act which espouses a vision of "developmental local government" based on a culture of community participation through relevant mechanisms, processes, and procedures. The ambition of the Act is to involve communities in all the policy stages (development, implementation, and monitoring and evaluation) in South Africa's Integrated Development Plans (IDPs), which are planning and strategic frameworks, for the short, medium, and long term, to help municipalities fulfil their developmental mandate.

Thus, at local government level there are a myriad of structures aimed at facilitating the involvement of other stakeholders and communities. These include representative structures like Ward Committees, Sector Forums, Ward Forums, Zonal Stakeholders Forums, Regional Stakeholders Networks, Citywide Stakeholders Forum, and Citywide Sector Networks. This is over and above *Izimbizo*, as described above. However, the involvement of communities appears more like consultation as opposed to effective participation in decision making, implementation, and monitoring. Many have observed that consultations tend to be confrontational and unconstructive with the end result usually being promises made by government. In addition, the turnaround times and timelines for delivery on issues that may have been raised tend to be long. Often times, there are no means to track if resolutions are indeed being implemented. There are also concerns around the IDPs: many observers argue that these are done by consultants and local governments impose IDPs to their jurisdictions without thorough discussions with those affected. In addition, people with disabilities, the aged, and women in rural areas in particular are not prioritised and their specific issues are not given sufficient attention.

Conclusion

It is important to emphasise that the road to true freedom in South Africa, and Africa in general, is through self awareness of the subservient position into which the African continent has been inserted by the global matrix of power; a strong aspiration to break loose from this chain through the acquisition of relevant endogenous-based knowledge and a commitment to fundamentally alter socioeconomic and political structures (which have been put in place to make it easy for Africa to be perpetually exploited and dominated) is needed. In essence, Africa, and South Africa in particular, must be cognisant of (and armed to contend with) what Adebayo Adedeji terms the Development Merchant System.[23]

Africa needs to free itself from the shackles of the hegemony of the West and from the bondage of its inferiority complex—of which all are a systemic creation of colonialism.

As previously alluded to, although colonialism ended and neo-colonialism may be ending, a phenomenon of "coloniality" has survived and continues to thrive to this day. And just as decolonisation underpinned the political liberation project across Africa, a process of "decoloniality" should be initiated for Africa to achieve epistemological freedom. The contention is that decolonisation did not decolonise the mind and free former colonial subjects from epistemological subjugation.

As aptly captured by Nldovu-Gatsheni (2013, 51), "one of the most powerful myths of the twentieth century was the notion that the elimination of colonial administration amounted to decolonisation of the world... The heterogeneous and multiple global structures put in place over a period of 450 years did not evaporate with the juridical-political decolonisation of the periphery over the past 50 years..."

In essence, the decolonial school of thought argues that Africans are in a predicament as they are trapped in a "post-colonial neo-colonised world," a term denoting the structural, cultural, discursive, and epistemological pattern of domination and exploitation created by Western modernity as it spread across the world (Ndlovu-Gatsheni 2013). Fanon (1963) asserted that more than just being simply concerned with political oppression and economic exploitation, colonialism by perverse logic "turns to the past of the oppressed people, and distorts it, disfigures it, and destroys it" (Fanon 1963, 67).

As such, pan-Africanists make the case that in order to free itself of the snares of colonial power, what Africa needs—and by implication South Africa—is to undertake a campaign of "decoloniality" which would go far beyond the aspirations of the decolonisation project. This would be an epistemic project aimed at freeing Africa from the grip of the pervasive Western world view and attaining a world where all knowledge would be able to shape the global cultural order. For Africa, and especially for

South Africa, there must be concerted effort towards Africanisation. That should involve the Africanising of the curricula, among other things. As argued in Gumede (2015e), the knowledge we consume, produce, and disseminate should assist in us—as Africans—to bring back pride in our identity, and to help us redeem our tempered souls as well as reclaim our lost glory and recover our stolen legacy.

Required changes, which are by definition fundamental, will not come easy as domestic and foreign capital and their cronies, who are comfortable with the current lopsided order, will fiercely resist change. The people must be mobilised, empowered economically, and incentivised to rise against the perpetuation of hegemonic control of the minority by other means. Just as it was during apartheid, progressive forces in South Africa must form solidarity with other progressive forces in the world to challenge the current impunity of capital, the excessive indulgences of the political class, the continuation of apartheid-like suppression of dissent by the state through force, the continued control of the land by a white minority, the emasculation of the education sector through a refusal to change the curriculum to reflect the true history of Africa, as well as the subordination of labour to capital and other forms of injustice. And to address psychosocial factors, the starting point has to be the unconditional acceptance that South Africa and the South African people are damaged.

Although South Africa appears to have aspects of what constitutes a developmental state, it is convincing that South Africa still has a long way to go towards becoming a fully fledged developmental state. As the African post-colonial development experience and the post-apartheid South African development experience show, complete liberation and thorough decolonisation as well as the reconfiguration of the global matrix of power relations are needed for South Africa to be a developmental state—the same applies for many countries, if not all countries on the African continent. For South Africa, the reconfiguration of state-market relations would be a prerequisite for a serious agenda towards a fully fledged developmental state.

Notes

1. Darly Glaser and other like-minded scholars (and politicians sharing the similar view) are likely to view my stance as "racial-nationalistic excesses" (see Glaser 2011). Glaser (2011:89) argues that "whites should be educated about past iniquities and encouraged to see that the better-off among them (even those born post-apartheid) have incurred obligations to the country's black poor as a result. However, the issue is not just "education."
2. Bantu Biko founded the South African Students' Organisation (SASO) in 1968 after he left the racially mixed National Union of South African Students—SASO restricted membership to black students only.
3. The Human Sciences Research Council (2000:227) defined social cohesion as descriptive term referring "to the extent to which a society is coherent, united and functional, providing an environment within which its citizens can flourish."
4. The successive post-apartheid administrations have pursued many initiatives aimed at strengthening social cohesion, including a strategy for social cohesion by the Zuma administration.
5. Mbembe (2001: 67) defines "foundational violence" as a form of violence that authorised the right of conquest and had an "instituting function" of making Africans its targets; "legitimating violence" is defined as a form violence that was used after conquest to construct the colonial order and entrench a colonial reality; and "maintenance violence" refers to violence infused into colonial institutions and cultures and used to ensure their perpetuation (Ndlovu-Gatsheni 2012).
6. Hart (2013:6) defines de-nationalisation as "alliances through which corporate capita defined the terms of reconnection with the global economy as well as to the forces unleashed in the process." She argues that "taken together, de-nationalisation and re-nationalisation define the contours of post-apartheid Africa's passive revolution" (9). The notion of de-nationalisation problematic is because it presupposes that there must have been "nationalisation" when, in fact, corporate capital in South Africa was never interested in domestic development, at least as far as Africans are concerned. The theoretical formulation of "reform bargain"—modifying Scott Taylor's "reform coalition"—that proposes a theoretical prism to understand post-apartheid South Africa is more appeal-

ing; so too are notions of "elite transition" and "compromise transition." I concur with Hart (2013:6) though that "neo-liberalism...is inadequate to the task" of understanding the post-apartheid South Africa.

7. Mbeki, T, *Punch*, November13, 2013.
8. Ndlovu-Gatsheni explains Global Matrices of Power as referring to a context or situation in which "the old colonial hierarchies of European versus non-Europeans remain in place and are entangled with the 'international division of labour' and accumulation of capital at a world scale." In other words, Africans still live under the "European/Euro-American exploitation and domination."
9. Refer to Library of Congress 1997.
10. South African History Online 2013.
11. Hendrik Verwoerd, South African Minister for Native Affairs before becoming Prime Minister (1958–1966) was speaking about government's education policies in the 1950s.
12. South African History Online 2013.
13. Ibid.
14. Mhone, G. 2004. 'Organisational and Institutional Implications of a Developmental State', Human Sciences Research Council paper, Pretoria: HSRC.
15. Wai Yip So, B. 2007. *Does China Follow the Path of Taiwan's Developmental State Model? The Rise of Hsinchu Science Park and Zhongguancun Science Park,* Department of Public Policy and Management, Taiwan: I-Shou University.
16. In the Mbeki administration, there were working groups which were made up of Cabinet Ministers and various leadership across society.
17. World Bank, 2005. 'Concept Note: Rethinking Social Policy'. World Bank conference in Arusha Tanzania (12–15 December 2005), http://worldbank.org/website/external/topics.
18. World Bank, 1997. *World Development Report.* Washington DC: World Bank.
19. Joel Netshitenzhe, the former Head of the Policy Unit in the Presidency in his opinion piece, gives extensive background and specific proposals on the envisaged long-range planning function in government. See, 'The shift is not ideological', *Mail & Guardian,* 31 October–6 November 2008, 23. Proposals for long-term planning took place during 20052008 and were implemented in 2009.
20. Organized labour comprised: the Congress of South African Trade Unions (Cosatu), National Council of Trade Unions (Nactu) and Federa-

tion of Unions of South Africa (Fedusa). Business was comprised of Big (white) Business and Black (African) Business – the two working groups for the business sector.

21. The debate about the functioning of Nedlac has not been resolved. However, Nedlac is achieving most of its objectives. Yet, some departments circumvent presenting to Nedlac on policy matters that should ideally be canvassed at Nedlac.
22. The National Gender Machinery is a constitution of all the key role players on gender equality and empowerment of women.
23. Adedeji, A. 2002. From the Lagos Plan of Action to the New Partnership for Africa's Development and the Final Act of Lagos to the Constitutive Act: Wither Africa? Keynote address to the African Forum for Envisioning Africa, Nairobi, Kenya, April 2629, 2002

Chapter 4

Evolution of Policy in Post-apartheid South Africa

> South Africa must and shall belong to all who live in it, black and white. She must and will be governed by an authority which derives its legitimacy from the will of all our people.
>
> OR Tambo, 1987, Longest serving president of the ANC

Introduction

It is through policy that there can be clarity of what is intended, and what is not intended, regarding a programme or an intervention. Policy ensures that tradeoffs made or to be made are clear. Without clear policy, implementation—actions that are undertaken to meet policy objectives—suffers. The Constitution of South Africa (1996) requires that a green paper, after a discussion document, should be drafted and, after inputs from the public, a white paper should be written to spell out policy for a particular issue. However, contrary to the dictates of the Constitution, there is a plethora of policy strategies and strategic frameworks, and very few green or white papers especially in the recent past (and many green papers never become white papers) become acts of parliament. I argue that part of the policy failure that this book identifies emanates from jumping an important stage—that of a policy—to strategies, plans, and so forth. Policy frameworks are a good and often necessary phase towards policies, but they are not policies.

I have defined public policy—drawing from literature, research, and practice[1]—as referring to "all formal and publicly known decisions of governments that come about through predetermined channels in a particular administration" (Gumede 2011a, 166). Policy implementation is the action or a combination of actions taken to execute the agreed policy objective, or programme (Gumede, 2011a). By arguing that there have been policy failures in post-apartheid South Africa, I mean that either inappropriate policies have been implemented or that the sequencing (or lack thereof) of policy reforms has been out of context. Policy failure is used as a shorthand, in this book, for policies that are either inappropriate or for which reforms did not happen, or reforms were not well sequenced. This book does not discuss policy implementation and related concepts such as planning, monitoring, and evaluation although parts of the book allude to these issues where pertinent.

In this chapter, I cover a wide spectrum of policies and strategies as well as programmes and projects that have shaped socioeconomic development since 1994 by focusing on initiatives that stand out. The analysis in this chapter examines policy directions pursued by the successive post-apartheid administrations: the Nelson Mandela administration, the Thabo Mbeki administration, and the Jacob Zuma administration—the brief caretaker administration of Kgalema Motlanthe is discussed as part of the third or Jacob Zuma administration. Given that I formally left government in 2009—though I continued working with some parts of government until 2011—I believe that I can write more authoritatively for the period 1994–2009.

In an effort to broadly answer the fundamental question that this book addresses—the issue of inclusive development—this chapter discusses the policy reforms at a macro level in particular. It discusses the various macroeconomic and/or political economy interventions since 1994. It also discusses social policy reforms and the changes that have taken place regarding the general wellbeing of South African society since 1994. Because of their extreme importance, education, skills development, health, and land reform are treated in more detail than other socioeconomic, development related issues.

The chapter argues that although South Africa has done relatively well in many respects, South Africa could have done far better in improving human development. More specifically, whilst the evolution of South African society has been getting closer to what was envisaged from 1994 to circa 2006, due to weak policy and/or lack of timely and ideal reforms, a number of aspects of societal development have not improved since 2006. The main argument advanced by this chapter, which is a build up to the main argument of the book as a whole, is that any initiative for socioeconomic development has to be premised on thoroughly conceptualised and well-articulated policy. Many initiatives have not delivered optimally because of unclear policies and sometimes contradictory policy options. Often, a cardinal question regarding policy—a "why"—does not get posed, and when it is posed it would seem it was not answered clearly. Equally important, not enough attention gets paid to context so as to reform policy. Public policy literature calls this "policy regime"—the inability to modify policy significantly even in the face of major changes in the context.

Background

The National Liberation Movement (NLM) had fought for about a century to eradicate colonialism and apartheid in South Africa. The victory against apartheid was effectively sealed in 1994. Nelson Mandela became the first president of the Republic of South Africa in 1994 as head of the Government of National Unity (GNU). Prior to that, particularly in the years leading up to 1994, the NLM had devised ideas on the kind of South Africa (and the economy) that would be pursued. In simple nomenclature, the main objectives of the NLM have been and continue to be the pursuance of the creation of a united, non-racial, non-sexist, democratic, and prosperous South Africa (ANC 1994). The outlines of, and the strategic path towards, the purported better life are thoroughly elaborated in the various documents of the ANC; documents such as the 1992 Ready to Govern discussion document, whose objectives were translated into the 1994 Reconstruction and Development Programme (RDP), as well as other macroeconomic documents adopted by the ANC-led government, fundamentally influenced by the pursuit of the National Democratic Society (NDS) as per the NDR.[2]

In 1994, the ANC came up with what it envisaged to be the main guiding policy framework for the post-apartheid South Africa: the Reconstruction and Development Programme (RDP). The RDP is the most comprehensive post-apartheid socioeconomic development framework in many ways —it covers all aspects of socioeconomic development policy. The RDP articulated what would be done in the economy, in social development, in industrial development, in small and medium enterprise development, wealth redistribution, nation building, and so on.

It is worth observing that the RDP, like Ready to Govern (R2G), and other documents of the ANC seem to be informed by the 1955 Freedom Charter. In fact, the Freedom Charter appears to be the natural fallback-position whenever there is a deadlock in policy and/or strategy and tactics of the ANC. An important debate should take place about the Freedom Charter especially now that South Africa has gone through two decades of democracy.[3] As hinted earlier, from an Africanist perspective, the Bill of Rights in the African's Claim should be the framework that South Africa uses to guide policy. Ivor Chipkin (2007) and others might differ because—among other things—the Africans' Claims "anticipated the Freedom Charter by more than a decade" (Chipkin 2007, 64). It is instructive that Chipkin (2007) hastens to highlight the major difference between the Africans' Claims and the Freedom Charter:

> There is an important difference between the Freedom Charter and the Africans' Claims. If the latter reflected a brief (and perhaps unexpected) engagement with liberalism, the Freedom Charter suggested the growing influence of Communists in the alliance, the rising importance of Marxist-Leninist concepts and terms and, most importantly, the emergence of the theory of the National Democratic Revolution as the pre-eminent expression of African nationalism in South Africa. (Chipkin 2007, 64)

Perhaps the debate should also entail a robust discussion of the theory of the NDR, as I attempt later. Gillian Hart (2013, 178) indicates that the "standard critique by the left outside the [Tripartite] alliance that the NDR operates first and foremost as an instrument of deception..." Devan Pillay (2011, 32) also raises critical questions about the NDR, and in particular that "the organised working class are being deceived – by their leadership, also implicated in patronage politics – into supporting the ANC against their own class interests, and some believe that the time has come to build a 'left opposition' outside the [Tripartite] alliance."

The debate on the NDR would, if it happens, have to revisit the views of the late Neville Alexander who wrote extensively and critically on the NDR—Neville Alexander (2012, 44) argued that "for the leadership of the NDR to be an integral part of a bourgeois government while pretending to conduct a revolutionary struggle against the capitalist system is mere political buffoonery" and he contends that "the class struggle would become brutal and unrelenting" (21) in South Africa. I am tempted to argue that, if the debate on the NDR takes place, perspectives on the South Africa that Steven Bantu Biko and Robert Mangaliso Sobukwe,[4] in particular, envisaged should also be part of that debate.

The debate would also have to reexamine the thesis of the Colonialism of a Special Type (CST), in particular because "the language of the NDR and its closely linked acronym CST originates from *The Road to South African Freedom*, an SACP document..." (Hart 2013, 175). Hart (2013, 174) is not alone in concluding that "the NDR shows no signs of giving way to socialism, as some of its proponents had confidently predicted." In fact, Norma Chaloult and Yves Chaloult (1979) and Peter Hudson (1986), among others, published papers critiquing the CST thesis and suggesting that it was not an appropriate characterisation of South Africa even in the 1950s/1960s. In addition, Nicholas Visser (1997) argued that the CST thesis would easily impress any person with little knowledge about South Africa because it obscures rather than explains the South African conundrum.

South Africa, and Africans in particular, should confront the question of what is becoming of South Africa. Moreover, was the NDR a correct theoretical basis for the liberation project? Similarly, was the CST an accurate conceptualisation of colonialism and imperialism that South Africa was experiencing? And, lastly, should it be the Bill of Rights in the Africans' Claims or the Freedom Charter or the Constitution or some other theoretical framework that forms the basis of post-apartheid South Africa going forward? Interestingly, with regards to the CST thesis, Jack Hicks (2004, 4), for instance, argues that "theories of internal colonialism miss the point that colonialism and imperialism are an integral part of the expansion of capitalism on a world scale."

POLICY AND PLANNING PRIOR TO 1994

Considerable policy thinking and planning took place in the NLM broadly, and the ANC in particular, before 1994—the issues discussed earlier bear testimony to that. The planning that took place in the NLM prior to the first democratic elections in 1994 is arguably well captured in the 1992 blueprint, *Ready to Govern*. Many practical initiatives were also undertaken, such as the training of those that were likely to be in the leadership of government. The training of "future leaders" so to speak continued even after 1994, and the training was extended to senior public servants who received scholarships to study abroad.

Capacity was assembled in the political space too. The ANC had many young researchers to assist with policy thinking. The Congress of South African Trade Unions (Cosatu) also had its own capacity. Most of the policy analysts/advisors that were in the ANC and Cosatu tended to end up in government, and when they "retire" from government mostly go into business. The South African Communist Party (SACP) has generally relied on its own leadership for ideas, and the SACP (or its predecessor, the Communist Party of South Africa) has had significant influence in the broader NLM—the NDR and CST are the two ideas that stand out, among many, that significantly shaped thinking in the NLM. The SACP's leadership also resulted in government, especially during the Jacob Zuma administrations. I have often wondered if the SACP really understands capital, especially, as I argue later, that the market has co-opted government in South Africa—and this happened at a time when the SACP's leadership was in government.

One of the important processes worth depicting as part of the plans and policy thinking prior to 1994 is the Macro-Economic Research Group (MERG), which was later transformed into a formal policy research outfit: the erstwhile National Institute of Economic Policy[5] (NIEP). MERG played a critical role in economic analysis, particularly in the understanding of the challenges facing the South African economy in the early years of the post-apartheid dispensation.

Policies and Strategies for Transforming South Africa

In 1996, an economic policy framework followed the introduction of the RDP. The Growth, Employment and Redistribution (GEAR) Macroeconomic Framework was intended, as an economic policy framework, to rescue an economy that was already falling apart and to stabilise the economy (Hirsch 2005). This was done in light of the double-digit inflation, double-digit interest rates, runaway budget deficit, negative growth rates, and a huge government debt prevalent in the late 1980s and early 1990s. The South African economy was effectively in a recession when the ANC came into office in 1994—the last period that South Africa had experienced uninterrupted economic growth was the 1960s.

In 2005, the government opted for another broader economic policy reform agenda through the Accelerated and Shared Growth Initiative for South Africa (AsgiSA). It was intended to accelerate the growth of South Africa's economy as well as accelerate wealth redistribution. The life of AsgiSA, however, was brief. The highlight of AsgiSA is that it aimed for equitable distribution of growth while ensuring skills development.

In 2010, AsgiSA was replaced by the New Growth Path. The New Growth Path (NGP) places emphasis on job creation, the need to create decent work, and, more specifically, it can be conceived of as a new policy orientation towards labour intensive approaches. The NGP aspired to grow employment by five million by 2020 and reduce narrow unemployment by 10 percent largely through a public infrastructure programme.

THE RECONSTRUCTION AND DEVELOPMENT PROGRAMME

The RDP remains the most important policy framework that was aimed at guiding the new government in policy making and implementation. The RDP has focused on meeting the basic needs of the majority. The main objectives of RDP were generally to create a strong economy to eliminate poverty and meet the basic needs of every South African irrespective of race or gender, to ensure a democratic society and a balanced regional economy in Southern Africa. The intention was to develop South Africa's human resources by building a strong economy and democratising the state and society at large. It envisioned a process of transformation that is people-centred and people-driven. It can be viewed as a renaissance in which economic development, popular participation, and respect for human rights are seen as integral components of the transformative process.

The ANC has understood that as a party in government, the success of the liberation struggle will be judged by its ability to address issues of poverty, unemployment, underdevelopment, and inequality. The RDP as the democratic government's development strategy sought to attain socioeconomic development while at the same time addressing the legacy of apartheid colonialism. As stated in the RDP discussion document, the ANC was tasked "to mobilise all people and country's resources towards the final eradication of apartheid...building of a democratic, non-racial and non-sexist future" (RDP 1994, 8). The RDP set out various socioeconomic commitments for delivery related to employment creation, housing, electricity, water, sanitation, health, education, infrastructure, and public enterprises. Chikulo (2003) indicates that during the 1994–1996 period, the RDP was viewed as the cornerstone of government's development policy —a yardstick against which the success of the government's development policy could be assessed.

There were five primary goals that were identified as essential to the socioeconomic transformation of the South African society (RDP 1994). These were:

- To create a strong, dynamic, and balanced economy in order to eliminate poverty and meet the basic needs of every South African;
- Develop human resource capacity of all South Africans;
- Ensure that no one suffers racial or gender discrimination in hiring, promotion, or training situations;
- Develop a prosperous, balanced regional economy in Southern Africa; and
- Democratise the state and society.

The primary vision of the RDP lies in the values it espouses and the strategic approach through which it proposed to achieve the National Democratic Revolution (NDR) towards the creation of a National Democratic Society (NDS). As indicated earlier, the NDS could be described in simple terms as a society that is free of poverty, racism, gender, and other forms of discrimination; a society that is prosperous and where its people exercise free will, free choice, and, in the economic philosophy of Amartya Sen (1999, 18), "people lead the kind of lives they value and have reason to value." As indicated above, there are both proponents and critics of the NDR and I have suggested that there must be a debate about it and its related philosophies.

Like some, Chikulo (2003) argues that as a development policy framework, the RDP had a number of shortcomings. Clearly, these objectives were overarching objectives which most societies that found themselves in the position of South Africa in 1994 would have pursued. The RDP was, however, and still is, criticised for being too broad and all-encompassing. For instance, Chikulo (2003) contends that the document looked more like a "wish list" than a strategy document focusing on opportunities and constraints. It has, in some quarters, been pointed out that the misplaced criticisms of the RDP are merely grandstanding at best and lacking knowledge of policy development at worst. Secondly, it made no attempt to set priorities or to assign responsibility for the implementation of each programme component. Thirdly, it lacked mechanisms for inter-departmental coordination. Finally, local government, which had been assigned the constitutional responsibility for promoting socioeconomic development, did not have adequate planning and implementation capacity. The possible downside of the RDP, perhaps in hindsight, is the setting of targets. This appears to be one specific weakness of the successive post-apartheid administrations—almost all set targets that are missed.

I have actually observed that the setting of targets is a challenge confronting governments the world over, except of course the margin by which South Africa misses the targets it sets appears worse compared with that of other countries. It baffles the mind that a wild target as halving unemployment by 2014 was set when the conditions for job creation were poor and no concurrent policy existed or was developed. It is even inexplicable to set a target of creating five million jobs by 2020 when the economy was entering a recession phase, and again no job creation policy existed or was devised. An important aspect of a job creation policy—the youth wage subsidy[6]—designed in 2007 could not be immediately implemented even after the pilot phase. In defence of the RDP, it never presented itself as the *policy* or *strategy*. It is, very explicitly, a policy framework. In other words, the RDP presents aspirations on what policies and programmes should entail and pursue.

Like other policies and programmes as well as other frameworks and strategies, the RDP set itself up for failure by specifying a number of wild targets. In 1994, the priority should have been to create a proper foundation for socioeconomic development. Of course a number of socioeconomic development initiatives had to start, given the deep legacy of apartheid colonialism. The RDP, strangely, set unachievable targets such as:

- The creation of 2.5 million jobs over a ten-year period;
- The building of one million houses by the year 2000;
- The connection to the national electricity grid of 2.5 million homes by 2000;
- The provision of running water and sewerage to one million households;
- The distribution of 30 percent of agricultural land to emerging black farmers;
- The development of a new focus on primary health care;
- The provision of ten years of compulsory free education for all children;
- The encouragement of massive infrastructural improvements through public works; and
- The restructuring of state institutions by 1997 to reflect the broader race, class, and gender composition of society.

The difficulty with setting targets is perhaps particularly the dates by which the targets would be met. As we will see in chapter 6, the targets are achieved but normally many years after the target year. The fundamental issue is to get the foundation right in order for targets to be achieved.

And a more critical issue is to have policy clarity which is commensurate with intended objectives and makes it feasible to achieve set targets.

Despite its shortcomings, however, the RDP played a critical role in inspiring hope for a better tomorrow amongst many South Africans, in particular the poor. As Munslow and Fitzgerald (1997, 57) aptly put it: "there is no doubt that the RDP played a pivotal role in ensuring the successful transition from separate development towards a more sustainable development future." Furthermore, the RDP's projects on basic needs provision would count among its successes. As discussed in later sections, a lot has been achieved with specific regard to the implementation of the government's priority on addressing the lack of access to basic social services as well as other important areas such as economic development.

THE GROWTH, EMPLOYMENT AND REDISTRIBUTION STRATEGY

The Growth, Employment and Redistribution Strategy (GEAR) became that strategy in 2006. The debate remains unresolved as to whether GEAR was the correct policy for South Africa's context at the time. The debate has remained ideological largely that GEAR was a Structural Adjustment Programme akin to the Bretton Woods Washington Consensus neo-liberal agenda. A useful debate should be on the kind of economic stabilisation programme that South Africa should have pursued if GEAR was not suitable. Many argue that South Africa or the government, in particular, had to succumb to international pressure and replace the RDP with GEAR. The proponents of this argument contend that the "socialist" RDP was not viewed amicably by international investors and as such the government had to shift to the "neo-liberal" GEAR.[7]

GEAR, in simple terms, was aimed at strengthening economic development, broadening employment, and encouraging the redistribution of wealth and increasing socioeconomic opportunities through structural reforms. Some of the major targets of GEAR were:

- an economic growth rate of 6 percent per annum by 2000.
- up to 400,000 jobs per annum.
- an increase of exports by up to 8 percent per annum.
- reduction of the budget deficit to below 4 percent of GDP.

However, there have been real differences over the question of macroeconomic policy and its potential effects. According to Chikulo (2003), GEAR was based on the assumption that the expansion of the private sector would have a substantial impact on the economy whilst the role of the state would largely be a facilitative one. There are many similar views on GEAR, which serve largely as a critique of GEAR. The gist of the critical views on GEAR is that it is a self-imposed SAP. SAPs are associated with IMF and WB, and the neo-liberal agenda. SAPs have a notorious history in sub-Saharan Africa in particular, as they resulted in low investments in human capital as a result of tighter fiscal and monetary policies.

Cosatu has been a foremost critic of GEAR. Knight (2001, 4) refers to a Cosatu policy document that argues that GEAR brought about deep cuts in government spending between 1996 and 1999. As a result, efforts to improve services to the poor suffered despite the continued reprioritisation of spending from the rich to the poor. GEAR failed to effectively attain many of its goals. Although changes in corporate tax levels, foreign exchange controls, and interest rates have yielded some degree of increased investment, many of the strategy's long-term targets were not met. Notwithstanding the weaknesses or failures, the most important objective of GEAR—that of macroeconomic stabilisation—was achieved.

As indicated earlier, Mathekga (2013) argued that GEAR brought the legitimacy of the ANC to the international community. Alan Hirsch's (2005) book concluded that GEAR was not only a good policy but that it achieved most of its targets. I share the view that a macroeconomic stabilisation policy or programme was necessary in the mid-1990s, but GEAR appears to have further entrenched inappropriate state-market relations that were obtained during the apartheid era. In hindsight, although it was important to stabilise the economy, the government should have ensured that the stabilisation programme took place under differently configured state-market relations. Another view contends that the actual problem that has constrained socioeconomic progress in South Africa relates to the negotiated political settlement—Alan Hirsch,[8] a former colleague in the Department of Trade and Industry and in the Presidency, is among those propagating this view. As discussed in chapter 3, it is indeed important to acknowledge that the kind of the political transition, which seems to have been the best option at the time, could not allow major changes in the status quo (also because of the much acclaimed *Sunset Clause* that apparently Joe Slovo brought to the negotiation table to resolve the impasse). However, I boldly argue that policies pursued since 1994 could have done better to advance the life and to improve the condition of an African in South Africa. If not much could be done in the first ten years of democracy, arguably more targeted policies could have been pursued ten years later and especially two decades after democracy when there is clear evidence that Africans predominantly remain at a disadvantage and that the entire South African society is undergoing rupture.

Like the RDP, however, and like other policy frameworks of the post-apartheid government, GEAR set unrealistic targets such as achieving an economic growth rate of 6 percent per annum by 2000 and creating 400,000 jobs per annum, amongst others. Although given the potential capacity of the South African economy in 1996 (and its global ranking), in hindsight, the focus could have simply been on macroeconomic stabilisation. In other words, the priority should have been to reverse the downward spiral of the economy first instead of aiming for farfetched targets. It would seem that the democratic government or the ANC in particular, always fell short of policy options although it had accurately diagnosed the challenges confronting South Africa.

GEAR was succeeded by AsgiSA, which was very short-lived as it was replaced by the NGP within about three years of its implementation. AsgiSA was not just a government programme but a national initiative supported by key groups in the economy. Launched in 2006, it prioritised government's commitment to halve unemployment and poverty by 2014. It was aimed at accelerating the growth of the economy and ensuring redistribution of wealth. One of its main components was the Joint Initiative on Priority Skills Acquisition (Jipsa), a partnership programme to address scarce and critical skills to meet the AsgiSA's economic growth objectives.

AsgiSA identified six "binding constraints" which were said to be preventing South Africa from achieving the desired growth rate:

- The relative volatility of the currency;
- The cost, efficiency, and capacity of the national infrastructure system;
- Shortages of suitably skilled labour, and the spatial distortions of apartheid affecting low-skilled labour costs;
- Barriers to entry, limits to competition, and limited new investment opportunities;
- The regulatory environment and the burden on small and medium enterprises; and
- Deficiencies in state organisation, capacity, and leadership.

Given the time it takes to effectively implement any policy, it is hard to assess the efficacy of AsgiSA, or the effectiveness of the NGP, which succeeded AsgiSA in 2010. The NGP was launched as an ambitious and imaginative government developmental framework broadly set to pursue economic growth and employment creation through an infrastructural development programme. It aimed to create five million jobs by 2015 and to reduce unemployment by 10 percent by 2020. Like GEAR, the

NGP is missing its targets. Indeed, there appears to be a general problem with the setting of targets. Often the diagnosis of the policy challenge is conclusive, but targets are usually unsubstantiated. This is, in itself, a problem of policy. Targets are set without clear policy choices that inform targets.

Lastly, it is hard to think of the National Development Plan[9] (NDP) as a policy document. It can be described as a consensus-building mechanism towards some envisaged end state, for which issues such as poverty, inequality, and unemployment would be drastically reduced. It might be worth indicating that there is value in such a vision, such as the one that the NDP presents, for South Africa. The diagnosis of the society and the economy is relatively robust but the proposed solutions, like in the NGP, do not address the identified policy challenges.

It is probably in the nature of governments not to focus on specific policy questions instead of attempting to address all challenges at once. The NDP does not deal with the practicalities of how it would be achieved; for instance, how would "sustainable communities" come about? As indicated earlier, the vision for the society should be clear and succinct. The NDP is rather longwinded and voluminous. It is also unclear whether the NDP responds to the legacy of apartheid colonialism. In fact, Hendricks et al (2013, 344) argue that "the main problem with the plan [NDP] is that it does not take account of colonial dispossession and the legacy of apartheid."

There are those who conclude that it will not work (see for instance, Sampie Terreblanche 2012) and there are those that are optimistic (see Adam Habib 2013). It could be that Adam Habib—as he details in his recent book—sees the NDP as a step towards a new "political settlement" and/or "social pact" emanating from new "political management" brought about by "astute leadership." Sampie Terreblanche—also in his latest book—argues that the "hyper-optimism" characterising the NDP is because "the NDP has not considered the historical trends of the past 130 years"—the National Planning Commission should have, according to

Terreblance (2012, 118), "concentrated on the unequal power relations, the unequal property relations, and the unequal opportunities that are making the new South Africa society a very unjust society—just as similar inequalities made apartheid South Africa a very unjust place." Interestingly, as indicated earlier, Lawrence Hamilton (2014, 124) restates Sampie Terreblanche's words as: "the elite compromise reified rather than enable the transformation of power relations that had been generated under and inherited from colonial and apartheid regimes and conditions."

State, Property Relations and Social Transformation

In 1998, the ANC—or the broader National Liberation Movement (NLM) —undertook what must be one of the most incisive probes into the South Africa economy and society in the *State, Property Relations and Social Transformation* discussion document. This discussion document made an important attempt at clarifying the NLM paradigm on the South African economy and society.

The following paragraph captures the essence of what was (to be) pursued in the post-apartheid South Africa:

> [South Africa] is pursuing the kind of state whose character is developmental. Development is about improving the quality of life; it is about equity and justice. As the RDP document asserts, development entails a growing economy in which redistribution is a critical element; it includes modernisation of the productive forces and a redefinition of production relations. It includes the preservation and development of human resources in the form of skills-training, job-creation and the provision of education, health services, infrastructure, an adequate social security system and so on. It is also about democracy and popular participation. (ANC 1998)

The discussion document also, for the first time, explains in detail the type of developmental state pursued by the NLM. The discussion document contends that the South African developmental state:

- should use the resources that it commands to ensure redistribution of wealth in the interest of the poor and disadvantaged.
- should put in place regulatory and other mechanisms that not only seek to obviate market failure, but also afford the state the capacity to intervene in a pro-active way to facilitate growth and redistribution.
- should also be able to strike the correct balance between state ownership of productive forces and private ownership, guided, *inter alia*, by the prerogatives of strategic interest, efficiency, technology-transfer, affordability of services and narrow cost-benefit considerations.
- And that the South African developmental state has to define and regulate its interaction with private capital in such a way that mutual benefit can be derived. This includes an industrial policy that helps direct private capital into critical sectors and a labour market policy that prevents super-exploitation and encourages skills development and workplace democracy. It includes offering aspirant black capitalists opportunities which in fact encourage the expansion of this class.

The main shortcoming I find in the discussion document is its inability to clarify the notion of a *mixed economy*. The mixed economy is a given. The fundamental issue is what kind of a mixed economy, and on the basis of which particular socioeconomic development model, is it pursued. The post-Cold War dispensation is characterised by mixed economies, but variegated mixed economies. The Indian mixed economy is a different mixed economy compared to, for instance, the Brazilian mixed economy. In India, a significant component of employment remains in the informal economy while in Brazil there is a greater degree of informalisation of jobs, as an example.

It was probably understandable in the 1990s that South Africa wanted to be known as a mixed economy. However, subsequent policy reforms should have provided better policy clarity on the balance between the state and the market. The decision to pursue a developmental state, with aspects of social democracy, as indicated in the 2007 Strategy and Tactics document of the ANC, could be conceived of as an attempt to spell out the type of mixed economy that South Africa desired. However, there was never a subsequent policy or framework that addressed this important policy question. As such, there remains policy confusion about public enterprises as well as the interface between the state and the market. It is also in this context that nationalisation or what is euphemistically termed "state intervention" has caused jitters from a policy perspective.

It is important the state-market relations are revisited. The notion of a mixed economy must be clarified. The state-market relations should be reconfigured to be in favour of development. The framework of a developmental state provides pointers, but the political leadership should lead the process of redesigning relations between the state and capital.

Governing in the Post-apartheid Dispensation

It would seem that although the ANC—or the broader NLM—had prepared for governing a democratic South Africa, policy thinking and capacity to govern was given insufficient attention. This was compounded by slow institutional reforms as the state machinery or the public sector bureaucracy was largely to remain untransformed for many years to come. Many years later, parts of the public sector remain poorly transformed. The lack of transformation in the economic sector is arguably linked to weak transformation in pertinent public sector areas. There are also views that the workings of the ruling party may have constrained the progress achieved.

Legislation introduced in the mid-1990s assisted in creating conducive conditions for transforming the public sector. However, transformation of institutions generally takes time, and transforming mindsets takes even longer. Overall, the new government—starting with the Government of National Unity (GNU)—did the best it could under the circumstances.

Governing in the post-apartheid environment remains a challenge. Governing is in fact quite difficult. Transformation of social institutions remains a challenge in South Africa. One of the most important social institutions that remains under transformed is the labour market. Combined with the reality of a poorly performing economy, South Africa suffers from one of the highest levels of poverty, unemployment, and inequality. This is an area of both social and economic policies that have limited the country's achievement of the targets set between 1992 and 1999.

The political environment itself, particularly during the 1990s and early 2000s, constrained the transformation project. The governing political party had to negotiate most of its policies, interventions, and initiatives with its alliance—Cosatu and SACP. The ANC, a social democratic party, had to be sensitive to the socialist-Marxist agenda of Cosatu and the leftist stance of SACP. Although the ANC acted alone in some instances, such as in economic policy, the implementation was lacklustre due to political cleavages that pitted the ANC against its alliance partners.

The relative political instability of the 1990s between the ANC and the Inkatha Freedom Party (IFP) added to the tension. However, the ANC was in a prime position to excel given the overwhelming political mandate gained from the 2004 elections—the ANC could have made a significant case for political, social, and economic reforms since this was ten years post democracy. From 2009, after the third democratic election, much more could have been achieved with regards to policy and programmes for radical socioeconomic transformation.

In hindsight, it was wise of Nelson Mandela to focus primarily on reconciliation and nation building. The most important transformation agenda of the post-apartheid South Africa, especially during the years of the GNU, had to be peace building. The RDP, as an example, could not be fully implemented because of the political problems—over and above those related to the fiscus, poor capacity to implement, and an underperforming economy, which had no muscle to support various aspirations of the RDP.

The ANC, or government in particular, had to contend with an important realisation that most of the goals set for the 1990s could not be met. As Hirsh (2005) argues, it was in that context that GEAR was introduced. As indicated above, the debate on GEAR remains ideological and therefore impossible to resolve. Another view could be that the introduction of GEAR was in essence a step towards shifting focus from reconciliation to sound economic management—*shift* is an operative word here, because there was no *change* per se. Nelson Mandela continued to focus on peace building, also backed up by Archbishop Desmond Tutu who chaired the Truth and Reconciliation Commission (TRC).

For a country with centuries of apartheid colonialism, reconciliation and peace building can be a lifetime process. The success of the TRC or its failures remains a matter of contention. However, the focus of this book is only on socioeconomic development. Juxtaposed with the Convention for a Democratic South Africa (Codesa) negotiations, the TRC played a far more important role. Codesa largely left white privilege—not white domination per se—unchanged.[10] The TRC had an important role of peace building, although it did not fully achieve its noble objective.[11]

Shifting from the Nelson Mandela to Thabo Mbeki administration, the Mbeki-led government initiated programmes aimed at improving the state of economy. Essentially, the South African economy was in a recession when the democratic government came to office. It was, however, fully stabilised by 2000 but the government did not implement further policy reforms until 2005. This is discussed in detail in the next chapter.

It should be acknowledged, in fairness to government, that numerous so-called microeconomic reforms were introduced in the late 1990s. However, clarity was never given regarding the reforms or which policy objectives were pursued with the reforms. For instance, an important area of economic policy—industrial development—was not vigorously pursued. South Africa's industrial policy still remains unclear.

With that said, it is safe to characterise the period of the late 1990s to early 2000s as focusing on the economy. This focus probably continues until today, except that it is difficult to infer the exact policy focus of government since the Thabo Mbeki era. To some extent, the post-Mbeki period finds the government trying to achieve plenty and please everyone. This is the challenge of governing a constitutional democracy such as South Africa. Of Mbeki, Noyoo (2015, 111) says:

> Mbeki seemed to encapsulate the various positive attributes of the more progressive leadership styles. One essential aspect that stands out in Mbeki's character which also epitomised his ability to balance his yearning for entrenching participatory democratic approach – where he encouraged a cross sections of South Africa's civil society to play a leading role in the governing of the country, on the other hand, and his capacity to be able to take decisive action, at critical moments, on the other. Mbeki did not shy away from being a leader when it mattered.

Besides the realisation that economic and social transformation has been slow, the "politics" factor further compounds the challenge of what to do. The economy is important; something must be done to foster its growth, sustenance, and redistribution. Poverty, inequality, and unemployment are the biggest challenges confronting South Africa. Rural development, land reform, and agricultural development have been poor. Race relations, national unity, and community integration are lagging. Health care, education, and skills development remain poor.

The point made by these rhetorical or polemical reflections is that governing in the later years of the post-liberation period has been more challenging. Marginal improvements are harder to achieve once progressive mileage has been gained. Having stabilised the economy, for instance, substantial and sustainable growth prove harder to achieve. Once poverty is reduced, it is harder to eradicate it completely. It is in this context that a radical transformation programme becomes critical.

Political Economy of Development Post-1994

The post-1994 period was most challenging in the 1990s for reasons mentioned above. As post-apartheid South Africa entered the second decade of constitutional democracy, the challenge of development became even more severe. The ANC, in its 2007 Strategy and Tactics, outlines actionable steps given the realisation that development was becoming more challenging; a developmental state, with aspects of social democracy, should be rigorously pursued.

The main political-economy factors worth discussing when considering the post-1994 period are: (1) the Mineral-Energy Complex (MEC) and land reform; (2) economic policy and empowerment; (3) labour market; (4) education and skills development; and (5) health reforms and wellbeing. Impacting on all these factors is an overarching political economy challenge of pursuing multiple objectives, at times conflicting from a policy perspective. This touches on one of the biggest challenges facing South Africa regarding development: namely, the sequencing of policy.

Addressing many major challenges, which governments justifiably have to do, is a question of how policy and reforms are sequenced. It would seem that South Africa, as argued above, kept the same "policies" long after the context or the policy challenge had changed. The obvious instance of this is the higher education sector. After the harmonisation and rationalisation of the higher education sector, a policy was never drafted to address the changed context that permitted more students to access higher education. Glaring realities following the dawn of democracy are yet to be addressed twenty one years later.

The Mineral-Energy Complex and Land Reform

The essence of the MEC is that there are advanced sectors that have developed around the mining, energy, and financial sectors. The MEC represents institutions that are centred on mining and mineral extraction bound together through the interaction of the state and domestic corporate capital. As Fine and Rustomjee (1996, 5) argued, "the Mineral Energy Complex (MEC) lies at the core of the South African economy not only by virtue of its weight in economic activity, but also through its determining role throughout the rest of the economy."

At the time of finalisation of the book, the MEC still required policy interventions to make it work for the South African economy. Taking the MEC as a given, the policy issue of determining ways of making it advantageous to the economy need to be addressed. The economy, therefore, would remain trapped in low growth rates if significant actions are not taken for the MEC—beneficiation is but one policy option. The fundamental issue about the MEC is that it maintains a structure of an economy that may not create value and jobs.

Land reform also remains a highly emotive issue in South Africa's transformation discourse. This is due to the brutal historic dispossession and transformation of the majority into wage-labourers. It is generally understood in the country that the survival of the apartheid system went hand in glove with the unjust dispossession of the majority African population and its subsequent subjugation.

Understandably, the advent of democracy brought with it a high societal expectation that the land issue would be resolved, thus ensuring that Africans become owners of land that could be used as a key asset in individual or communal socioeconomic development (through food security, sustainable livelihoods, and commercial enterprises). The government responded with a Land Reform Programme (LRP) based on three main tenets: tenure reform, redistribution, and restitution.

It is important to note that the land question remains a fundamental issue in policy making, economic growth objectives, and socioeconomic development. If for no other reason, land reform is necessary to correct the wrongs of the past because productive land was stolen from Africans during the process of colonisation. As a requisite step to decolonisation, therefore, relevant land should be restored to its owners. I reiterate that redress in South Africa has to start by recognising the historical experience of apartheid colonialism.

Economic Policy and Economic Empowerment

Given the repulsive history of apartheid colonialism, it became important that an economic redress programme be established. Such programmes have been implemented in many countries, and Malaysia is lauded as one good example for successful economic empowerment. If well conceptualised, and informed by a clear policy, an economic empowerment programme can play a significant role in levelling the economic playing field. Within the South African context, it is somewhat strange that despite being in the majority, Africans beg to be economically empowered. Nonetheless, it is important that redress programmes, especially in the economic sphere, are clearly articulated and the policy succinct. An economic empowerment programme could, for instance, be informed by a policy to expand the middle class or to create new industrialists or to improve wellbeing. However, an economic empowerment programme that aims to do all three or more is unlikely to succeed. In addition, the context should determine a suitable economic redress programme; as the context changes, policy should adjust accordingly.

In 2003, the government conceived Black Economic Empowerment (BEE). Black Economic Empowerment was intended to transform South Africa's race and gender relations as well as to deracialise the economy. Whereas there were criticisms levelled against the new initiative as a new form of discrimination, government and other critical voices have defended the integrity of BEE, referring to it as an integral and necessary legislative framework. Whilst BEE was considered too narrow and leading to the enrichment of a few politically connected individuals, it was later reformed into Broad-Based Black Economic Empowerment (BBBEE). The goal of BBBEE was to redistribute wealth across as broad a spectrum of South African society as possible (Presidency 2013). Whilst, "narrow based" empowerment measures focused only on equity ownership and management representation, BBBEE includes elements such as human resource development, employment equity, enterprise development, preferential procurement, and investment, ownership, and control of enterprises and economic assets; it takes into account people with disabilities, women, and considers rural places.

BBBEE is officially defined by government as "an integrated and coherent socioeconomic process that directly contributes to the economic transformation of South Africa and brings about significant increases in the numbers of African people that manage, own, and control the country's economy, as well as significant decreases in income inequalities" (Presidency 2013). The economic empowerment legislation aims to promote racial equality as well as the designated groups (Africans, Coloureds, Indians, and Chinese, who are considered South African citizens). Evaluation criteria are established and businesses earn points based on the criteria when dealing with government. Points can only be accumulated when businesses "empower" previously disadvantaged groups.

The Broad-Based Black Economic Empowerment Bill was introduced along with the BEE strategy document outlining measurement criteria or the use of a "balanced scorecard" approach for gauging success, setting targets, formalising guidelines and codes, and the establishment of an Advisory Council, including use of financial support measures aligned with the strategy (Presidency 2013). The 2003 Broad-Based Black Economic Empowerment Act and Codes of Good Practice on Black Economic Empowerment (released on November 1, 2004 and gazetted on February 9, 2007) are among the sets of legislation to promote economic empowerment. An Interpretive Guide was added in June 2007. These have served as guides for Codes of Good Practice, dealing mostly with ownership and management aspects as well as BBBEE Charters that set sector-specific targets. Additional Codes of Good Practice have since been introduced, primarily to respond to complex issues relating to BBBEE that needed to be resolved: namely, complex structures, broad-based ownership schemes, fronting practices, and verification agencies.

All of these policy documents are outcomes of rigorous consultative processes between government, the private sector, and civil society; they are largely informed by the contributions of the Black Economic Empowerment Commission that informed the initial economic empowerment programme as well as shaped by the views of the Presidential Black Business and Big Business Working Groups, The Trade and Industry Chamber of the National Economic Development, and the Labour Council, among others (Presidency 2013). The initial process for an economic empowerment programme was developed by the BEE task team set up by the South African Department of Trade and Industry (DTI).

Because of BBBEE, South African companies dealing with government or public enterprises are now required to be "empowered" as required by preferential procurement legislation. Government, as the largest buyer of goods and services in the economy, appears to have recognised its responsibility to leverage its purchasing power in the supply value chain in support of previously disempowered groups. The government uses (or misuses) the tendering process as a mechanism to open economic opportunities to previously disadvantaged groups, particularly women and black people. The government introduced a point-scoring system that awards business on the basis of a combination of price and preference for targeted groups. Although there are no applicable direct financial penalties to non-BEE compliant businesses (Presidency 2013), the system ensures that procurement managers and buyers favour businesses that are compliant since that enhances their own BEE scorecard under the preferential procurement element provisions.

The government has also established a set of financial mechanisms intended to support BBBEE and the transfer of wealth into black hands. The government recognised that the financing of BBBEE is important for the economy and that BBBEE must have a credible financing component in order to proceed (Presidency 2013). The financing of BBBEE is particularly important in ensuring that investment funds are not diverted into asset transfers and economic outflows. In response to this economic prerogative, the government appears to be revising many of its incentives and enterprise support measures to promote broad-based economic empowerment. According to the Presidency (2013), the government created, in 1998, a National Empowerment Fund, which is a trust to hold equity stakes in state-owned enterprises and other private enterprises on behalf of historically disadvantaged persons, while providing historically disadvantaged persons with the opportunity to, directly and indirectly, acquire shares. The Trust was also created to promote and support business ventures pioneered and run by historically disadvantaged persons. The government also leverages both private sector and state funds to support economic empowerment. This includes financial support from the Department of Trade and Industry and its various agencies, including Khula and the Industrial Development Corporation (IDC) and offerings from the Land Bank, the Development Bank of Southern Africa, and other financial development institutions (Presidency 2013).

That said, it has become clear that the current approach to black economic empowerment has been deficient. Moeletsi Mbeki (2009)—the brother of the former president of South Africa—observes, as an example, that BEE has become both the core ideology of the black political elite, and it is the driving material and enrichment agenda, which is to be achieved by maximising the process of reparations that accrue to the political elite. In addition, as captured in Gumede (2015c, 243) "critics of the B-BBEE argue that the process of economic empowerment is characterised by dishonesty and corruption to the effect that powerful government officials illegally become beneficiaries of B-BBEE. There is also a view among critics of the economic empowerment programme that B-BBEE promotes narrow-based transformation."

There are other numerous initiatives within the scope of economic empowerment that focus on the development and promotion of small, micro, and medium enterprises (SMMEs). Since 1996, there have been various programmes and legislation for the development and promotion of SMMEs. Similar to BEE and even BBBEE, policy was never explicit:

SMMEs could be for economic growth, job creation, or the advancement of welfare. Since 1998 government has been unclear in addressing the fundamental questions regarding policy and various policy reforms promoting SMMEs. As I have argued, there is no a priori reason why SMMEs should perform better than large enterprises (Gumede 2004). This highlights the paramount importance of policy clarity on any socioeconomic development initiative. Similarly, why should a government own a firm in the form of public enterprises or youth development initiatives? Policy remains fuzzy (Gumede 2011d).

Lastly, economic development also involves economic growth and other positive changes in society. A good example would be a job-creating economy. South Africa could have performed better and ensured more economic development. Besides the MEC constraint discussed above, the patterns of ownership of the South African economy imply that many people would remain economically excluded. Industrial policy should have ensured better economic development. The government has been reluctant to choose the "winners," which is what industrial policy is about. South Africa remains with policy frameworks instead of proper policies in many important policy areas—the notion of Industrial Policy Strategy Framework is confusing from a policy analysis viewpoint. The policy framework or strategy should inform policy. Ideally, countries should avoid policy frameworks and strategies and focus on policy options. South Africa in particular needs clear policies in many areas, instead of policy frameworks or strategies. Arguably, the 1990s needed policy frameworks and strategies but after some period of strategies and policy frameworks, clear policy and or reforms become paramount.

The Labour Market

Major efforts have been made by the state and its institutions to accelerate job creation for previously disadvantaged citizens. Comprehensive employment strategies have been consolidated into integrated and coherent policy documents designed to facilitate the attainment of employment. These employment strategies have been underpinned by an integrated and interconnected set of employment promoting policy frameworks and projects for target groups expected to be principal beneficiaries of the programme.

Efforts have been made by the ANC-led government to transform the skewed and discriminatory character of the South African labour market. The democratic government introduced laws that would impose minimum conditions of employment in order to recognise and promote worker and trade-union rights, address ongoing discrimination in the labour market, and correct the demographic imbalance in the workforce resulting from apartheid policies, practices, and its legacy (Godfrey, Maree and Theron 2006).

According to Godfrey, Maree, and Theron (2006), the need to rebuild a fractured and uneven labour market has provided a great impetus to all labour reforms, all of which give special attention to worker and labour rights. Collective labour rights have found prominence with the inclusion of worker and trade-union rights in Section 23 of the Constitution of the Republic which affirms that "everyone has the right to fair labour practice." Labour reforms include the establishment of the National Economic Development and Labour Council (Nedlac) and the radical transformation of labour legislation that is encapsulated in the enactment of the Labour Relations Act, the Basic Conditions of Employment Act, the Employments Equity Act, and the Skills Development Act—and the institutional arrangements and statutory bodies which give effect to them.

These labour reforms have focused on the provision of equal rights to all employees, the protection of organisational rights (including the right to strike and picket on all socioeconomic matters, and the rights of trade unions to access information from the employer), and the democratisation of the workplace through the establishment of a centralised system of collective bargaining, workplace forums, as well as sanctioning the right for worker participation in all decision-making processes of the workplace. The government's labour policy largely intended to maintain peace in the labour sector, to countervail high unemployment rates (particularly amongst Africans, women, and people with disabilities), to improve skills training and employee productivity, to improve workplace safety, and to extend social securities to workers. These provisions of the law were purposed to promote fair employment practices, orderly and equitable collective bargaining, and the regulation of industrial action, and therefore demonstrate government's commitment to collective labour rights and worker rights through organised labour.

There have been complaints from the business sector that certain aspects of the labour legislation have invariably produced unanticipated consequences (i.e., retrenchments and low employment rates) largely because they do not promote the much needed flexibility at an enterprise level—for example granting the right to employers to "hire and fire," the right to deploy workers more freely, and to set wage levels at a rate more appropriate to productivity levels (Clarke, Godfrey, and Theron 2002). The government, however, maintains that its policy approach is aimed at balancing the protection of minimum standards and the requirements of labour market flexibility. South African labour legislature has introduced flexibility by allowing a greater scope for variation/negotiation while at the same time increasing statutory regulation (Godfrey and Theron 2006). It has simultaneously prioritised the protection and enforcement of revised basic employment standards, and the establishment of rules and procedures for the variation of these standards.

So linked to both the notion of the MEC and the economy, as discussed above, is a labour market that has been characterised by both policy failure and government failure. The fundamental challenge of development that has confronted post-apartheid South Africa is the inability of the economy to create jobs. This labour market failure has nothing to do with regulation as some argue. It also has very little to do with skills as most people have argued that the problem is lack of skills and poor education. The real problem has been on the demand side: employers do not want to employ graduates and /or give them in-service training, for reasons only known to the employers (including the public sector).

Compounding the unemployment challenge is a very small informal sector. This might very well be linked to government's perspective regarding the informal economy. Regardless, many developing countries, including African countries, have a vibrant informal economy. Of importance to the informal economy is its structure and organisation. In other words, the issue is about the kind of informal economy a country has as opposed to whether it has one.

The informal economy is different, conceptually, from what the government termed *second economy*. There is merit in addressing both the second economy, which is one of South African peculiarities, and the informal sector. Even in the sphere of the so-called second economy it is not clear what the government has done or is doing. What was unveiled as a second economy strategy needed to be followed by clear policy articulating options for improving the second economy and/or linking it to the so-called first economy.

EDUCATION AND SKILLS DEVELOPMENT

Democratic South Africa inherited an extremely poor education and skills regime along with a skewed and biased system profoundly shaped by severe gaps in skills attainment along racial and gender lines (McGrath and Badroodien 2004). According to McGrath and Badroodien (2004), South Africa inherited an education system for which the curricula and research and teaching were fashioned to produce graduates that would serve a labour market that was rigidly separated by race and gender; the system was attributable to racial segregation in South African universities and was legislated with the passing of the Extension of University Education Act in 1959. South Africa's education and training has also failed to respond to the pressing socioeconomic needs of the country.

Since 1994, the government has undertaken numerous initiatives to transform South Africa's education and training system so that it reflects the best ideals, values, and practices of a burgeoning democratic South Africa that responds to growing socioeconomic needs of the country. The government has introduced a myriad of education and training interventions in order to do so.

The 1995 White Paper on Education and Training entrusted the state with the responsibility of creating opportunities for citizens to develop their capabilities and potential. It also charged the state with the responsibility of ensuring education transformation, the "redress of educational inequalities among those sections of people who have suffered particular disadvantages," and the commitment to the principle of "equity" so that all citizens have "the same quality of learning opportunities" (National Department of Education 1995, 21–22).

The Constitution provides the overarching ideals for a national policy on basic education and higher education. It gave birth to the 1996 National Education Policy Act, the 1996 South African Schools Act, and the 1997 Higher Education Act. The 1996 National Education Policy Act became an overarching framework for education transformation and reinforced the need to democratise and transform the national education system, as well as to have an integrated, coherent, and coordinated system that serves the needs and interests of all the people of South Africa and upholds their fundamental rights (Republic of South Africa 1996). Specific to basic education transformation aspirations, the South African Schools Act 1996 asserted that a new schooling system would "redress past injustices in schooling provision, provide an education of progressively high quality for all learners...advance the democratic transformation of society...[and] contribute to the eradication of poverty and the economic wellbeing of society" (Republic of South Africa 1996). The Education White Paper 3 of 1997 and the 1997 Higher Education Act called on the higher education sector to play a key role in the move towards achieving "political democratisation, economic reconstruction and development, and redistributive social justice aimed at equity" (National Department of Education 1997).

And finally, the government also introduced a set of skills development legislation together with the National Skills Development Strategy, which sought to achieve a skills revolution in enterprise training (McGrath and Badroodien 2006). According to McGrath and Badroodien (2006), these created an institutional framework that understood skills building as a collectively-derived input that the market mechanism would not be able to achieve effectively on its own. The policy framework on skills development intended to develop critical skills for sustainable growth, as well as promote employability and sustainable livelihoods for designated groups, including new entrants by helping them participate in accredited work, as well as integrated learning and work-based programmes.

Turning to skills development in particular, the National Skills Development Strategy (NSDS) came about as an initiative by the democratic government to address education and training inefficiencies that were legacies of colonialism (McGrath and Badroodien 2006). More specifically, the NSDS intends to develop a culture of high quality, lifelong learning, as well as foster skills development in the formal and informal economy.

It is argued that the first version of the NSDS represented a very ambitious attempt to radically transform enterprise training in South Africa (McGrath and Badroodien 2004). According to McGrath and Badroodien (2004), the new institutional environment was structured largely around learnerships and Sector Education and Training Authorities (SETAs). In addition, there are numerous pieces of legislation that have been enacted in order to give impetus to skills development in South Africa:

- South African Qualifications Authorities Act of 1995.
- Skills Development Act of 1998.
- Skills Development Levies Act of 1999.
- Employment Equity Act of 1998.
- Further Education and Training Act of 1998.

The South African Qualifications Act established authorities to oversee and implement the National Qualifications Framework (NQF), register qualifications, and monitor and promote high standard qualifications (National Department of Labour 2001). According to the Department of Labour (2001), the establishment of National Standard Bodies (NSBs), and Education and Training Quality Assurance Bodies (ETQAs) through the Act enabled the South African Qualifications Authorities to oversee the NQF implementation and to monitor the quality of training given by providers according to the standards and qualifications on the NQF. NSBs were established to recommend standards and qualifications to the South African Qualifications Authority (SAQA) for registration on NQF. ETQAs, accredited by SAQA, are responsible for monitoring the quality of training provisions.

The Skills Development Act (SDA) aims to create a more educated and trained workforce to improve the employability of people, to build entrepreneurial skills for productive citizenship, and to increase investment in education and training in business (National Department of Labour 2001). According to the Department of Labour (2001), it provides the institutional framework to devise and implement national, sector, and workplace strategies. The SDA integrates strategies within the NQF of SAQA by training and developing programmes that provide workers with nationally recognised qualifications. It provides the financing of skills development through a levy-grant scheme and the National Skills Fund (NSF) and also aims to provide and regulate employment services that will help new entrants to the labour market, the unemployed, and retrenched workers find work.

The Skills Levies Act introduces a levy payment system in which the skills levies paid by employers are used to fund skills development (National Department of Labour 2001). For firms that pay in access of R25,000 per annum in remuneration, 1 percent of the total remuneration is collected by the South African Revenue Service (SARS), 20 percent of which is used by the National Skills Fund for national priority projects, and 80 percent by SETAs (10 percent of which is used for administrative purposes and the rest is refundable to compliant firms).

The 1998 Further Education and Training Act aims, among other things, to create a vibrant, accessible, and high quality Further Education and Training (FET) college system that imparts the kind of skills and knowledge needed by South Africans to be productive while keeping abreast with modern technology that meets the country's pressing human resource needs as well as encouraging lifelong learning and contributing towards development (McGrath and Badroodien 2004).

The NSDS, in essence, seeks to achieve its goals through a system of co-ordinated functions giving effect to governing policies (National Department of Labour 2001). There are, however, valid concerns that the core elements of the new system might have been too ambitious for the current South African context (Mayer and Altman 2006). It is argued that the problem with the policy direction of the late 1990s is that the lessons learnt are more attuned to a first-world country.

With regard to basic education, it could be argued that the main goal of the 1996 South African Schools Act was to de-racialise education and create race-blind policies throughout the system. In accordance with the1996 Education White Paper (National Department of Education 1996) on the organisation, governance, and funding of schools, the 1996 South African Schools Act calls for a new structure of school organisation, which should create the conditions necessary for developing a coherent and flexible national system that redresses past inequity, eliminates inequalities in the use of public resources, and ensures an improvement in the quality of education across the system.

In addition, the 1996 South African Schools Act sought to unify the fragmented education departments into one department and to make education compulsory for all learners regardless of race. In accordance with the Act, the minister of education, in 2006, declared deserving schools "no-fee schools." The South African government has also been introducing various curriculum reforms since 1994. Curriculum 2005

(C2005) outcomes-based education (OBE) was implemented in the school curricula as a competence-based learning and teaching methodology aimed at facilitating learners' strategic and technical skills until 2010. Some of the identified outcomes of such a system included ensuring that learners identify and solve problems and make decisions using critical and creative thinking; work effectively with others as members of a team, group, organisation, and community; organise and manage themselves and their activities responsibly and effectively; collect, analyse, organise, and critically evaluate information; and communicate effectively using visual, symbolic. and/or language skills in various modes. The rationale for such a curriculum within a new democracy makes not only political but also economic sense with the country's aspirations to establish itself as a strong, globally competitive knowledge economy.

Where it has worked, OBE has worked relatively well but generally there have been many challenges with the curriculum owing to insufficient teacher training, unsatisfactory teacher-learner ratios, lack of availability of learning materials and other resources, as well as language barriers. The government introduced the National Curriculum Statement (NCS) after OBE—then the Revised National Curriculum Statement, and in 2012 a Curriculum Assessment Policy Statement (CAPS) was introduced. Similar to the frequent changes in the Further Education and Training (FET) colleges—FET colleges were changed to be Technical Vocational Education and Training (TVET) colleges in 2014—there are many endless changes in general education. It might be better to improve on what exists than to frequently change without a comprehensive overarching policy.

Regarding higher education, the higher education sector has also undergone (and continues to undergo) transformation. Education White Paper 3: A Programme for the Transformation of Higher Education (National Department of Education 1997a) outlines a framework for transforming the higher education system to serve a new social order, meet pressing national needs, and respond to new realities and opportunities.

The important objectives in line with the vision of the National Plan on Higher Education (National Department of Education 2001c) include: achieving equity and diversity in the South African higher education system; producing graduates needed for the social and economic development of South Africa; promoting research; and restructuring the institutional landscape. The most recent thinking on further transforming the higher education sector (and perhaps correcting errors committed earlier) is contained in the 2013 White Paper for Post-School Education and Training.

Similar to other education sub-sectors, the higher education system inherited from the apartheid era was one characterised by inequity, fragmentation, and inefficiency, with thirty-six public higher education institutions (twenty-one universities and fifteen technikons), separated along racial lines (Breier and Mabizela 2008). For some reason the government opted for restructuring the higher education landscape by merging institutions. Two phases of restructuring occurred between 2004 and 2005, which saw the emergence of new terms of reference and institutional arrangements for institutions. For instance, universities not required to merge with any other institution remained "universities" (such as those that merged with or rather incorporated other universities); some technikons were transformed into "universities of technology;" some universities were merged with technikons and became "comprehensive institutions;" and two national institutes for higher education were established in Mpumalanga and the Northern Cape. The 2013 White Paper for Post-School Education and Training recommends that the two national institutes for higher education in Mpumalanga and the Northern Cape be converted to two new universities.

OTHER EDUCATION TRANSFORMATION INITIATIVES

Acknowledging the challenge of poverty and underdevelopment faced by the majority of South Africans, the Education White Paper 5 on Early Childhood Development (National Department of Education 2001a) highlights that children raised in poor families are most at risk of infant death, low birth weight, stunted growth, poor adjustment to school, increased repetition of school grades, and dropping out of school. This was cited as a strong enough case for the National Department of Education to set up an action plan to address the early learning opportunities of all learners, especially those living in poverty. The government's objective has been to increase access to and improve the quality of early learning and development programmes particularly for poor children.

The government is implementing a number of other programmes such as Adult Basic Education and Training (ABET) and a mass literacy campaign. These programmes are geared primarily towards eradicating illiteracy; they have been made available to adults seeking to finish their basic education while offering learning tools, knowledge, and skills under nationally recognised qualifications. Furthermore, acknowledging the dire impact of apartheid on special needs education, a policy to transform the education sector was effected in 2001 through the publication of Education White Paper 6: Special Needs Education: Building an Inclusive Education and Training System (National Department of Education 2001b). During apartheid, the segregation of learners on the basis of race was extended to incorporate segregation on the basis of disability and thus special schools were organised according to two segregating criteria: race and disability. Schools that accommodated white disabled learners were well resourced, while the few schools for African disabled learners were systematically under-resourced resulting in only 20 percent of learners with disabilities being accommodated in special schools (National Department of Education 2001b). For this reason, the National Department of Education, now as National Department of Basic Education, continues to drive the policy on special needs education, outlining how the education and training system must be transformed to accommodate the full range of learning needs and the mechanisms that should be put in place.

ADVANCING HEALTH AND WELLBEING

The challenge of the provision of social services in South Africa is largely similar in many cases, and it is largely a legacy of apartheid colonialism. Undoing the legacy of apartheid colonialism is taking a long time. In addition, as this book demonstrates, there is a challenge that relates to policy and policy reform. Redressing the legacy of apartheid colonialism, with regards to social provisioning, requires robust and appropriate policies. Like in education and other areas, there are policy constraints that have limited the extent to which South Africa is addressing the legacy of the apartheid health care system.

Health care administration was fragmented during the apartheid dispensation. For instance, there were fourteen separate health care departments for the different racial groups, the homelands, and self-governing territories. The transformation that had to take place in the health care space was guided by the Constitution which requires of the state to take "reasonable legislative and other measures within its available resources, to achieve the progressive realisation of each of these rights." In particular, Section 27.1 of the Constitution indicates that "everyone has the right to have access to health care services, including reproductive health" (Cullinan 2006).

Numerous policies have been pursued in order to redress the legacy of apartheid with regards to health care in South Africa. Of note are the policies that ensured access to health care by children, pregnant mothers, the aged as well as those with disabilities or the poor in general. The other set of policies focused on improving the public health care system which was in a dire state on the eve of democracy—this remains as a severe challenge, implying an inability of policy or policy reforms to reconfigure the public health care infrastructure. This is not to say that other challenges such as poor implementation have not limited progress with regards to health care. The prevailing argument is that a weaknesses in policy and policy reform pose as more pressing in nature than other challenges that may have shown socioeconomic transformation.

Although there has been commendable progress in health care, as in other areas of socioeconomic development, this progress would have been more notable had there been effective policies or if policy reforms were sequenced accordingly. More pressingly, implementation requires a coherent set of policy reforms if policy is to meet its desired objectives. The necessary institutional reforms that have taken place since 1994 could have delivered better results had they been informed by appropriate policies or policy reforms.

Increasing access to health care was a starting point; it became apparent that access needed to be expanded because of the discriminatory and exclusionary apartheid system. Other policies and programmes such as those that target specific diseases such as HIV, AIDS, and tuberculosis appear to have ameliorated the health care challenge that relates to the "burden of disease."

However, the major policy issues relating to equity were not sufficiently addressed. As such, twenty years since the dawn of democracy, the two-tier health care system remains. The recent policy of National Health Insurance (NHI) is intended to address this critical challenge. The NHI is primarily aimed at making significant changes and improvements in the health care system as well as promoting equity, fairness, and social solidarity. The main objective of the policy is to ensure that all South Africans have full access to appropriate, efficient, and quality health care services. This policy is planned to be phased over a period of fourteen years and is said to require significant changes in the existing service delivery infrastructure, administrative structures, and management systems (National Department of Health 2013). In particular, the NHI's objectives are:

- to improve access to quality health services for all South Africans, irrespective of whether they are employed or not;
- to pool risks and funds so that equity and social solidarity will be achieved through the creation of a single NHI fund;

- to procure services on behalf of the entire population and efficiently mobilise and control key financial resources; and
- to strengthen the under-resourced and strained public sector in order to improve the health system's performance.

The fundamental political economy issue pertaining to wellbeing in South Africa is social policy. This important and overdue policy can significantly improve the health profile of the country. Like the poor economic policy, social policy has not played its extremely important role. It is also in this context that South Africa has very high unemployment—the labour market, as a social institution, has not transformed. Government has, quite understandably, prioritised social provisioning. However, access to basic services, social pensions, and strengthening social capital requires a robust social policy that should guide interventions regarding the social wage in particular. In essence, it is about the society that is envisaged. Also of importance is that there should be an appropriate interface between social policy and economic policy. The obvious candidate for that is the labour market.

CONCLUSION

This chapter has discussed the evolution of the South Africa's policy environment from the perspective of what was initially envisaged for society. Although South Africa has done relatively well in many respects, it could have done better. The point that this chapter makes is that the evolution of South African society from 1994 to approximately 2006 has been close to what was envisaged. However, from about 2006—due to weak policy and reforms—a number of aspects of societal development have not improved.

Therefore, because of weak social policy, wellbeing has not advanced to satisfactory levels—many people remain in unemployment and poverty and are unhappy and unsatisfied with weak social capital, which also impacts social cohesion. Policy or appropriate reforms would have stood

South Africa in good stead in advancing wellbeing. While bigger issues of power relations, property relations, and the global order would take a lifetime to address, policy can be reformed and implemented readily to ease the pain that many South Africans are enduring.

NOTES

1. I spent about 10 years doing policy work in government and I have been teaching public policy since leaving government in 2009.
2. Hart (2013) extensively covers the various views on the NDR, especially critics like Neville Alexander. Ivor Chipkin (2007) explains the NDR in detail and Devan Pillay (2011) presents a concise history of the NDR and its relevance in the Zuma dispensation.
3. Besides an argument by Peter Hudson (1986:7) that the Freedom Charter is a "notoriously ambiguous document", Albert Luthuli (1963:151) confesses that – because inputs from the branches came very late – "it was not too possible for the National Action Committee to circulate the draft carefully. The result is that the declaration in the Charter is uneven."
4. According to Motsoko Pheko (2012), regarding the Freedom Charter, Sobukwe viewed the Freedom Charter as a "colossal fraud ever perpetrated upon the exploited and degraded people... It is a product of the slave mentality and colonialist orientation."
5. The National Institute of Economic Policy (NIEP) played an important role in shaping economic policy in South Africa, perhaps more in critiquing policies than in formulating them.
6. During the finalisation of this book, government passed a law—Employment Tax Incentive Act (2014) —to implement a wage subsidy. The wage or employment subsidy was originally proposed as part of a National Health Insurance programme in 2005; proposals were developed and suggested the design and implementation thereof were approved by Cabinet in 2007. From a financing perspective, employment subsidisation was critical because of the high unemployment. Other proposals included the Risk Equalisation Fund, the Solidarity Fund.
7. This view was pronounced among formations such as Cosatu and individuals such as Patrick Bond and Ashgar Adelzadeh.
8. Alan Hirsch wrote a newspaper article on this—see: http://www.iol.co.za/news/special-features/was-jujus-criticism-of-madiba-justified-1963939.
9. The NPC, originally established to work with the Ministry of Planning in the Presidency, formulated the *National Development Plan: Vision 2030*, adopted at the ANC's policy conference in 2012. The Plan determines the future that South Africa should aim towards and it proposes a social pact for the *Vision 2030*.

10. Frank Meintjies (2013) argues that "CODESA did nothing to rearrange economic power. It was silent on the need for ownership changes in major corporations. It sent no message about the need to reverse injustice in land ownership."
11. Nahla Valji (2004) and Mahmood Mamdani (2000) are renowned critics of the TRC. Valji (2004), for instance, argues that the TRC's failure to deal with the issue of race was an "ironic silence" because economic discrimination and various forms of human rights violations were motivated by racism. Among other issues, Mamdani (2000:59) views the use of a Latin American commission's design as problematic because "the Latin American analogy obscured the colonial nature of the South African context: the link between conquest and dispossession, between racialised power and racialised privilege, between perpetrator and beneficiary."

Chapter 5

Nation Building

> I believe that perhaps we should answer this question honestly and deal with the consequences of an honest response.... our answer to the question whether we are making that requisite progress towards achieving the objective of nation building would be no! A major component part of the issue of reconciliation and nation building is defined by and derives from the material conditions in our society which have divided our country into two nations, the one black and the other white.
>
> Thabo Mbeki, 29 May 1998, First democratic deputy president of South Africa and 11th President of the ANC

Introduction

This chapter deals with the *national question*: an issue that has been largely avoided in the post-apartheid dispensation in South Africa. By a national question, simplistically, it is implied that there is appropriate balance of power and influence among all population and ethnic groups in a nation state. Ernest Renan[1] (1882, 892), writing in the context of a "French nation" argues that "the essence of a nation is that individuals have many things in common, and as well as all forgot [forget] many things." Joseph Stalin (1953), however, defined a nation as "a historically constituted, stable community of people, formed on the basis of a common language, territory, economic life, and psychological make-up manifested in a common culture."[2]

Eric Hobsbawm (1962, 53), in explaining the French Revolution, argues that France "provided the first great example of the concept and the vocabulary of nationalism."[3] Benedict Anderson (2006), who has put the theorisation about notions of nation, nationalism, and national identity back on the agenda in the 1980s, defines a nation as "an imagined political community—and imagined as both inherently limited and sovereign... the nation is always conceived as a deep, horizontal comradeship" (Anderson 2006, 8). Language, culture, and similar factors are critical in the imagination of a political community as complementary efforts in nation building. Nationalism, though, refers to loyalty based on nationality—it could be an association premised on commonality of language, religion, ethnicity, or such.

The starting point, in any discussion of the (post-apartheid) South African "nation" should be a reflection on the three key periods in the South African history that have shaped the post-apartheid society so far:1652–1795, 1795–1870, and 1948–1994. The first period (1652–1795) represents colonial exploits by the Dutch and their particular type of colonialism that used commercial entities such as the Dutch East Indian Company (DEIC). It was during this time that the Cape of Good Hope (present day Cape Town) gradually became a place of trade and stopovers en route to Asian colonies and spice markets.[4]

The period 1795–1870 represents the ascent (and eventual colonialism) of the British initially on the Cape and eventually South Africa as a whole. It was during this period that the development of mining, financial institutions, and other activities gained momentum.[5] The period between 1948–1994 represents a time when the Afrikaner nationalists were in power and formally installed an apartheid system. The end result of the white minority rule was that land belonging to African peoples was confiscated (through the Land Act of 1913), their movement across the country was restricted, and they were legally forced to live in so-called Bantu areas based on their ethnic classification (as per the Population Registration Act of 1950, Group Areas Act of 1950, Prohibition of Mixed Marriages Act of 1949, Black Homeland Citizenship Act of 1970, and Reservation of Separate Amenities Act of 1953), and the education system was configured to favour whites (as per the Bantu Authorities Act of 1951 and Bantu Education Act 1953).[6]

It is therefore important to appreciate that when discussing a post-apartheid South Africa and a South African society, one is attempting to understand and analyse a system of over 350 years of systematic oppression and dispossession. The era of apartheid, its legislation, and institutions through which the [apartheid] ideology was implemented left a legacy of persistent poverty and extreme inequalities that spans over 300 years. As a result, post-apartheid South Africa is confronted with massive "accumulated disadvantages," which can only be sustainably addressed collectively.[7] Therefore, any change to previous oppressive laws and twisted logic of the apartheid system is [was] bound to be an exercise in the creation of something not only new but strikingly new to both victims and perpetrators.

Major Shifts in South African Society

It is critical to first and foremost understand that early African kingdoms and socioeconomic development were interrupted by European slavery, colonialism, and apartheid rule. However, when outlining what constitutes major shifts in South African post-apartheid society, two events are at least worth brief attention: the unbanning of anti-apartheid political parties and the Convention for a Democratic South Africa (Codesa) and the creation of a new Republic of South Africa.

UNBANNING OF ANTI-APARTHEID POLITICAL PARTIES

South Africa was a country under a four-year State of Emergency (1989–1993); however, the last sitting apartheid head of state, FW De Klerk, announced the unbanning of the African National Congress (ANC), Pan-Africanist Congress (PAC), and other liberation movements like the Black Consciousness Movement and the United Democratic Front.[8] The landmark speech by the then president of apartheid South Africa, FW De Klerk, unleashed many changes in society including, but not limited to, how the different races would interact both at a political level and at a social level.

Indeed, the unbanning of political parties ushered in a new era from a legal and political perspective. It must be mentioned that FW de Klerk did not just, overnight, decide to permit political activism—there were a series of events, including numerous discussions with the ANC leadership. In fact, the discussions, characterised by Willie Esterhuyse as "talks about talks," date as far back as the 1980s.[9] The "secret negotiations" played a critical role in nudging FW de Klerk towards permitting political activism and releasing political prisoners.

EVOLVING A NEW SOUTH AFRICA

According to Gumede (2015f, 137–138), "some of the key defining features of post-apartheid South Africa emanated from the Convention for Democratic South Africa (Codesa) meetings. Codesa I and II highlighted two pivotal points: the future of South Africa's political stability rests on an understanding that no one party wins the battle, but rather negotiations set South Africa's post-apartheid narrative and system, and the transition from dictatorial and oppressive apartheid rule would be done in a manner that sought to maintain certain institutions and rights of the minority, while also recognising the historical injustices visited on Africans over centuries. The Codesa negotiations were, therefore, an attempt to systemically create an environment and decision making processes through which a "new" South Africa could be agreed upon."

Codesa negotiations started on December 20, 1991, and many tragic and challenging events would unfold over the preceding two years.[10] For example, the general secretary of the South African Communist Party, Chris Hani, was assassinated by right-wing elements. Initially and ultimately, not all liberation movements participated in the negotiations. The Inkatha Freedom Party (IFP) attempted to circumvent the process in order to introduce new policy debates (e.g., the formal and legal recognition of the amaZulu monarch and monarchy under His Royal Highness King Goodwill Zwelithini kaBhekuzulu.[11]) Lastly, it is important to acknowledge that that the road to negotiations was paved over many years by the various players, both in the Afrikaner community and within the liberation movement.

From Interim to Final Constitution

One of the lasting legacies of the Codesa meetings was that an interim South African constitution was drafted which would later become the Republic of South Africa's 1996 Constitution. The 1996 Constitution is one of the hallmarks of the post-apartheid South African society. The 1996 Constitution is pivotal in the making of the post-apartheid society because it serves as the "foundation" on which citizens interact with the state and other democratic institutions of government, as well as find recourse for other non-political matters. For instance, the 1996 Constitution best captures the aims and objectives of a post-apartheid society when it states that,

> We, the people of South Africa, Recognise the injustices of our past; Honour those who suffered for justice and freedom in our land; Respect those who have worked to build and develop our country; and believe that South Africa belongs to all who live in it, united in our diversity. We, therefore, through our freely elected representatives, adopt this Constitution as the supreme

> law of the Republic so as to heal the divisions of the past and establish a society based on democratic values, social justice and fundamental human rights; Lay the foundations for a democratic and open society in which government is based on the will of the people and every citizen is equally protected by law; Improve the quality of life of all citizens and free the potential of each person; and Build a united and democratic South Africa... (Republic of South Africa 1996, 3)

Given the nature of the political settlement and the complexities of the transition, any narrative of the so-called post-apartheid South African society, has to reflect on the Codesa negotiations and the eventual end product of that era—the 1996 Constitution. However, as indicated in the first chapter, many people view the transition and consequently Codesa as an elite pact—that Codesa resulted in an elite transition where the elite made compromises that have constrained the speed with which inclusive development is taking place in post-apartheid South Africa. There is a context to this, as many have explained. Vincent Maphai (1993, 255), for instance, argued that "the negotiation process was underpinned by at least two major factors: first, that by the late 1980s both the ruling National Party and the ANC believed that the country had reached a stalemate. The second factor is the endemic political violence which emanates largely, though not exclusively, from right-wing elements."

NARRATIVES OF UNITY

Part of the early post-1994 narrative of trying to unify or allow South Africans to view one another as joint owners of the Republic of South Africa was the investment in soft-power politics by government and other non-government entities. Key defining moments in this regard were sporting events such as the 1995 Rugby World Cup, the 1996 African Nations Cup, and subsequent sporting events as well as active creation of new symbols of unity such as the national anthem, the coat of arms, and the flag.

As part of an attempt to inculcate African-ness, or South African-ness in particular, Thabo Mbeki—then as the Deputy President of the new South Africa—gave a moving rendition at the launch of the new Constitution (in Parliament), invoking being an African. Thabo Mbeki, in the 1996 speech "I am an African," described being South African fundamentally in historical terms; but it appears that, though lauded by many, the speech was not helpful in directly dealing with the national question. If taken for granted that anyone can view himself as "African," could that translate into a South African nation in South Africa? It seems to me that the idea of a South African nation is still farfetched if the basic ingredients of nationhood (such as feelings of oneness, socio-cultural affinity, and institutionalised framework of unity) remain patchy or nearly absent in some instances. Other requirements for building social cohesion and national harmony such as education, cross-cultural mingling, and equitable access to material and economic opportunities continue to be absent in post-apartheid South Africa. For instance, many institutions of higher learning continue to reinforce the divisions of the past as they are racially configured both at the student and faculty levels. Although the old slogan of "white only" schools has been removed, inadequate economic resources have successfully excluded many of the previously disadvantaged groups from accessing such institutions. This abnormality calls for a pragmatic public policy intervention, which sadly, has been missing.

In a letter (dated June 22, 2013) addressed to the Concerned Africans Forum, Thabo Mbeki argued that a discussion on the *national question* has been based on the understanding that such a *solution* [to the national question] would derive from the achievement of related and interconnected objectives:

- the equitable (non-racial) sharing of **political** power, through the establishment of a democratic system;

- the equitable (non-racial) **economic** sharing of wealth and income, and therefore the eradication of poverty and the elimination of race, gender and geographic disparities and imbalances in this regard;
- the actual **social** integration of the South African population, (across the colour-line), given the very visible colour and racial identities of this population; and,
- the development of a common (non-racial) **psychological** sense of common national identity, and therefore a shared patriotism.

I have been outlining key historical events and highlighting certain key soft-power events. I now turn to a discussion of the events described thus far as they are aimed at fostering positive power dynamics. The power dynamic in question firstly relates to *moral capital.* While the apartheid system came to be reviled and rendered obsolete by the anti-apartheid movement and other forces in the late 1980s, one of the greatest weapons or powers gained by the post-apartheid government, led by the ANC, was moral capital. Kane (2001, 7) describes moral capital as having "moral prestige—whether of an individual, organisation or a cause—in useful service."[12] This capital was best exemplified by the late president of South Africa who received much international and local support premised on his moral capital.

This aspect of power (i.e., moral capital) hinges on the fact that society, firstly voters and non-political actors, trusts government or non-governmental institutions. This form of power has been cited as being needed for building trust among members of society or institutions.[13] It banks on citizens' ability to trust that government, civil service, and business entities have their best interests at heart and will not be taken for granted.

It can be argued that the post-apartheid South African society, especially post-1994 to 2009, was characterised by national government and political leaders being the primary custodians of moral capital. However, as South Africa was entering its second decade of democracy, numerous signs of weakening moral capital were showing. Some cite the declining number of non-voting eligible citizens, increases in service delivery protests, escalating concerns about the enrichment of politicians at the expense of citizens, failure of government institutions to deliver quality education and health care as well as other problems that create mistrust in government authority.

Another undocumented viewpoint suggests that the situation is not that dire. Given that the new South Africa is only twenty-one years old, one should not expect miracles. Given the various historical cleavages characterising South African society, it is expected to take a longer period to create a South African "nation." An alternative view also argues that the service delivery protests are an indication of an effective, functioning democracy. In addition, freedom of expression, especially for the media, the independence of the Office of the Public Protector, and the increasing number of political parties augur well for efforts towards forming a South African "nation."

The second power dynamic that exists within the post-apartheid society is twofold: namely, *capital/financial resources* and *governmental power* in the form of public policy. While political power might have become more democratised after the 1994 elections, numerous commentators highlight that financial or capital power still resides with white minority business and the middle class. For instance, although inequality is a function of an under-transformed labour market and a skewed structure of the economy, the entrenched legacy of apartheid colonialism has ensured that it increases or remains very high. Taking the historical experience of apartheid colonialism as paramount, it is not surprising that white privilege remains stark. While this understanding of power has been greatly challenged by the ascent of the so-called black middle class, the nature and ability of this middle class to effect wider socioeconomic development has cast much doubt on whether white financial capital was affected in any manner post 1994.[14]

With regard to public policy—government power—the post-1994 government has pursued two interventions: formulation of socioeconomic policies to advantage or attempt to improve the material condition of blacks (Africans in particular), and the utilisation of national resources gained from the taxation of individuals and businesses to effect socioeconomic change. Gumede (2008a, 16) argued that "in essence, as recent targets and objectives imply, (social) policy making in South Africa has been about addressing the challenge of poverty and underdevelopment as well as building national unity." Therefore, the post-apartheid policy narrative and outputs have been geared at attempting to deal with the socioeconomic shortfalls inherited from the apartheid regime.

However, the government's inability to create a democratised form of shared capital and financial resources has resulted in unequal relations between white and black South Africans. With financial resources still being predominantly the preserve of whites, unequal power relations still characterise the working, living, and even social environment.[15] The inability to ensure that blacks are able to share the riches of the country through access to gainful employment has meant that they are still dependant largely on government's ability to provide quality education and support grants. In instances for which job opportunities abound, skills mismatch and lack of requisite capacity and experiences often deny Africans access to such jobs. This problem is particularly acute for youth, many of whom are currently out of school and unemployed.

Furthermore, poor relations between a largely white private sector and black government have fostered an environment of mistrust and the inability to work together to invest in the wellbeing of citizens. Lastly, the post-1994 dispensation's inability to deliver much needed services has created a situation where citizens no longer believe that government agencies and departments work for their good. In fact, the government elite come across as simply the agents of global capital.

The Making of Post-Apartheid South Africa

Based on the abovementioned, a few questions arise. For instance, what is the likelihood that citizens shift their trust from government institutions to non-governmental entities while government grapples with the various socioeconomic challenges? Would South Africans give way to their frustrations and revolt? In addition, what perception do black South Africans have of South African corporations, especially the large private sector? Such questions point towards salient factors that constrain the making of a South African nation. Some of these critical factors are discussed in the next section.

Race Still Matters

Despite the major strides made by both government and the broader society, the unfortunate issue of race still permeates South African society. Interestingly, the late Bernard Magubane (1979)[16] described South Africa as a society characterised by a hierarchy of wealth and social power whereby whites are at the top and blacks are at the bottom. Magubane (1979) further explained that even though South Africa's racial stratification was inherent in the colonial setup, it could not be divorced from capitalist economic development. As he aptly puts it, "in a racist-capitalist power structure, capitalist exploitation and race oppression are inextricably linked" (Magubane 1979, 16). It would seem not much has changed. Former president of the ANC, Albert Luthuli, posed a pertinent question that remains relevant even in this day: Whose is South Africa.[17]

The recent report by the Institute for Justice and Reconciliation explains that,

> The relationship between race and class in South Africa paints a picture of class segregation with racial inflections. The majority of the poor continue to be black and segregated from the multiracial, urban middle class. This pattern is witnessed on the geographical landscape of South Africa, where our cities may demonstrate

> increasing racial integration, but townships and rural settlements continue to be poor, black and segregated as was intended by apartheid planners. This finding is important for racial reconciliation in South Africa and points to the need to address the relationship between material and social exclusion that results in the segregation of many poor black South Africans from interracial middle-class city spaces[18] (Wale 2014, 24).

It is indubitable that the post-apartheid society has yet to properly deal with the phenomena of race at both a social and economic level. While it cannot be denied that the legal and tangible racial aspects that began with British imperialism and worsened with Afrikaner nationalism have been slightly addressed, the real effects of racial inequality and systematic racism at an economic level are yet to be properly attended to.

ECONOMIC DEMOCRATISATION, NON-EVENT

It is also clear that the South African government is yet to develop an appropriate economic policy that addresses challenges such as youth unemployment, poor entrepreneurial support and financial assistance, inadequate use of rural areas for development, poor spatial planning for township economic development, and other avenues that can be exploited to accelerate development.

The issue of economic opportunities, however, is more pressing. Although the South African economy has done relatively well since 1994, the benefits of economic growth have been unequally shared across society. Despite the numerous political economy interventions unpacked in the preceding chapter, the economic development needed by the vast majority of South Africans is still a work in progress. If government and the private sector are able to combine their financial and human capital, perhaps the problem of economic development will be better addressed. Yet, the defining characteristic of the post-apartheid society pertaining to economic development is a society that is unable to compete with other developing nations, one that performs poorly on the job creation front, and is unable to use its natural resources to effectively deal with poverty and inequality.

Disappearing Moral Capital

One of the emerging characteristics of a post-apartheid South Africa is the phenomena of citizens increasingly losing trust (moral and social) in the governing party and various government institutions. While it has been shown internationally that the relationship between citizens and governments is often fraught with strained relations, the pace at which citizens are losing moral and social trust in the ANC is evidenced by:

(1) decreasing numbers of ANC voters.
(2) frequent violent protests against local and national authorities/institutions, due to the poor service delivery record.
(3) the ever increasing spectre of the ANC spawning or experiencing new breakaways (e.g. United Democratic Movement, Congress of the People and more recently the Economic Freedom Fighters) as well as the cleavages in the Tripartite Alliance (i.e. ANC, SACP and Cosatu).

These and other examples, whether in civil society in the form of political parties or ordinary protesting citizens, paint a picture of a society that is deeply at odds with the party in power and probably a society at odds with itself. Furthermore, it shows a picture of a society that is quickly beginning to believe that government is not its protector or agent in achieving its socioeconomic aspirations. Thus, would South Africa ever be a nation or are the various developments sketched above militating against the making of a South African nation?

Towards a South African Nation

Ivor Chipkin (2007), as indicated in chapter 1, discusses whether South Africans exist. Chipkin (2007, 175) concluded that "if South Africans were not a nation, they were, nonetheless, already some kind of people. The issue therefore: Who was [is] eligible for citizenship and who was [is] not. At stake were [are] the limits of the political community." It might very well be that Chipkin inevitably reaches this conclusion because his definition of a "nation," decidedly and conveniently, ignores the importance of cultural artifacts in a make-up of any "nation." Also, as captured by Ndlovu-Gatsheni (2013, 154), Chipkin (2007, 2–3) defines a nation as "a political community whose form is given in relation to the pursuit of democracy and freedom." I am more persuaded by Ndlovu-Gatsheni's formulation in his recent book that "for South Africa, the challenge was [is] how to mould the various ethnic and racial groups into a stable nation of diverse but equal citizens" (Ndlovu-Gatsheni 2013, 155). Incidentally, in interrogating the national question, Neville Alexander (1986, 66) argued that "there is no inherent contradiction between the postulate that nations are normal modes of existence of capitalist and socialist social formations and the almost universally recognised fact the nation state is outmoded in terms of development of the forces of production on a world economic scale."

Given that Renan (1882), Stalin (1953), Hobsbawm (1962), and Anderson (2006) state that it would make sense to think of a nation as involving both arte-facts and mental-facts, it is therefore problematic to think of a "nation" as simply a people pursuing democracy and freedom, especially in the context of South Africa and its political history. This is not to downplay African nationalist struggles which unquestionably brought about new "nations."

It is also important to acknowledge that "nations" may have existed long ago, particularly in the African continent, before the emergence of "print-capitalism" to use Anderson's nomenclature. I also want to argue that most literature, especially by leading scholars on nationalism is questionable in ignoring the African experience: could it be that Inkosi Shaka kaNandi[19] was a nationalist in pursuit of an "African nation." Also, we must not deceive ourselves into conflating citizenship and belonging to mean the existence of a "nation."

It might very well be that South Africa has succeeded only, to some extent, in state-building. Nation building, not state-building, can be viewed as the strengthening of unity, coherence, functionality, and pride in a nation state—in a speech at the National Assembly on May 29, 1998, during the debate on reconciliation and nation building, Thabo Mbeki defined nation building as "the construction of the reality and the sense of common nationhood which would result from the abolition of disparities in the quality of life among South Africans based on the racial, gender and geographic inequalities we all inherited from the past." For post-apartheid South Africa, it will be more meaningful and relevant to see a nation as a community that shares a lot in common, acknowledges and respects its repulsive political and economic history of deprivation through systematic restitutionary, reconciliatory, and restructuring measures, and equitable sharing of resources. As it stands, "democracy," especially liberal democracy, is insufficient!

The current order unquestionably perpetuates the injustices of the past, especially in areas of control over economic and intellectual resources. Thus, the nation building project appears to be falling apart in South Africa. It is debatable whether South Africans share similarities as those critical aspects of nation-building such as commonality of values, culture, language, shared psychological and emotional affinity are conspicuously missing among the various groups that currently inhabit the country. Arguably, the repulsive political history and the ramifications of apartheid colonialism make it difficult to build a "South African nation."

As previously indicated, South Africa, a creation of apartheid colonialism, has so-called different races: whites, coloureds, Indians, and Africans. The African nationalist struggles in South Africa should have focused on improving the lot for Africans—non-racialism, especially the artificial "rainbow nation," is insufficient, if not a complete myth (as some have put it). Neville Alexandre has made a case for the importance of non-racialism—understood as "race" categories becoming irrelevant—for the *national question*. Alexander (2013, 35) actually believed that the primary task facing South Africans was "to learn and to teach one another how to live in a democratic, non-racial society based on anti-capitalist economic and humanistic social and cultural principles." He was probably optimistic. The myth of the "rainbow nation" has been unravelling for a while and seeds of rapture have been planted.

Africans continue to suffer in the land of their forefathers, while whites hold the grip on the land's wealth and resources. Ndlovu-Gatsheni (2013, 175) writes that "South Africa is a typical example where a movement of black people that started with a liberatory agenda was, by the mid-1950s, gravitating toward an emancipatory project having been hijacked by both white and black liberals." It is therefore not an exaggeration to argue that South Africa appears to be drifting further away from being a "nation." It seems highly unlikely that we can have the celebrated French revolution that Renan (1882) and Hobsbawm (1962) discuss given the ANC's role in our body politic in trying to bring about a "South African nation." I wonder, however, if a South African specific cultural revolution is farfetched. While South Africa may not be able to drastically change the political transition it embraced, which might have been ideal under the then circumstances, South Africa could change its destiny through honest acknowledgment of the limitations of the political transition and the evolving dispensation.

The ANC—in its 1997 discussion document subtitled "The National Question in South Africa"—makes a startling self-defeatist, if not convenient and absurd, claim that "the national question can never be fully resolved." On the contrary, with visionary political leadership that is committed to positive social change as well as conscious and articulate citizens, the national question can be resolved. If the reality of the consequences of past injustices is duly and comprehensively acknowledged by the perpetrators, a deliberate elaborate agenda for the construction of a "South African nation" could be formulated and implemented.

Beyond the simplicity of acquiescence to the Constitution as a numinous path to nation building and a stable South Africa, the path to sustainable development lies in the agenda of building a nation where the uniqueness of the various nationalities and ethnicities, in terms of historical realities of land ownership and its appurtenances for example, cultural specificities, arte-facts and mental-facts, access to justice and opportunities, and mutual respect are taken seriously. An agenda for nation building in South Africa will also require institutional frameworks and political processes that are geared towards the promotion of social cohesion, inclusion, and socio-economic and political integration of all inhabitants of the country. Besides, a deliberate programme of socialisation must be pursued that will see the heirs to apartheid-inspired accumulation of wealth, appreciating the injustices of the past, having their mind de-racialised and reconstructing the damaged and subjugated minds of Africans to have confidence in the essence of their being as subjects, rather than objects of history.

Ideas and Perspectives for a New Nation

As indicated in the preceding chapter, the policies and programmes for inclusive development and for imagining a new "South African nation" have been shaped by three main ideas and perspectives: the Colonialism of a Special Type (CST) thesis, the two-stage theory of the National Democratic Revolution (NDR), and the Freedom Charter. These three ideas and perspectives have been questioned by many. Among the main concerns is that these ideas and perspectives might have been informed by inaccurate theorisation or they were relevant for those particular contexts. My fundamental challenge is the overemphasis on non-racialism that consequently blurs the historical experience of apartheid colonialism.

This preoccupation with non-racialism discounts the fact that Africans suffered historical injustices of apartheid colonialism of which the ramifications are still pronounced even after two decades of political independence. As many have argued, South Africa appears stuck in the bourgeois democracy phase—the first stage of the NDR. As Peter Hudson (1986) predicted, national [bourgeois] democracy would most likely lead to a consolidation of capitalism than a transition to socialism. South Africa seems to have what Bernard Magubane (1979) terms as a "racist-capitalist power structure." In such a reality, the focus should have been specifically the liberation of Africans, including their economic standing instead of "bettering lives of all."

It is therefore important to rethink the main ideas and perspectives that have informed the socioeconomic transformation programme for South Africa. Writing in the late 1950s and early 1960s, Luthuli (2006, 76) made a point that "the basic point at issue in South Africa is the question of ownership." It is in this context that many people argue for the de-racialisation of the means of production. Other political economy interventions, as the next chapter shows, can only scratch the surface.

The obsession with class analysis should be countered by the disturbing reality that race remains a salient factor in South Africa and that, as Magubane (1979, 17) presented, "African workers are confined to a marginal, yet indispensable, role by fraud, violence, and a system of institutionalised racism that protects the white masters of the world." White privilege continues to loom large in South Africa. As indicated earlier, efforts towards constructing and imagining a "South African nation" have to prioritise restitutionary, reconciliatory, and restructuring measures and ensure equitable sharing of resources. This is not to say that class analysis is wrong. My view is that we are dealing with a race question. At issue is the de-racialisation of the South African economy. The next chapter and the concluding chapter deal with this fundamental issue.

CONCLUSION

Indeed, the post-apartheid South African society is fundamentally different to the one shaped by draconian laws and policies of the apartheid regime. Yet, while the draconian laws and repulsive policies of the British Empire and National Party were eradicated with democracy, the South African post-apartheid society is grappling with the socioeconomic effects of the centuries of systemic racism and the abuse of blacks (and Africans in particular) and is yet to fundamentally change in order to be considered a just and equitable society.

As for becoming a nation, South Africa seems to be drifting further away and at the expense of Africans. A close examination of "related and interconnected objectives" that former president Thabo Mbeki enumerated in his letter to the Concerned Africans Forum suggests that most of those objectives are far from being achieved. Malcolm Ray, in a lecture at the University of Johannesburg on July 2, 2012, argues that "despite the merits of constitutional liberties—equally conferred on *all* citizens [in South Africa] since 1994—the various strands of identity politics that coalesced under the national flag, sensualised in emblematic or iconographic forms of 'rainbow' nationalism during the 'honeymoon period' of the post-liberation transition, have yet to be built up, elaborated, and translated into durable propositions of national unity." The closing chapter discusses possible interventions towards making South Africa, at minimum, an inclusive society and thereby getting closer, hopefully, to resolving the national question.

NOTES

1. Renan, E. 1882. What is a Nation? Conference Faite en Sorbone, March 11, 1882, Oeuvres, Completes.
2. Stalin, J. 1953. 'Marxism and the National Question', in *Works*, Moscow, vol. 2, 300–381.
3. Hobsbawm, E. 1962. The Age of Revolution: Europe: 1789–1848, Vintage Books, New York.
4. South African History Online. *Dutch East India Company (DEIC)/VOC.* Accessed on November 29, 2014, http://www.sahistory.org.za/topic/dutch-east-india-company-deicvoc.
5. Aartsma, H. 2008. *Early history of the Cape Colony, South Africa.* Accessed on November 29, 2014, www.south-africa-tours-and-travel.com.
6. *Apartheid Legislation in South Africa.* Accessed on November 30, 2014, http://scnc.ukzn.ac.za/doc/HIST/Apartheid%20Legislation%20in%20South%20Africa.htm.
7. Gumede, V. 2008a. Public policy making in a post-apartheid South Africa: A preliminary perspective. *Africanus.* 38 (2), 723.
8. South African History Online. F.W. de Klerk announces the release of Nelson Mandela and unbans political organisations. Accessed on the 30 November 2014, http://www.sahistory.org.za/dated-event/fw-de-klerk-announces-release-nelson-mandela-and-unbans-political-organisations.
9. Esterhuyse, W. 2012. *Endgame: Secret Talk and End of Apartheid,* Tafelberg, Cape Town
10. Thompson, L. 2000. *A History of South Africa.* Jonathan Ball Publishers.
11. Ibid.
12. Kane, J. 2001. *The Politics of Moral Capital.* Cambridge University Press, Melbourne.
13. Sison, A.J. 2003. The Moral Capital of Leaders: Why Virtue Matters. New Horizons in Leadership Studies Series.
14. Khunou, G. What Middle Class? The Shifting and Dynamic Nature of Class Position. Accessed on November 27, 2014, http://resep.sun.ac.za/wp-content/uploads/2013/10/Khunou-Main-Article-Black-middle-class-.pdf.
15. The South African Civil Society Information Service. 2013. Prof.SampieTerreblanche: White South Africans Will Have to Make Some Sacrifices. Accessed on November 23, 2014, http://sacsis.org.za/site/article/1749.

16. Magubane, B.M. 1979. *The Political Economy of Race and Class in South Africa.* Monthly Review Press: New York.
17. Luthuli, A.J. 1963. *Let my people go.* London: Fontana.
18. Wale, K. 2014. *Reflecting on Reconciliation: Lessons from the past, prospects for the future.* Institute for Justice and Reconciliation, Cape Town, 24.
19. There is a prevailing view that Shaka should be named as Shaka kaNandi, not Shaka kaSenzangakhona, because Nandi played a more critical role in Shaka's ascendance to kingship while Senzangakhona was not fully supportive.

CHAPTER 6

SOCIAL AND ECONOMIC TRANSFORMATION

POLICIES AND PROSPECTS

> We have, at last, achieved our political emancipation. We pledge ourselves to liberate all our people from the continuing bondage of poverty, deprivation, suffering, gender and other discrimination.
> Nelson Mandela 1994, First democratic president of South Africa and 10th President of the ANC

INTRODUCTION

In this chapter I deal with the policy making approach discerned since 1994 and the socioeconomic transformation that has taken place. Over and above research on public policy issues, I draw extensively from the approximately ten years I spent in policy making and policy analyses portfolios I was involved with when I was in government. I have also been involved with teaching public policy since I left government in 2009.[1] The chapter also makes use of the works I have published over the years on policy making in South Africa (see Gumede 2008a, Gumede

2011a, Gumede 2013a, Gumede 2013b, Gumede 2014a and Gumede 2015a) and draws on a recently published book of mine.

A macro-level evaluation of the broad policy reforms since 1994 points out that the South African government has made concerted efforts to deal with the historical socioeconomic challenges; however, much still needs to be done to get the country to the envisaged post-apartheid society. Significant achievements have been registered, for instance, in the expansion of access to education, health care, housing, and basic services. Moreover, South Africa has established institutions to transform society. However, there are fundamental policy constraints that have limited economic performance and the general wellbeing of society. There are also overarching constraints that have to do with state-market relations and the global order. This chapter narrowly examines policies and policy reforms.

Institutional Mechanisms in Policy Making and Implementation

An important political economy question about South Africa's policy making processes is: are there mechanisms to encourage wider stakeholder participation in policy making? To answer this fundamental question satisfactorily, it is necessary to examine knowledge sharing networks and public participation networks, as well as the inclusion of parliamentarians, researchers, the broader civil society, citizens' forums, traditional leaders, and so on. In addition, the analysis also concerns itself with the form of the involvement of the stated stakeholders.

From 1998 to 2010, one of the key institutions besides Parliament in the policy making landscape in South Africa was the Policy Coordination and Advisory Services (popularly known as the Policy Unit) located in the Presidency. It not only dealt with policy making and its various components such as policy analysis, policy coordination, and policy advice, but included medium to long range planning and government-wide monitoring and evaluation. In brief, the Policy Unit provided research, analytical, advisory, policy, project, programme, and strategic support to the Presidency and government as a whole on matters of socioeconomic development, justice, governance, and international affairs. It comprised six main policy sectors: economic, social, justice, crime prevention and security, international relations, and governance and administration. There were three additional sub-units: monitoring and evaluation, planning, and special programmes (which dealt with issues related to gender, disability, and children's rights). There was also a youth directorate dealing with youth development issues. Mirroring policy sectors were the five Forum of South African Directors-General (FOSAD) Clusters.

The Policy Unit worked closely with the FOSAD Clusters and acted as a link between the Cabinet, its committees and the respective FOSAD Clusters. The Cabinet had committees that mirrored the clusters with one exception: there were two committees mirrored by one policy sector (i.e., the economic sector). Arguably, this was primarily the function of further prioritisation of economic development, especially in the Thabo Mbeki administration. Essentially, all other economic matters were dealt with through the normal economic sector Cabinet committee whilst critical issues were handled by the investment and employment Cabinet committee. Such critical matters included restructuring of state-owned enterprises. It may be worth noting that there were various inter-ministerial committees for each of the Cabinet committees. For instance, there was an inter-ministerial committee on the restructuring of state-owned enterprises. The Policy Unit was part of all such inter-ministerial committees such as those on social security and retirement reforms, the second economy, and so on. I was involved in a number of these structures during my tenure in the Presidency's Policy Unit (2001–2009).

My definition of public policy is informed by the periods I spent in various ministries of government and the literature. Public policy is "all formal and publicly known decisions of governments that come about through predetermined channels in a particular administration" (Gumede

2011a, 166). A recent book by Ndangwa Noyoo deals with policy-making in the Mbeki era. Noyoo (2015, 3) argues that:

> the Mbeki era was instrumental in putting South Africa on a firm footing in regarding to modernity and modern governance...Mbeki has sought to create a firm platform where the post-apartheid state could be launched. It can thus be speculated that Mbeki was quite clear, in his mind, as to what kind of a society he wanted South Africa to be, namely, a well-functioning democratic and modern African society." With regard to policy making in particular, Gumede (2008a, 14) makes the point that the hallmark of Mbeki's administration was "the involvement and or participation of non-state actors....

The post-apartheid government, at a national level, and provincial governments continue to experiment with functions pertaining to coordination, planning and monitoring, and evaluation. The thinking and analytical work that took place from 2005 culminated in recommendations regarding an institutional architecture that aimed at improving the functioning of government—one particular recommendation related to establishing a planning commission. The Jacob Zuma administration implemented many of the recommendations made—the jury is still out on whether the Jacob Zuma administration reorganised the state appropriately. One thing seems obvious: the disbandment of the Policy Unit in 2010 and the creation of planning, monitoring, and evaluation ministries might have been a big mistake. Policy thinking and coordination appear to have been compromised, even though, paradoxically, the Presidency has more capacity in the various new ministries created by the Zuma administration and in the private offices of the President and the Deputy President. It is worth highlighting though that the Zuma administration established Ministerial Committees and Implementation Forums consisting of directors-general to coordinate the fourteen outcomes (previously twelve were unveiled in 2012).

Economic and Social Development

Much has been achieved with regard to the implementation of the government's priority on addressing the lack of access to basic social services. However, as the forthcoming discussion indicates, much more needs to be done in ensuring that "Better Life for All."

Statistics South Africa (Stats SA) data and government records show an impressive progress achieved in ensuring that people have access to basic services such as clean water sources despite the fact that many people are still without access to piped (tap) water.[2] The challenges of service delivery remain unabated. Progress is mixed at best and disappointing at worst, as discussed in chapter 2. For instance, there was a decline in the percentage of households with electricity between 1996 and 2001. The 2011 figures look relatively good even for access to electricity as is shown in table 9.

There remain, however, significant backlogs. From the 2011 data, 10 percent of households do not have access to a flush toilet and 7.3 percent of the total households do not have a toilet at all as is shown in table 9. Table 9 provides apt reasoning for the increased public protests that have increased significantly post 2007. It is also worth highlighting that South Africa's social assistance programme—the cash transfer system —has quite considerably raised the income level of those in the lower socioeconomic quintiles, as illustrated in table 10. The 2010/11 data shows approximately 15 million people which constituted more than 3.2 percent of GDP received social grants. This figure rose to 15.6 million in 2011/12 and latest data indicates that, during 2014/15, about 16.6 million people receive social grants (Ministry of Monitoring and Evaluation 2014). The majority of grant recipients relate to the child support grant—this grant is provided to children in need up to the age of fifteen years (it is expected that children below age eighteen would, over time, also receive the child support grant as per the means test). The requirement age for the old-age pension for men was also reduced to 60 years.

The challenge with the social assistance programme is its financial sustainability and possible unintended consequences. Although it is stabilising as a share of the GDP, it is still very high (over 3 percent). As for the unintended consequences, the fundamental issue relates to the type of society South Africa desires to be. Ideally, like in Brazil and India, there should be more people in gainful employment than on social assistance. The grants, however, especially in the context of a small informal sector, play an important role in mitigating the severe hardship endured by those in need. As some of the findings on poverty suggest, the grants could have played an important role in cushioning against the global economic recession.

STABILISED YET UNTRANSFORMED ECONOMY

Democratic South Africa's economy has been growing relatively faster than it has in decades. The economy has since stabilised despite South Africa beginning to record stagnating growth levels as a consequence of the global economic recession and poor economic management.

The GDP per capita has been increasing at an impressive rate particularly since 1996. The GDP per capita is an important indicator—despite its shortcomings—of the standard of living in a society. Whereas the GDP per capita was declining from 1980 to 1994/95, South Africa has seen marked improvements in economic growth since 1994. During the period 1994–2004, growth averaged about 3 percent which is a considerable improvement on the decade prior to 1994 when growth averaged 1 percent per year.

Since 2004, growth has exceeded 4 percent per year, reaching about 5 percent in 2005. One point worth highlighting is that although the GDP improvement (per capita) cannot be entirely attributed to macroeconomic stabilisation alone, it coincides with key macroeconomic interventions, in particular GEAR. For an economy to perform well, macroeconomic stabilisation is a prerequisite.

As table 11 shows, the GDP, and not the per capita incomes per se, has been performing relatively well. Looking at the recent period, after the macroeconomic stabilisation programme of the 1990s, GDP has averaged about 3.5 percent—barring the recent global economic recession. However, the expected jobs have not been forthcoming despite the economy creating a relatively good number of jobs in the growth period of 2005–2008.

Although South Africa's GDP performance could be celebrated, it has not performed well enough given the size of its economy within a comparative context. Looking at comparable countries such as Botswana, India, Brazil, and Malaysia, South Africa's economic performance has been low. The low GDP growth rate supports the point that it is not only the global economic recession that has lowered South Africa's economic performance, but the GDP decline began after its highest point in the post-apartheid dispensation in 2006.

The ten-year period (1996–2006) shows no significant economic policy reforms undertaken effectively, as argued in chapter 4. Macroeconomic stabilisation was achieved through GEAR around year 2000. The obvious next policy or strategy step would have been the one focusing on accelerating GDP growth, which should have happened around 2002. There was, arguably, a significant policy reform lag because AsgiSA began in 2005. Because it takes some time for any policy to gain traction, AsgiSA would have started to deliver optimally around 2008. However, the recall of former President Mbeki created a state of flux and relative instability in the public sector that resulted in the immediate resignation of former Deputy President, Phumzile Mlambo-Ngcuka, and others who were championing AsgiSA.

There was an exodus of critical technocrats and policy gurus such as Joel Netshitenzhe who left government in 2009. I left the presidency in 2009 too—I, however, also spent a year as a Special Advisor in the State-Owned Enterprises Portfolio of the Department of Public Enterprises during November 2010–October 2011. The caretaker administration of

Kgalema Motlanthe from mid-2008 to mid-2009 maintained relative stability and continuity. However, the politics of that specific period made governing more challenging. It would seem that it was always understood in the ANC that Kgalema Motlanthe was temporarily holding reigns for Jacob Zuma (who had become president of the ANC, replacing Thabo Mbeki, in December 2007). My recollection of this period, during my interactions with Acting President Kgalema Motlanthe and Acting Deputy President Baleka Mbethe, was uncertainty. Many important, especially major, decisions were not taken.

During 2009 and 2010, there were many changes in government exacerbating the state of flux and relative instability. The new ministries, which had been conceptualised during the Mbeki administration, were introduced in 2009—the Ministry for Planning and the Ministry for Performance Monitoring and Evaluation. These two ministries or functions were meant to strengthen the functioning of government in order to deliver on the mandate of the RDP. It should be noted that the proposals were mainly about strengthening coordination, planning and monitoring, and evaluation—at an institutional level, the proposal was for the establishment of a Planning Commission and definitely not the Ministry for Planning and the Ministry for Performance Monitoring and Evaluation. The process of rethinking the organisation and capacity of the state began in 2005 when President Mbeki led the process of ameliorating the organisation and structure of government including the requisite capacities necessary to ensure that derived objectives were met. This process of rethinking culminated in the revisiting of the notion of South Africa becoming a developmental state.

Back to the economy, the point that I am making is that GDP growth in South Africa could have remained higher and perhaps even increased further if the correct reforms were implemented on time. The relative instability, and sometimes confusion, during 2008–2009 further compounded the challenge, as not enough attention was paid to economic policy and/or policy reforms during this critical time. Just as AsgiSA was making headway, it was replaced by the NGP. Since 2006, a consistent medium-term policy direction has been lacking. As table 11 shows, South Africa's GDP starts to decline from about 2006.

It could be argued that a recession in South Africa was inevitable from 2009 because of its own poor economic management especially in light of the mismanagement of public finances from about 2008–2009. Compared to similar economies, the relatively low rate of GDP growth has meant that fewer jobs are created. In fact, the South African economy, unlike economies of India and Brazil, has shed many jobs.

GDP projections appear to substantiate the view that the poor economic performance has little, if anything, to do with the global economic recession. South Africa's annual percentage changes in GDP will continue being lower than its counterparts, namely emerging markets including sub-Saharan Africa as an economic region.

Underemployment and Unemployment on the Rise

As indicated above, one of the most critical challenges facing the government or the South African society is the creation of employment and the fight against poverty. The government's goal was to reduce unemployment by at least half between 2004 and 2014, with a maximum of 14 percent in 2014. However, the economy's employment performance has not adequately met society's needs. The number of jobs created has lagged behind the demand for jobs. The recession and overall poor economic management has not only resulted in job insecurity and losses but a number of newly created precarious and poor quality jobs.

An unemployment rate of 25.2 percent in the first quarter of 2012 compared to 23.9 percent in the fourth quarter of 2011 was recorded by Stats SA (2012); this is considerably high by global standards. The 2011 Census revealed an unemployment rate of 28.9 percent (Stats SA 2012). Using the expanded definition of unemployment, unemployment stands at approximately 40 percent reflecting high volumes of discouraged job seekers. For the period 2000–2008, South Africa's unemployment rate averaged 26.3 percent reaching a historical high of 31.2 percent in March 2003 and a relatively low 23 percent in September 2007 (Stats SA 2012). The majority of the unemployed are mostly women and youth in rural areas who are low skilled or poorly educated, and for whom demand has been shrinking due to changes in the domestic structure of production of the economy. A large number of graduates are also unemployed. As discussed in Gumede (2013b), there were over 3 million of those in the 18–25 age bracket who were classified as Not in Employment, Education or Training (NEET) in 2010.

South Africa is further faced with the complexities relating to an uneven labour market environment, the changing nature of work, lack of labour market measurement instruments, and serving multi-class service beneficiaries such as vulnerable workers and unemployed job-seekers. The fragmented nature of South Africa's labour market, increasing informality, casualisation, and externalisation of the labour market has worsened the job crisis and economic status of the ordinary working class. Millions of workers are trapped in informal, temporary, involuntary part-time, or casual work that offers few benefits and limited prospects for advancement. This is the case particularly for youth, women, and immigrants who constitute the biggest chunk of South Africa's workforce.

EDUCATION: IMPROVED ACCESS BUT POOR QUALITY

Although significant achievements have been made in turning apartheid education around in the first decade of democracy, many challenges still remain (Bloch 2006). According to Kraak (2008), this has been evident in increased access to education, headcount enrolment in schools, investment by government and the private sector in education, and institutional rationalisation processes and regulation.

The changes pursued in the education sector have resulted in great strides. The government has made some progress in the expansion of education access, particularly improving access for disadvantaged groups. Progress is also visible in the different sectors, as presented in the 2008 Review of National Policies for Education in South Africa by the OECD. For instance, the OECD noted that government's achievements in the space of fourteen years were commendable and that it is understandable that some of the policy goals have not yet been realised.

In this instance, data from the Towards a Fifteen Year Review (2008) indicates that education participation has increased since 1994, especially in the case of primary schooling. This is attributed to those interventions geared towards increased access. In terms of the 2002–2007 enrolments growth for the age group 7–15, the enrolment of five-year-olds improved from 40 percent to 60 percent; the improvement for six-year-olds was 70 percent to 88 percent, and 96 percent to 98 percent for 15-year-olds.

Data from the Department of Basic Education's 2010 Education Statistics in South Africa Report shows relatively high gross enrolment rates (see table 12): 94 percent for the foundation phase (grades 1 to 7), 86 percent for the senior phase (grades 8 to 12) and an overall 91 percent for grades 1 to 12. In essence, South Africa has been successful in facilitating access to primary and tertiary education, particularly for girls. Using the MDG for 2015, the country has achieved its goal.

Further corroborating this point, the OECD report indicates that South Africa is close to achieving universal basic education with 96.6 percent enrolment for the age group 7–15 years with almost all children of school-going age entering school and the majority reaching the end of Grade 9.

In support of reports such as the OECD report, table 12 shows improved access to education between 2001 and 2011. Although the numbers of those not attending school are still high, the percentage of those attending has increased from 71.5 percent in 2001 to 73.4 percent in 2011, while the percentage of those not attending school has decreased to 26.6 percent in 2011 from 28.5 percent in 2001. There are also increases in percentage shares, in terms of attendance, for all types of educational institutions except pre-school as table 13 shows. In the ten year period 2001–2011, there has been an increase of about 100,000 university students. This reiterates the point that the numbers of those seeking higher education increases over time in any society and as such more universities are needed.

In terms of enrolments, it is noted that the extent to which the higher education system can actually produce highly skilled graduates is predicated on three important factors: the number of school "graduates" that qualify for entry into higher education institutions; the number that choose to enter higher education institutions; and the number that complete their qualifications (Breier and Mabizela 2008). However, the quality of Grade 12 school-leaving passes is said to be questionable.

Other important areas are literacy and numeracy. Various datasets and publications show a steady increase in the literacy rate. The 2012 Development Indicators (Presidency 2012) show that, according to General Household Surveys, the literacy rate has increased from 70.7 percent in 2002 to approximately 80 percent in 2009. Although there are improvements, much still needs to be done to ensure that the illiterate 20 percent may be literate. Bloch (2009) shows that despite the fact that South Africa has higher levels of educational spending than most countries, it is amongst the worst performing countries internationally on literacy and numeracy.

Despite improved literacy rates and access to education, it remains evident that key historical factors continue to constrain and limit the successful transformation of the education sector. It is becoming increasingly apparent that South Africa's education institutions remain untransformed. An emerging consensus indicates that the quality of education is poor and the curriculum is ill-structured—a legacy of the Bantu education system. Chapter two discussed the disappointing average years of schooling relative to expected years of schooling, implying that there are indeed many challenges with education in South Africa.

Recent data from the latest census highlights the reality that access to education, not to mention the quality of the education system, remains a challenge. For instance, the number (at above 5 million) and the share of those not attending school remains very high. Also of importance is the slow progress of rolling out early learning. Lastly, although the enrolment of Africans in higher education institutions has increased, detailed analysis of data reveals historical disparity in participation rates among population groups. The total gross participation rate remains roughly the same at approximately 15.7 percent in early to mid-2000 and increased marginally to 16.18 percent in 2007. Although the numbers of those enrolled in higher education have been increasing, the participation rates for the African student population do not seem to be increasing at any significant rate.[3]

Of concern is that qualified graduates are struggling to find employment. Moleke (2006) found that the majority of the unemployed fall under the categories of Africans, females, graduates of humanities and the arts, and graduates from the so-called historically black universities. It would seem that the problem of graduate unemployment has worsened with graduates from commerce and even science and engineering finding it difficult too.

The unification of the education system and standards also remains an issue. The two-tier education system is accentuated by an increasing share of those attending a private education system. Also, it remains to be seen whether the approach adopted while restructuring the higher education landscape was appropriate or not. The Higher Education Monitor of the Council on Higher Education (CHE 2007) has reflected on a number of pertinent issues relating to the challenges confronting the higher education landscape. Overall, the picture looks bleak but there is some progress especially in the context of proposals contained in the 2013 White Paper for Post-School Education and Training.

HEALTH CARE: IMPROVED ACCESS BUT EQUITY REMAINS A CHALLENGE

The challenge of the provision of social services in South Africa is largely similar in many cases, and it is largely a legacy of the apartheid system. Undoing the legacy of the apartheid system is time consuming. In addition, however, there is a challenge that relates to policy and or policy reform. Redressing the legacy of apartheid, with regards to social provisioning, requires robust and appropriate policies. Like in education and other areas, there are policy constraints that have limited the extent to which South Africa is addressing the legacy of the apartheid health care system.

In a nutshell, health care administration was fragmented during the apartheid dispensation. For instance, there were fourteen separate health care departments for the different racial groups, the homelands, and self-governing territories. The transformation that had to take place in the health care space was guided by the Constitution which requires state to take "reasonable legislative and other measures within its available resources, to achieve the progressive realisation of each of these rights" (Bill of Rights, section 25.5). As indicated earlier, Section 27.1 of the Constitution indicates that "everyone has the right to have access to health care services, including reproductive health" (Cullinan 2006).

Increasing access to health care, like in education, was a starting point. It was evident that access needed to be expanded because of the discriminatory and exclusionary apartheid system. However, the major policy issues that had or have to do with equity were not sufficiently addressed. As such, two decades since the dawn of democracy, the two-tier health care system remains. Shisana (2011) states that the two-tiered financing health care system in South Africa has led to a situation where more state resources are used to cater for fewer South Africans that can access private health care systems, while the under-resourced public health sector caters for the majority of the country's population. According to Shisana (2011), South Africa spends 8.3 percent of its GDP on health, yet 4.1 percent of this GDP is spent on the private health sector which caters to only 16.2 percent of the total population; 4.2 percent of this is allocated to public health which covers 84 percent of the population.

The recent policy of National Health Insurance (NHI) addresses this important challenge. The NHI is primarily aimed at making significant changes and improvements in the health care system. It aims at promoting equity, fairness, and social solidarity in the health care system. The main objective of the policy is to ensure that all South Africans have full access to appropriate, efficient, and quality health care services. This policy will be phased over fourteen years and would require significant changes to the existing service delivery structures and administrative and management systems (National Department of Health 2013).

This important and overdue policy can significantly improve the health profile of the country. There are, however, some critical risks with any health insurance policy. In many instances countries implement Social Health Insurance (SHI), often with the plan of graduating it to NHI. SHI can be a good start, particularly if a country needs to first get the public health care system right and to pool and equalise risks. As previously mentioned, the health care system remains a two-tier system: an efficient and well-funded private health care system and an inefficient and poorly funded health care system. Conceptually, it is difficult to talk about equity.

Another major policy issue regarding any health insurance is that income through gainful employment is critical. It is difficult to imagine a successful implementation of an NHI without some form of subsidisation in a context of very high unemployment rate. It is in this context that an argument is made that a SHI coupled with wage subsidy would prove a better policy option. The starting point, and perhaps policy emphasis, should have been on fixing the ailing public health sector; this could have been done with a better focus on risk equalisation for a significant period of time in order to avoid running into financial constraints that can compromise a noble policy.

The health care challenge has been even more pronounced in rural areas. For instance, although 43.6 percent of the South African population lives in rural areas, they are served by only 12 percent of the doctors and 19 percent of nurses. Also, it is reported that of the 1200 medical students graduating annually, only about 35 of them end up working in rural areas in the longer term. Furthermore, 21.3 percent of households in metropolitan areas belong to a medical aid in comparison to 5 percent of households in rural districts. In comparison, the infant mortality rate is 32.6 per 1000 live births in urban areas compared to 52.6 on average in rural areas (Human Resources for Health 2012, 34–35).

South Africa is dealing with a severe "burden of disease," like many countries in the developing world. For instance, tuberculosis (TB) infections are very high in South Africa. Also, and equally challenging, is that HIV prevalence levels remain very high. Although it is reported that HIV prevalence has stabilised since 2009, at a national antenatal prevalence of about 30 percent, it is still very high. With regards to infections, despite of the treatment given to HIV-infected individuals, the number of infections seems to be increasing. Table 14 shows that the infection rates increased from 4 million in 2002 to over 5 million in 2012.

It would seem that the trend for HIV incidence shows a decline from 2006. In terms of HIV prevalence, women aged 15–49 and adults of same age, there are marginal increases over time. With regards to youth (15–24) the trend is that HIV prevalence is declining (from 13.6 percent in 2002 to 8.7 percent in 2012).

Also, although mortality rates are improving, the challenge remains severe. The United Nations (UN) estimates suggest that under-5 mortality rates have declined between the period of 2000 to 2011 from a 74 per 1000 live births to 47 per 1000 live births (which is indeed a significant improvement). This is probably linked to a decline in HIV/AIDS infections and ameliorated sanitation systems. There is a noteworthy decline in the transmission of mother to child HIV infections. Although inroads are being made, table 15 suggests that it is unlikely for South Africa to reach the set MDG target for child mortality by 2015.

Table 15 also demonstrates that the trend for life expectancy has been marginally increasing, incidentally from 2006, which is year when HIV prevalence and infection rates started to stabilise.[4] The death rate also begins to decline from 2006. As indicated above, the challenge of mortality remains significant and the under-5 mortality rate is still very high despite the trend indicating decline over time.

There are other challenges regarding health care. For instance, there is a serious shortage of health care workers. For an example, the World Health Organisation (WHO) in 2003 estimated that above 60 percent of the posts in the health sector were vacant; this included over 4,000 vacancies for general practitioners and 32,000 vacancies for nurses in all provinces. It is argued that besides the international migration of health care workers, there is an incorrect distribution of health care workers favouring the private health sector. Many well-trained medical practitioners are employed in private hospitals, which serve a minority of the country's total population. Thus, the development and functioning of public health care is further undermined by this uneven distribution of health care workers. Furthermore, the quality of health care provided is also undermined by this shortage. The government is aware of this challenge and efforts are underway to address it.

Conclusion

This chapter has reviewed social and economic transformation since 1994. It began with a discussion of the policy making approach in the post-apartheid dispensation. The overwhelming conclusion is that South Africa has achieved relatively significant social and economic development in the two decades of democracy. The economy had stabilised by mid-2000 and social development improved, albeit marginally.

From a policy perspective, South Africa has fallen significantly short. The necessary reforms in the economy have been weak because of poor policy development and a lack of vision. In the area of social development, the lack of the social policy has constrained the advancement of wellbeing. Broadly speaking, South Africa has been effectively stagnant following robust reforms of the 1990s. Implementation has proven to be particularly poor when policies are inappropriate or weak.

The answer to South African woes is policy and/or policy reforms particularly in the economy. The strategies and programmes introduced since mid-2000s have not addressed the policy constraints that compelled the need for policy reforms. Therefore, more policy thinking should be exercised for both social and economic transformations. And, most importantly, policy should be in pursuit of an agreed upon economic vision through national consensus. Robust and clear policies should still advance the wellbeing of South Africans, even in the context of twisted state-market relations and a lopsided global order. The government, at least through moral persuasion, should navigate the currently inappropriately configured state-market relations to make some gains in economic and social development for the majority of the population. The next chapter makes proposals how to take South Africa forward faster.

Table 9. Access to Services and Type of Dwelling South Africa, 1996–2011.

Type of main dwelling	1996	2001	2011
Formal	65,1	68,5	77,6
Informal	16,2	16,4	13,6
Traditional	18,3	14,8	7,9
Other	0,4	0,3	0,9
Household basic services			
Piped water (tap)	80.3	84.5	91.2
Electricity (lighting)	58.2	51.4	84.6
Toilet facilities			
Access to a flush toilet	82,9	82,3	90,6
Bucket toilet	4.7	4,1	2,1
No toilet	12,4	13,6	7,3

Source: Based on the 2011 Census data.

Table 10. Social Assistance, 2000–2011.

Grant type	2000/01	2002/03	2004/05	2006/07	2008/09	2009/10	2010/11
Old Age Grant	1 900 406	1 943 348	2 124 984	2 195 018	2 390 543	2 546 657	2 678 554
War Veterans Grant	5 617	4 638	2 963	2 340	1 500	1 216	958
Disability Grant	655 822	840 424	1 293 280	1 422 808	1 286 883	1 264 477	1 200 898
Foster Child Grant	66 967	83 574	195 454	400 503	474 759	510 760	512 874
Child Dependency Grant	33 574	42 355	86 917	98 631	107 065	110 731	112 185
Child Support Grant	1 111 612	1 998 936	4 165 545	7 863 841	8 765 354	9 570 287	10 371 950
Total	**3 773 998**	**4 913 275**	**7 869 143**	**11 983 141**	**13 026 104**	**14 004 128**	**14 877 419**
Growth Rate	40.4%	23.4%	21.5%	9.5%	5.2%	7.5%	6%
Grant-in-aid	10 107	12 625	25 667	31 918	46 069	53 237	58 413

Source: 2012 Development Indicators.

Table 11. Gross Domestic Product: South Africa and Other Countries, 2000–2010.

	2000	2001	2002	2003	2004	2005	2006	2007	2008	2009	2010
SA	4.2	2.7	3.7	2.9	4.6	5.3	5.6	5.5	3.6	-1.5	2.9
Botswana	5.9	3.5	9.0	6.3	6.1	1.6	4.5	4.8	2.9	-4.9	7.2
Brazil	4.3	1.3	2.7	1.1	5.7	3.2	4.0	6.1	5.2	-0.6	7.5
India	4.0	5.2	3.8	8.4	8.3	9.3	9.3	9.8	4.9	9.1	9.7
Malaysia	8.9	0.5	5.4	5.8	6.8	5.3	5.8	6.5	4.7	-1.7	7.2

Source: 2011 Development Indicators.

Table 12. Gross Enrolment Ratios by Gender and Level of Education.

Gender	Primary phase: Grade 1–7	Secondary phase: Grade 8–12	Overall: Grade 1-12
Female	92 %	89 %	91 %
Male	96 %	83 %	91 %
Total	**94 %**	**86 %**	**91 %**

Source: Gumede (2013b, 73).

Table 13. Access to Education in South Africa, 2001–2011.

Education	2001		2011	
	Number	Percentage	Number	Percentage
School attendance				
Yes	13 727 893	71.5	13 837 961	73.4
No	5 463 823	28.5	5 023 110	26.6
Type of educational institution				
Pre-school	575 936	4.2	128 719	0.9
School	12 584 818	91.7	12 862 961	92.9
FET college/College	191 234	1.4	359 228	2.6
University/Technikon	315 592	2.3	410 063	3.0
ABET	26 505	0.2	22 730	0.2
Other	33 809	0.2	57 883	0.4
Public or Private				
Public	13 028 486	94.9	11 924 285	92.7
Private	699 407	5.1	934 480	7.3

Source: Statistics South Africa (2012).

Table 14. HIV Prevalence Estimates and the Number of People Living with HIV, 2002–2012.

Year	Prevalence			Incidence	HIV Population
	Women (15-49)	Adult (15-49)	Youth (15-24)	(Adult 15-49)	(millions)
2002	15.9	15.1	13.6	1.26	4.00
2003	16.0	15.1	12.8	1.25	4.10
2004	16.1	15.1	12.0	1.28	4.18
2005	16.2	15.1	11.4	1.32	4.25
2006	16.4	15.2	10.9	1.29	4.34
2007	16.5	15.3	10.5	1.21	4.46
2008	16.7	15.4	10.1	1.12	4.59
2009	16.9	15.5	9.7	1.03	4.74
2010	17.1	15.6	9.3	0.98	4.88
2011	17.2	15.7	9.0	0.95	5.01
2012	17.3	15.8	8.7	0.87	5.13

Source: Statistics South Africa (2012).

Table 15. Fertility and Mortality Levels, 2002–2012.

Year	Crude birth rate	Total Fertility Rate (TFR)	Life expectancy at birth			Infant Mortality Rate (IMR)	Under-5 mortality	Crude death rate	Rate of natural increase (percent)
			Male	Female	Total				
2002	24.5	2.71	50.0	55.2	52.7	63.5	92.9	13.9	1.05
2003	24.2	2068	49.5	54.4	52.1	62.6	91.9	14.6	0.96
2004	23.6	2.61	49.3	53.9	51.7	60.1	89.3	15.0	0.86
2005	23.1	2.56	49.4	53.6	51.6	58.0	85.4	15.2	0.79
2006	22.8	2.53	50.2	54.6	52.5	55.6	80.9	14.6	0.82
2007	22.6	2.53	51.7	56.1	54.0	53.6	76.7	13.5	0.91
2008	22.5	2.52	53.3	57.6	55.5	50.8	72.3	12.6	0.99
2009	22.3	2.51	54.6	58.8	56.8	49.1	68.5	11.8	1.05
2010	22.2	2.50	55.5	59.5	57.6	47.1	65.2	11.5	1.07
2011	21.6	2.44	56.1	60.0	58.1	45.1	62.1	11.3	1.03
2012	21.0	2.39	56.8	60.5	58.7	43.5	59.5	11.0	1.00

Source: Statistics South Africa (2012).

Notes

1. Some of the ideas presented in this chapter are as a result of heated class discussions with my students, both at the University of Johannesburg and at the Graduate School of Public and Development Policy (renamed the School of Government) at the University of Witwatersrand. I have also benefited from facilitating sessions on behalf of the Public Administration Leadership and Management Academy (now the National School of Government) of the South African government.
2. According to the 2011 Census there were about 1,265,907 people without access to piped water, of which 1 234 087 were Africans—this supports the view that most of the socioeconomic challenges confronting society remain predominantly problems of Africans.
3. Refer to Kraak (2008) and Steyn (2009).
4. It should be mentioned, however, that Statistics South Africa estimates are much higher than my own estimates (as presented in Chapter 2) and those of the UN (as presented in the 2013 Human Development Report).

Chapter 7

Towards an Inclusive Society

> Indeed, since 1912, this organisation [the ANC] has worked consistently to rid South Africa of colonialism, oppression, apartheid, racism, tribalism and sexism. The organisation continues with its nation-building task, informed by the teachings of founding leaders like Pixley ka Isaka Seme who emphasised unity and spoke out about the need to eradicate the demons of racism and tribalism.
>
> Jacob Zuma 2012, 12th President of the ANC

Introduction

The book has deliberated one of the most pressing issues about post-apartheid South Africa: after two decades of political independence, how close or far is the South Africa we observe to the society that was envisaged by the liberation project? If an assessment of the developments is approached within the prism of the notion of inclusive development in the context of the pursuit of a democratic developmental state, the answer is an unequivocal *far*.

Essentially, the book's concern was inclusive development: development that involves those that were previously excluded and oppressed.

The social and economic transformation—in a context of a country with over 350 years of apartheid colonialism—has to ensure that "all Africans fully participate in ownership and government" as Albert Luthuli (1963, 81) put it. Again as Luthuli (1963, 78) aptly characterised the South African conundrum, this is because "the Act of Union virtually handed the whole of South Africa over to minority of whites, lock, stock and barrel." Bernard Magubane (1979, 1) puts it differently, if not better, when he says "the plight of the black people of South Africa is intimately bound up with the history of white settlement in their lands."

An important discussion of the national question aided in the analysis is consideration of other relevant issues that could have fallen outside the scope of analysing social and economic inclusion. As I have argued, the key issue for South Africa is the wellbeing of Africans. The notion of development, as adopted by the book, is explicated by Claude Ake (1996, 125) as "the process by which people create and recreate themselves and their life circumstances to realise higher levels of civilisation in accordance with their own choices and values—development is something that people must do for themselves."

This book has taken for granted that a developmental state in South Africa means a *democratic* developmental state, as characterised by Omano Edigheji (2005).[1] In other words, over and above all the attributes for a developmental state, the state must also be democratic. Arguments have been made that developmental states that have existed before, both in Asia and Africa in particular, were not democratic. The Scandinavian developmental states are advanced social democracies. It, therefore, means that South Africa cannot be expected to be similar to any developmental states that have existed before.

As Mkandawire (2001a) has explained, a country's "circumstances" shape the kind of a developmental state it can be or become. It is in this context that I argue that the notion of a developmental state should be viewed as a framework instead of attempting to copy the developmental state "model" of another country. In fact, a developmental state as a framework guides the work of a serious government concerned about development—if a government can attain the various attributes of a developmental state then the hopes of that society would be realised, thus ensuring an inclusive development. Therefore, a developmental state is discernible simply by observing the people of that particular society.

Also, the desired developmental state in South Africa is a democratic developmental state notwithstanding some prevailing notions that apartheid South Africa could have been conceived as a developmental state. In other words, apartheid South Africa was a *separatist* developmental state given the philosophy of separate development that was pursued under apartheid colonialism and imperialist capitalism. Unlike post-apartheid South Africa, the apartheid state ensured *underdevelopment* of the African instead of advancement. In this context, apartheid colonialism was premised on a *predatory* state. White domination, the fundamental character of apartheid colonialism and the capitalist-imperialist system, implied that South Africa, before 1994, had a destructive developmental state if the notion of a developmental state can at all be considered where apartheid colonialism or similar obtains.

Lastly, the book also concludes that South Africa is still quite far from becoming a nation. While the advent of democracy saw the abolition of the draconian laws and repulsive policies of the British Empire and National Party, the South African post-apartheid society is grappling with the socioeconomic effects of centuries of systemic institutionalised racism and abuse of Africans; in order for South Africa to be considered a just and equitable society, this is yet to fundamentally change. Regardless of the constitutional provisions for nation building in South Africa, racist and ahistorical comments[2] such as the ones occasionally made by key figures of the apartheid regime can only succeed in fanning the ember of anger, disgust, and revenge, where possible. The form of relations that exist between the various peoples that constitute a geographical space significantly matter for nation building. It is in this context that I have argued, in chapter 5 in particular, that for post-apartheid South

Africa, it will be more meaningful and relevant to see a nation as a community that, among other things, acknowledges and respects its repulsive political and economic history of deprivation through systematic restitutionary, reconciliatory, and restructuring measures and, more importantly, equitable sharing of resources.

CONCLUDING REMARKS

Chapter 1 provided a broad sense of what was envisaged for a democratic South Africa. Highlights of some of the main policy documents of the ANC and the broader National Liberation Movement give a good sense of what was envisaged. A broad review of the various strategies, frameworks, and programmes in chapters 4 and 6 illustrated the evolution of policy thinking that has shaped socioeconomic inclusion in South Africa since 1994. While what was envisaged appears clear, the strategies, from a policy perspective, pursued have thus far fallen short. The main message of the book as a whole is that socioeconomic inclusion still has a long way to go.

Among the main points advanced by this book is that inappropriate policies and/or delayed reforms have constrained the extent to which socioeconomic inclusion has been pursued. The main argument of the book can be misunderstood—I have observed that particularly in the public discourse the point I make regarding policy constraints gets misunderstood or misinterpreted. For clarity, this main argument does not preclude other issues, such as state capacity and implementation challenges, from constraining socioeconomic progress in South Africa.

The basis of my argument is that the fundamental constraint to socioeconomic development is primarily inappropriate policies—it is difficult to implement inappropriate policies. In other words, even within the constraints imposed by the global socioeconomic and political environment, South Africa could have done better with regards to socioeconomic inclusion. Notwithstanding unfortunate current state-capital relations in South Africa as elaborated, correct policies and appropriately sequenced reforms could create better socioeconomic inclusion.

The fundamental development challenge confronting South Africa was adequately analysed in the 1990s, but the policy remedies are not addressing that fundamental challenge (i.e., the reconfiguration of the society to ensure that South Africa becomes a nation or has a semblance of a nation). In addition, the centrality of the apartheid colonialism experience appears to not have gained prime position in policy thinking. Policies should focus on undoing the repulsive political past and redress the deeply entrenched legacy of apartheid colonialism, the ramifications of the capitalist imperialist system, and the colonial apartheid agenda. Any policy should take the experience of apartheid colonialism as a point of departure. It is in this context that socioeconomic development has, to a very large extent, been constrained by policy failure. As argued in chapters 4 and 5 in particular, the policy failure in question involves incorrect theorisation or theories that gave precedence to non-racialism when the fundamental developmental challenge required that Africans be prioritised in the post-apartheid development agenda.

A brief synopsis as presented in the book is that South Africa has been or is pursuing inappropriate policies in redressing apartheid colonialism. The various political economy and development interventions since 1994 have been *general* rather than specific when tackling the ramifications of apartheid colonialism. The successive post-apartheid administrations were seemingly preoccupied with growing the economy and pursuing a broad socioeconomic development agenda instead of focusing on policies directly affecting victims of apartheid colonialism, which would ensure effective social and economic inclusion. To be clear, policies are considered inappropriate or weak if they do not take account of particular contexts. Since 1994, there has been changes in the global environment and domestic context yet policy changes or shifts (i.e., reforms) and their sequencing have remained stagnant, especially since the mid-2000s

(Gumede 2015a).[3] South Africa has not sufficiently confronted apartheid colonialism directly.

Chapter 2 examined development dilemmas in order to depict the intractable socioeconomic challenges that South Africa must address in order to be a fully inclusive society. While chapter 3 provided theoretical reflections, chapter 4 discussed policy reforms at a macro level in particular. It discussed the various macroeconomic interventions, social policy reforms, and the changes that have taken place regarding the general wellbeing of the South African society since 1994. Chapter 5 dealt with the *national question* within the context of social and economic inclusion. Chapter 6 discussed the evolution of South Africa's policy framework in its quest to transform society.

Policy Options

Given the emerging verdict of the book, the question arises as to what should be done to ensure effective social and economic inclusion in South Africa. I argue that transformation of societies requires far-reaching if not radical interventions. Without a doubt though, South Africa has only scratched the surface since 1994. The fundamental answer to the challenges confronting South Africa is policies that reconfigure the society as a whole in order to ensure effective social and economic inclusion. The following sections propose possible policies that can realign the country at the least towards the envisaged post-colonial and post-apartheid society. South Africa has become a post-apartheid corporatist neo-colonial state.[4]

Economic Policy for Economic Transformation

In order to realise human development, South Africa has to honestly reassess its socioeconomic achievements since 1994. Perhaps the accumulation regimes that were adopted in the past are part of the problem and not necessarily solutions—*primitive accumulation*, as Marxists would put it, has taken a different form and shape in South Africa, as on the

African continent as a whole. Currently, South Africa still battles with one of the central economic questions of wealth distribution.

Capitalism has been and remains cruel. Whilst many countries have experienced sizeable economic growth, many citizens are still living in abject poverty while a small minority reap the benefits of redistributive growth. Despite sustained growth levels in different phases of the lifecycle of the economy, we have not made a dent in improving human development; instead we have been bewildered by unsustainable poverty levels, joblessness, weak economic growth, and rising inequality. South Africa has to urgently address both underlying and structural causes as well as the distressing consequences in order to reduce uncertainty and insecurity in the life of Africans particularly.

Because reconfiguring society is a complex undertaking, South Africa needs a new mix of policy instruments that would ensure that the economy grows substantially and, most importantly, that the economy creates jobs.[5] In other words, over and above a robust social policy, South Africa needs an economy that works better for society—not a society that adjusts to the so-called needs of an economy. To achieve this, South Africa requires an agile and capable developmental state. This is actually the case for the whole of the African continent: agile and capable developmental states are critical if not indispensable if Africa is to pursue the right policies for the benefit of all of Africa's people.

South Africa's biggest threat would be government and policy failures to transform the structure of its economy. This view is supported by Edigheji and Moyo (cited in Edigheji 2010), who contend that South Africa is unlikely to achieve its developmental state agenda because of its Minerals-Energy-Complex (MEC), de-industrialisation, as well as slack agrarian and land reforms. Seeraj Mohamed (2010), among many others, has made similar points, in particular, that the post-apartheid South African economy has remained in crisis because of neo-liberal policies that resulted in internationalisation, financialisation, and de-industrialisation. The question of the structural transformation of South

Africa's economy therefore remains central to the debate on South Africa's developmental trajectory.

As indicated in chapter 1, the South African economy has, in the recent past, been the main obstacle to social and economic transformation at two levels. The structure of the economy has remained relatively unchanged from the predominantly MEC bias as well as in terms of ownership patterns. Secondly, the South African economy, after stabilising in the 1990s, has been unable to take off like its peers (such as India, Brazil, Malaysia, and Mauritius). These issues have been acknowledged by many people in South Africa, including by the National Planning Commission (NPC) and the ANC. Therefore, it is simply a matter of reshaping economic policy to address the conundrum facing the South African economy. Over and above policies for the economy, including a robust industrial policy, South Africa should have a clear vision for the economy. In other words, South Africa needs an explicit economic model or approach that would be agreed upon by all relevant role players. It is not enough that South Africa is a mixed (and capitalist) economy. In fact, as argued in Gumede (2013b), South Africa should have used the opportunity presented by the 2008–2009 global economic recession to craft its own socioeconomic development model. Gumede (2011b) makes a similar point with regards to Africa as a whole.

The second most important issue for social and economic transformation is employment. South Africa needs to resolve the challenge of unemployment in general, and specifically youth unemployment which has reached crisis proportions. This is a broader economic policy issue and narrowly a labour market issue. The restructuring of the economy should alleviate unemployment challenges. Bearing in mind that employment creation and poverty challenges will continue to be the most pressing development challenges in the twenty-first century, it becomes essential to explore a development path that prioritises multi-faced strategies.

Firstly, the ideal development path should optimise development within productive and labour intensive sectors for the creation of jobs and poverty alleviation. One of the main problems in boosting the pace of employment growth is that, although South Africa has faced a shortage of capital and an abundance of labour, past development strategies have often favoured capital-intensive rather than labour-intensive investment. Agricultural policies, for example, have often favoured production by capital-intensive and land-intensive farmers and trading companies instead of targeting the needs of small farmers and landless labourers (Gumede 2014a). In this respect, a multi-pronged macroeconomic strategy must recognise the necessity to re-orientate the entire national development strategy so that it becomes more employment intensive.

Secondly, the labour market should function differently in order to fully address the unemployment challenge. The demand side of the labour market, firm behaviour in particular, requires more attention. In other words, the private sector must play ball in efforts towards reducing unemployment. Youth training programmes play an important strategic role in ensuring that workplaces become places of structured learning, experiential learning, and in-service training thus increasing the chances of youth employment in key sectors. The government should scale-up learnership agreements for unemployed graduates and out-of-school youth with employers. These agreements should focus on building entrepreneurial and business skills for the long-term establishment of new youth co-operatives and youth-driven small and medium enterprises. As Gumede (2013b) argued, the challenge of youth classified as Not in Employment, Education or Training (NEET) must be prioritised.

It is obvious that the private sector is instrumental in providing unemployed graduates with workplace training/experience through graduate programmes and vacation work. The requirements on experience, especially for graduates, should also be revised. Broadened options must be created to ensure that the youth acquire relevant work experience prior to them formally entering the labour market. A set of active labour market type interventions should be devised to increase the probability that graduates are absorbed by the labour market.[6] Skills development initiatives designed to transfer high level technical skills and facilitate work experience for unemployed matriculants and tertiary graduates with the aim of securing them meaningful employment in strategic sectors in the economy are paramount. Also of importance is the creation of more opportunities for matriculates to study at tertiary levels, and second chances for the youth that fall through the cracks should be created.

On a broader level, the informal economy should not be discouraged. India, for instance, has an informal economy that is effectively above the formal economy. As a temporary cushion, the informal sector plays an important role in alleviating unemployment and poverty. It is also critical that basic livelihoods (e.g. spaza shops) for those on the lower rungs of society are protected and supported where feasible. To address unemployment, a consensus is needed on the vision for the economy. The consensus argued for here is dissimilar to the wide-ranging 2030 National Development Plan of the NPC. The vision that should inform the South African economy going forward should be more focused on restructuring, if not de-racialising, the economy and creating jobs.

The government should also continue to support and promote community-based enterprises (cooperatives), and micro and small enterprise development amongst South Africans, and should be targeted at rural and unemployed youth and women particularly. It is acknowledged that the proportion of people employed in small businesses in South Africa is much lower than in most other countries. As the business sector is recognised as an important engine of economic growth and job creation in South Africa, a renewed commitment by government needs to be made to improve the efficiency of a range of factors in the regulatory environment that may hinder the development of small businesses. The creation of new African-owned and African-controlled enterprises should be a key component of the strategy for job creation and economic empowerment (Gumede 2006). Of utmost importance is ensuring that entrepreneurial South Africans have access to capital and/or credit, business development support, and procurement opportunities.

Social Policy for Social Inclusion

The gains on social development and/or social welfare in post-apartheid South Africa are commendable, although inadequate. Besides wide reaching challenges as indicated by the data discussed in chapter 2, South Africa is confronted with the task of improving the quality of social services—various government reports also highlight this challenge. Therefore, as Gumede (2008b) argued, the implementation of social upliftment programmes should be improved by ensuring a comprehensive social protection programme. Education and skills development should be improved as well as health care services. These are challenges that all developing countries face in one way or another.

Improving the quality of education, as well as industrial skills development, remains a particularly essential component of any human development strategy. Skills are essential to improve productivity, income, and access to employment opportunities. Yet, a striking feature of most poverty reduction strategies, for instance, is the absence of vocational education and training (ILO 2003) even though the vast majority of those living in poverty cannot afford and have no access to training opportunities. Rising educational and skill levels are vital in overcoming many of the barriers that exclude and limit disadvantaged (poorer) workers in the labour market. Integrating measures to stimulate the demand for labour and improving the responsiveness of the supply side of the labour market remains a significant pillar in efforts to boost the earning power of the poor, and to enhance the growth potential of the economy.

As indicated earlier, to successfully transform society, as Mkandawire (2001b, 12) contends, "collective interventions directly affecting transformation in social welfare, social institutions, and social relations" are critical. In other words, social policy should transform social welfare, social institutions, and social relations. It can be argued that social policy—if it exists—has not been successful in transforming social institutions and social relations. The labour market is one of the critical social institutions that remain significantly under-transformed. Broadly speaking, there is merit in the argument that social relations remain largely untransformed too.

It is in this context that South Africa needs to rethink its social policy. We should also think of social policy "as an instrument for ensuring a sense of citizenship...which is in turn a prerequisite for sustained economic development" as Mkandawire (2001b, 12) argues. Social policy should work in tandem with economic policy towards advancing wellbeing—both subjective and objective wellbeing. Therefore, the rethinking of social policy should be undertaken jointly with improving economic policy. These policies can only work in the context where South Africa has a clear vision for its economy and society.

Way Forward

As chapter 3 theorises, post-apartheid South Africa is facing a fundamental challenge that characterises the African post-colonial development experience and the global South broadly. There are different interpretations why South Africa is unable to achieve effective social and economic inclusion: one school of thought simplistically blames the ANC or the ANC-led government, while another attributes the seeming paralysis and miasma to the repulsive political history of South Africa. A third school of thought basically argues that South Africa has not attained complete liberation; there are many other relatively simplistic views that list factors such as poor implementation, corruption, lack of skills, and so on, for a relatively poor development record in post-apartheid South Africa.

The numerous explanations provided for the rather mixed performance of successive post-apartheid governments, result in recommended solutions that do not address the fundamental challenge facing South African society. The solutions I suggest, too, mainly tinker with the fundamental challenge in the margins. South Africa requires a complete overhaul of the current configurations of the state-market relations. However, it is difficult for South Africa to successfully do this because of the "global matrix of power" and the "development merchant system," both which pursue interests that are contrary to the development of the African continent as the works of Sabelo Ndlovu-Gatsheni, Issa Shivji, Thandika Mkandawire, Amina Mama, Samir Amin, Patricia McFadden, and Adebayo Adedeji, among others, indicate.

This does not mean that the ANC or the ANC-led government has not made mistakes or disaffected the post-apartheid development experience. As the book has argued, part of the main difficulty facing the ANC is that it embraced concepts and theories that may no longer be applicable, if not outright wrong. As discussed in chapters 4 and 5, the notion of Colonialism of a Special Type is questionable—colonialism is colonialism and settler colonialism is simply settler colonialism, and colonialism affects the African more than anyone else. Similarly, the seeming departure from the 1943 Africans Claims to the 1955 Freedom Charter might have resulted in many ideological compromises that have made it difficult to implement robust socioeconomic policies for inclusive development. This point also applies to the influence of Marxist ideologies in the thinking within the ANC from 1950s in particular—the same can be said about many other foreign ideologies that the ANC uncritically embraced. Ayi Kwei Armah, Chinweizu Ibekwe, and Valentine Mudimbe, among others, question the relevance of Marxism in Africa for an example. It could be argued also that the two-stage theory of the National Democratic Revolution may no longer be applicable. It could very well be that two decades of political independence are enough to revisit theories and perspectives that guided the developmental agenda since 1994.

The South African post-apartheid governments seem, so far, to have failed to adapt and finetune key policies to the needs of the time, particularly from 2006 onwards. Other stakeholders have inadequately fulfilled their role of shaping and informing policy instead of criticising the government. The African youth remains a loser (Gumede 2011c). It is obvious that government and social partners should be paying added attention to the plight of youth. Currently, it is the youth that is revolting against political patronage, corruption, and ineffective policies. It is the youth that is at the forefront of attacks on foreign nationals and public service delivery protests.

It is a given that any government that is serious about socioeconomic development would strive for clear policies that address the challenges at hand. In the case of South Africa, the challenges are precipitated by apartheid colonialism and compounded by the capitalist imperialist system. In addition, without attributing the inability to transform society squarely to the past, the power relations that shaped the historical experience of apartheid colonialism must be recognised, especially the centuries of structural and systemic underdevelopment. The policy constraints faced by South Africa are rooted in the limitations imposed by the global order.

To emphasise, the fundamental challenge facing post-apartheid South Africa is the manner in which state-market relations are structured—mainly in favour of the market and capital. The neo-liberal paradigm that has shaped post-apartheid policies has further entrenched unequal power relations and ensured that government is captured by capital, making it difficult to pursue radical reforms. To significantly move forward, the state-market relations should be titled in favour of the development project. Although some scholars suppose that class has overtaken race as a key issue in South Africa, the starting point should be an acknowledgement that race remains far more pronounced than class in South Africa.

The imperative of advancing human development to ensure socioeconomic inclusion would require that the state take a lead in not privileging capital over people. The policies and policy reforms that have been pursued since 1994 have been relatively ineffective because of the unbalanced relationship between the state and the market. Policies have tended to subordinate development and privilege the market. Therefore, the policy reforms that the book has argued for need to privilege development.

However, without complete decolonisation and de-imperialisation of the global order, South Africa—like the rest of the African continent and the global South broadly—can only achieve so much. I echo the views of Hein Marias (2010), Gillian Hart (2013), and Adam Habib (2013) that a political settlement is overdue—a settlement that will favour the people instead of capital. The proposed new political settlement should heed Amartya Sen's advice that policy makers should focus on "suffering humanity" in order to avoid "inflaming the minds."[7] The minds appear to be already inflaming and the suffering remains unabated, particularly for the African in South Africa.

I also pose a challenge to all of us, and particularly to Africans in South Africa, to decolonise our minds. To decolonise our minds, we must return to our "roots," so to speak. Africans are known to be respectful, kind, caring, forgiving, tolerant, and compassionate people who despise individualism, self-aggrandisement, senseless competition, and all that is affecting a fellow human being. Africans have, arguably, allowed themselves to learn many wrong things from Europeans. Africans should rid themselves of inappropriate thought patterns that have resulted in rampant corruption and many other social ills. What is needed is thought liberation, thought leadership, and higher levels of critical consciousness (as argued in Gumede 2015e).[8]

Lastly, as far as the national question is concerned, all South Africans should better understand the repulsive history of this beautiful but troubled country. Because we all have to coexist, we have to find means to live together and build a better future for our children. Is a "common political citizenship" that Mahmood Mamdani (2012) makes reference to—in the case of Nyerere's Tanzania—farfetched in South Africa? Is a new social pact, which many argue for, impossible? What should the beneficiaries of the colonial and apartheid regimes do differently? Would South Africa ever be a fully fledged nation?

NOTES

1. Edigheji (2005:6) argues that a democratic developmental state should hold principles of electoral democracy and ensure citizen participation in development and governance structures and processes.
2. FW de Klerk is reported to have said on CNN in 2012 that the apartheid regime was only "morally repugnant in a qualified way." Dave Steward, Executive Director of the FW de Klerk Foundation, also states in a January 16, 2015 article, that despite the apartheid regime, South Africa is much better than other African countries which did not experience apartheid.
3. Gumede, V. 2015. Millennium Development Goals: Towards a post-2015 Development Agenda for South Africa, in Nyoka, A and Hofmeyr, J (eds), *Breaking the Mould: Prospects for Radical Socio-Economic Transformation*, 2014 Transformation Audit, Institute for Justice and Reconciliation, Cape Town.
4. A "corporatist state" refers to a state that is influenced, if not captured, by business interests. It is a state that is not (sufficiently) concerned with socio-economic transformation. A corporatist state, different from the neo-liberal state, is fundamentally characterised by privileging capital over people—a neo-liberal state is generally understood as a state that pursues neo-liberal economic policies. Often, a corporatist state functions within neo-liberal principles, but it is not necessarily a neo-liberal regime. The notion of corporatist state is useful because it distinguishes the character of the post-apartheid state and disagrees with the notion of a neo-apartheid state as some have characterised South Africa's state.
5. As Seekings and Natrass (2005) explained, the main fundamental challenge we face is unemployment, especially youth unemployment.
6. Government passed the Employment Tax Incentive Act (2014)—to implement the youth wage subsidy—which should go a long way in addressing youth unemployment.
7. Sen, A. 2009. *The Idea of Justice.* Allen Lane: London.
8. Thought leadership is about a leadership orientation that is underpinned by developmental ideology that is historically nuanced, culturally sensitive, influentially and contextually grounded. It is a form of leadership that is based on progressive ideologies, beliefs, orientations with significant pragmatic and impact appeal. By implication, thought leaders are

individuals who can decipher phenomena needing attention and have the capability to think through possible solutions to advance the human condition. Thought liberation, however, connotes a psychosocially liberated mind—a psychology and wellbeing that is free of inappropriate thought patterns. And critical consciousness is about higher levels of socio-political and cultural awareness.

Bibliography

Adedeji, A. 1979. Statement to the Economic and Social Council of the United Nations. Second Regular Session, July 12, 1979, Geneva.

———. 2002. From the Lagos Plan of Action to the New Partnership for Africa's Development and from the Final Act of Lagos to the Constitutive Act: Wither Africa? Keynote address to the African Forum for Envisioning Africa, Nairobi, Kenya, 2629 April 2002.

Africa Commission. 2009. Global Financial Crisis calls for Action. Africa Commission Newsletter, Issue 5, February 2009.

Africa Development Bank. 2009. Africa and the Global Economic Crisis: Strategies for Preserving the Foundations of Long-term Growth. Paper Prepared for the 2009 Annual Meeting of the African Development Bank (May 13–14, 2009, Dakar, Senegal).

———. 2010. Assessing Progress in Africa toward the Millennium Development Goals: MDG Report 2010. Available from: http://www.afdb.org/fileadmin/uploads/afdb/Documents/Publications/MGDS20 2010 20Eng.pdf.

Africa Focus. 2009. Africa: Global Economic Crisis. March, 2009. Available from: http://www.africafocus.org/docs09/gec0904b.php.

African Monitor. 2009. Dialogue on Africa's Response to the Global Financial Crisis.Available from: http://www.africanmonitor.org/Site/index2.php?option= com_content&do_pdf=1&id=109.

African National Congress. 1978. Mandela and our Revolution. 30 September. Available from: http://www.anc.org.za/show.php?id=26 10 on November 29, 2014.

———. 1994. Re*construction and Development Programme: A Policy Framework.* Johannesburg: Umanyano Publications.

———. 1998. The State, Property Relations and Social Transformation. *Umrabulo* 5. 3rd Quarter. Available from: http://amadlandawonye.

wikispaces.com/1998, +ANC,+State,+Property+Relations,+Social +Transformation. Accessed on November 29, 2014.

———. 2007a. ANC 52nd National Conference Resolutions. Available from: http://www.anc.org.za.

———. 2007b. Strategy and Tactics: Building a National Democratic Society. Available from: http://www.anc.org.za/docs/pdf.

———. 2010. Economic Transformation Discussion Document for the 2010 National General Council. Available from: http://www.anc.org.za/docs/discus/ 2010/economicq.pdf.

———. 2012. Economic Transformation, Land Policy Proposals, Available from: http://www.anc.org.za/docs/discus/2012/landpolicyproposals_june2012g.pdf.

Ake, C. 2000. *Democracy and Development in Africa.* Maryland: Brookings Institution.

Alexander, N. 2013. *Thoughts on the New South Africa.* Auckland Park: Jacana Media.

Alexandra, P. 2010. 'Rebellion of the poor: South Africa's service delivery protests – A preliminary analysis'. *Review of African Political Economy,* 37 (123): 25–40.

Amin, S. 1972. 'Underdevelopment and Dependence in Black Africa: Historical Origin.' *Journal of Peace Research,* 9 (2): 105–120.

———. 1997. *Capitalism in the Age of Globalisation: The Management of Contemporary Society.* Cape Town: Zeb Books.

Amsden, A. 1989. *Asia's Next Giant: South Korea and Late Industrialization,* New York: Oxford University Press.

ANCYL, 2012. 'The Freedom Charter an irreplaceable beacon of hope The ANC Youth League's message on the centenary of the African National Congress in January 2012'. *Politicsweb.* Available from: http:www.politicsweb.co.za/party/the-freedom-charter-an-irreplaceable-beacon-of-hop. Accessed on April 20, 2015.

Anderson, B. 2006. *Imagined Communities: Reflections on the Origin and Spread of Nationalism,* London and New York: Verso.

Asante, M. 2007. *An Afrocentric Manifesto: Toward an African Renaissance.* Cambridge: Polity Press.

Bagchi, K.A. 2000. The Past and the Future of the Developmental State. *Journal of World Systems Research*, 11(2): 398–442.

Barret, C., Carter, M., and Little, P (eds). 2006. 'Understanding and Reducing Persistent Poverty in Africa: Introduction to a Special Issue.' *Journal of Development Studies*, 42(2):167–177.

Bhorat, H., and Van der Westhuizen, C. 2010. 'Poverty, Inequality and the Nature of Economic Growth in South Africa.' In Misra-Dexter, N., February, J. (eds), *Testing Democracy: Which Way is South Africa Going?* Cape Town: IDASA.

Biko, S.B. 1996. *Steve Biko: I write what I like. A selection of his writings.* Randburg: Ravan Press.

Blas, J. 2009. 'Poor still hit by high food prices.' *Financial Times* March 19, 2009.

Brown, J. 2015. *South Africa's Insurgent Citizens: On Dissent and the Possibility of Politics.* London: Zed Books.

Bloch, G. 2006. *Building Education beyond Crisis.* Johannesburg: Development Bank of Southern Africa.

———. 2009. *The Toxic Mix.* Cape Town: Tafelberg.

Bond, P. 2011. 'South African splinters: from 'elite transition' to 'small-a alliances.' *Review of African Political Economy*, 38 (127): 113–121.

Breier, M. and Mabizela, M. 2008. 'Higher Education.' In Kraak, A. and Press, K. (eds), *Human Resource Development Review 2008: Education, Employment and Skills in South Africa.* Cape Town: HSRC Press.

Buccus, I., Hemson, D., Hicks, J. and Piper, L. 2007. Public Participation and Local Governance. *Journal on Public Participation in Governance.* Available from: http://www.cpp.org.za/docs/reports/2007/lg-report0507.pdf.

Bunting, B. 1975. *Moses Kotane - South African Revolutionary.* London: Inkukuleko. Available from: www.marxists.org/subject/africa/bunting-brian/kotane/. Accessed on April 20, 2015.

Capehart, T., and Richardson, J. 2008. Food Price Inflation: Causes and Impacts. Congressional Research Service: Report for Congress, Library of Congress. Available from: http://opencrs.com/document/RS22859.

Castells, M. 1997. *The Rise of the Network Society, Volume I.* London: Blackwell.

Centre for Development and Enterprise. 1999. Policy-making in New Democracy: South Africa's Challenges for the 21st Century, Johannesburg: Centre for Development and Enterprise.

Centre for Development Report. 2008. Land Reform in South Africa: Getting Back on Track, CDE Report No 16, 2008. Available from: http://www.cde.org.za/images/pdf.

Centre d' Economie de la Sorbonne (CES), Available from : http://ces.univ-paris1.fr.

Chaloult, B.N. and Chaloult, Y. 1979. 'Internal Colonialism Concept: Methodological Considerations.' *Social and Economic Studies*, 28(4): 8599. Available from: http://www.jstor.org/stable/27861779. Accessed on April 16, 2015.

Chibber, V. 2002. 'Bureaucratic Rationality and the Developmental State.' *American Journal of Sociology*, 107(4): 951–989.

Chikulo, B. 2003. Development Policy in South Africa: A Review. *PMN Bulletin:* X (2).

CHE (Council on Higher Education). 2007. *Higher Education Monitor: A Case for Improving Teaching and Learning in South African Higher Education.* Pretoria: CHE.

Chipkin, I. 2007. *Do South Africans Exist? Nationalism, Democracy and the Identity of the People.* Johannesburg: Wits Press.

Cohen, J. and Peterson, S. 1999. *Administrative Decentralisation: Strategies for Developing Countries.* West Hartford, CT: Kumarian Press.

Constitutional Court of South Africa Judgement, CCT 100/09, 2010. Available from: http://www.saflii.org.za/za/cases/ZACC/2010.

COSATU. 2006. Political Resolutions of the 9th National Congress. Available from: www.cosatu.org.za/docs/resolutions/2006/resolutions.htm. Accessed on April 16, 2015.

Cronin, J. 2008. 'The future of the state: A two-tier Cabinet is on the cards.' *Mail & Guardian*, October 24–30.

Cross, E. 2009. The *Cost of Zimbabwe's Continuing Farm Invasions.* Cato Institute: Economic Development Bulletin, 12.

Cullinan, K. 2006. Health services in South Africa: A basic introduction. *Health-e News Service.*

Cummings, S., and Nørgaard O. 2004. 'Conceptualizing State Capacity: Comparing Kazakhstan and Kyrgzstan.' *Policy Studies*, 52(4): 685–708.

Daniel, J., Naidoo, P., Pillay, D., and Southall, R. 2010. *New South African Review 1: 2010: Development or Decline?* Johannesburg: Wits University Press.

———. 2011. *New South African Review 2: New Path, Old Compromises?* Johannesburg: Wits Press.

De Jager, N., and Meintjes, C. 2013. 'Winners, Losers and the Playing Field in Southern Africa's 'Democratic Darlings': Botswana and South Africa Compared.' *Politikon*, 40(2): 233–253.

Department of Economic Development. 2010. The New Growth Path Framework. Available from: http://www.economic.gov.za/communications/51-publications/151-the-new-growth-path-framework.

Department of Education. 1996. 'White Paper 2 on the Organisation, Governance and Funding of Schools.' *Government Gazette Notice 130. No. 16987, 14 February.* Pretoria: Government Printers.

———. 1997. 'White Paper 3 on A Programme for Higher Education Transformation.' *Government Gazette Notice 1196 No. 18207 24 July.* Pretoria: Government Printers.

———. 1998. 'White Paper 4 on A Programme for the Transformation of Further Education and Training.' *Government Gazette Notice 2188 No. 19281, 25 September.* Pretoria: Government Printers.

———. 2001a. 'Education White Paper 5 on Early Childhood Education: Meeting the Challenge of Early Childhood Development in South Africa.' Pretoria: Government Printers.

———. 2001b. 'White Paper 6 on Special Needs Education: Building an Inclusive Education and Training System.' Pretoria: Government Printers.

———. 2001c. *National Plan on Higher Education.* Pretoria: Government Printers.

———. 2003. 'Plan of Action: Improved Access to Quality Basic Education for All.' Pretoria: Government Printers.

Department of Basic Education. 2012. *Education Statistics in South Africa 2010.* Pretoria: Government Printers.

Department of Health. 2003. *Essential Health Care for All South Africans: An Investigation into the Adequacy of Public Health Financing and the Equity of Provincial Health Resource Distribution.* Pretoria: Government Printers.

———. 2007. *A Policy on Quality in Health Care for South Africa.* Pretoria: Government Printers.

———. 2012a. South Africa joins the world in commemorating World Malaria Day on 25 April 2012. Available from: http://www.doh.gov.za/docs/misc/2012/ malariaday2012.pdf.

———. 2012b. *South Africa's National Strategic Plan for a Campaign on Accelerated Reduction of Maternal and Child Mortality in Africa.* Pretoria: Government Printers.

———. 2013. *National Health Insurance: The First Eighteen Months.* Pretoria: Government Printers.

Department of Higher Education and Training. 2013. *White Paper for the Post-School System.* Pretoria: Government Printers.

Department of Labour. 2001. *An Introduction to the Skills Development Strategy.* Pretoria: Government Printers.

Department of Land Affairs. 1997. *White Paper on South Africa Land Policy.* Pretoria: Government Printers.

Department of Land Reform and Rural Development. 2012. *Land Reform Discussion Document.* Pretoria: Government Printers.

Department of Public Service and Administration. 1995. *White Paper on the Transformation of the Public Service.* Pretoria: Government Printers.

Deutsch, K. 1969. *Nation-Building and Social Communication: An Inquiry into the Foundation of Nationality.* Cambridge, Massachusetts and London: MIT Press.

Dikeni, L. 2012. *South African Development Perspectives in Question*, Johannesburg: Real African Publishers.

Du Plessis, W.J. 2011. 'African Indigenous Land Rights in a Private Ownership Paradigm.' *PER*, 14(7): 46.

Economic Commission for Africa. 2012. Economic Report on Africa. Addis Ababa.

Edigheji, O. 2005. *A Democratic Developmental State in Africa. A Concept Paper.* Johannesburg: Centre for Development Studies.

———. 2007. *The Emerging South African Democratic Developmental State and the People's Contract.* Johannesburg: Centre for Policy Studies.

Edigheji, O. 2010. *Constructing a Democratic Developmental State in South Africa: Potentials and Challenges.* Cape Town: HSRC Press.

El-Beltagy, K. 2009. Global Economic Crisis. Available from: http://pathways.cu. edu.eg/news/news/uf/30/30293_4MPED-03-04.pdf.

Esterhuyse, W. 2012. *Endgame: Secret Talk and End of Apartheid*, Cape Town: Tafelberg.

Evans, P. 1995. *Embedded Autonomy: States and Industrial Transformation.* Princeton: Princeton University Press.

———. 2007. *In Search of the 21st Century Developmental State.* Berkeley Campus: University of California.

Fanon, F. 1963. *The Wretched of the Earth.* Grove Press: New York.

Fine, B., and Rustomjee, Z. 1996. *The Political Economy of South Africa: From Minerals-Energy Complex to Industrialisation.* Boulder, CO: Westview Press.

Finn, A., Leibbrandt, M., and Woodland, I. 2009. 'Income and Expenditure Inequality: Analysis of the NIDS Wave 1.' Database Discussion

Paper No. 5. Available from: http://www.nids. uct.ac.za/documents/discussion-papers/96-nids-discussion-paper-no05/file. Accessed on February 22, 2013.

———. 2013. 'Mobility and Inequality in the First Three Waves of NIDS'. Cape Town: SALDRU, University of Cape Town. SALDRU Working Paper Number 120/ NIDS Discussion Paper 2013/2. Available from: http://www.nids.uct.ac.za/documents/discussion-papers/181-income-inequality-and-economic-mobility/file. Accessed on February 22, 2013.

Fiske, E.B., and Ladd, H.F. 2005. *Educational Aspirations and Political realities. Elusive Equity Education Reform in Post-apartheid South Africa.* Cape Town: HSRC Press.

Food and Agricultural Organisation. 2009. The Right to Food and the Financial and Economic Crisis. Submission to the United Nations Conference on World Financial and Economic Crisis, United Nations General Assembly, June 24–26, 2009, New York.

Food and Agriculture Organization. 2011. World Hunger and Poverty Facts and Statistics, State of World Food Insecurity Hunger Notes. Available from: http://www.worldhunger.org/articles/Learn/Number_of_hungry_people_in_the_world.

Freedom to Learn. 2013. A look at South African Education. Available from: http://www.freedomtolearn.co.za/standards

Frye, I., Farred, G., and Nojekwa, L. 2011.'Inequality in South Africa.' In Jauch, H. and Muchena, D. (eds), *Tearing Us Apart: Inequalities in Southern Africa.* Rosebank: OSISA.

Gelb, S. 2003. *Inequality in South Africa.* Johannesburg: The EDGE Institute.

———. 'Macroeconomic Policy Development: From Crisis to Crisis.' In Freund, B. and Witt, H. (eds), *Development Dilemmas in Post-Apartheid South Africa.* KwaZulu Natal: University of KwaZulu Natal Press.

Glaser. D. 2011. 'The New Black/African Racial Nationalism in SA: Towards a Liberal-Egalitarian Critique.' *Transformation,* 76: 67–94.

Godfrey, S. 2003. 'Workers Protection: An Update on the Situation in South Africa: A Country Study', with M Clarke and J Theron.

Report to the International Labour Organisation, Geneva. Available from: http://www.ilo.org/wcmsp5/groups/public/---ed_dialogue/---dialogue/documents/genericdocument/wcms_205380.pdf

Godfrey, S., and Theron, J. 1999. 'Labour Standards Versus Job Creation? An Investigation of the Likely Impact of the New Basic Conditions of Employment Acton Small Businesses.' In *Development and Labour Monographs 1/99*, Institute of Development and Labour Law, University of Cape Town.

Godfrey S., Maree, J., and Theron J. 2006. 'Regulating the Labour Market: The Role of Bargaining Councils.' *Industrial Law Journal.* 27 (4): 731–752.

Government of the United States of America 1997. A Country Study: South Africa. The Library of Congress: Federal Research Division. Washington. Available from: http://lcweb2.loc.gov/frd/cs/zatoc.html.

Green, D. 2009. *A Copper-Bottomed Crisis? The Impact of the Global Economic Meltdown on Zambia.* Oxfam: Oxford.

Greenspan, A. 2013. Financial Times. October 25, *Financial Times.*

Gumede, V. 2000. 'Import Demand Elasticities for South Africa: A Co-integration Approach.' *Journal for Studies in Economics and Econometrics*, 2(1): 21–38.

———. 'Export Elasticities for South African Manufacturing – A Time-Series Approach.' *Studies in Economics and Econometrics*, 27(1): 39–55.

———. 2004. 'Export Propensities and Intensities of Small Manufacturing Enterprises in South Africa. Small Business Economics.' *An International Journal*, 22(5): 379–389.

———. 2006. 'Small and Medium Manufacturing in South Africa: Constraints and Opportunities.' In Roberts, S. (ed), *Sustainable Manufacturing.* Cape Town: Juta Academic Press.

———. 2007. 'Is Government Optimally Poised to Achieve Set Objectives and Targets in Time?' *Service Delivery Review Journal*, 5(3): 48–51.

———. 2008a. 'Public Policy Making in a Post-Apartheid South Africa – A Preliminary Perspective.' *Africanus: Journal of Development Studies*, 38 (2): 7–23.

———. 2008b. 'Social Protection in Latin America and Africa. Institute for Africa's Development. Cornell University, Africa Notes, Summer 2008.

———. 2008c. 'Poverty and Second Economy Dynamics in South Africa: An Attempt to Measure the Extent of the Problem and Clarify Concepts.' Development Policy Research Unit Working Paper 08/133. University of Cape Town.

———. 2010. Developmental States Remain a Pipedream in Africa. *The Thinker: Journal of Progressive Thought,* 19: 36–37.

———. 2011a. 'Policy making in South Africa.' In Landsberg, C. and Venter, A. (eds), *South African Government and Politics* (4th ed). Pretoria: Van Schaik.

———. 2011b. 'The Role of Public Policies and Policy Makers in Africa: Responding to Global Economic Crises.' In Lee, D.R. and Ndulo, M. (eds), *The Food and Financial Crises in Sub-Saharan Africa: Origins, Impacts and Policy Implications.* CABI International.

———. 2011c. *Social and Economic Inclusion in Post-Apartheid South Africa. Transformation Audit.* Cape Town: Institute of Justice and Reconciliation.

———. 2013a. 'Socio-Economic Transformation in Post-Apartheid South Africa: Progress and Challenges.' In Ngcaweni, B. (ed), *The Future We Chose: Emerging Perspectives on the Centenary of the ANC.* Pretoria: AISA Press.

———. 2013b. 'Public Sector Reforms and Policy-making: A Case of Education in an Emerging Developmental South Africa.' In Kanjee, A., Nkomo, M. and Sayed, Y. (eds), *The Search for Quality Education in Post-apartheid South Africa.* Pretoria: HSRC Press.

———. 2013c. 'African Economic Renaissance as a Paradigm for Africa's Socio-Economic Development.' In Kondlo, K. (ed.), *Perspectives in Thought Leadership for Africa's Renewal.* Pretoria: AISA Press.

———. 2014a. 'Land Reform in Post-Apartheid South Africa: Should South Africa follow Zimbabwe's Footsteps?' *International Journal for African Renaissance Studies,* 9(1): 50–68.

———. 2014b. 'Poverty and Poverty Lines in South Africa.' In Bhorat, H., Kanbur, R., Hirsch, A. and Ncube, M. (eds), *Oxford Companion to the Economics of South Africa*, Oxford: Oxford University Press.

———. 2015a. 'Millennium Development Goals: Towards a post-2015 Development Agenda for South Africa.' In Nyoka, A. and Hofmeyr, J. (eds), *Breaking the Mould: Prospects for Radical Socio-Economic Transformation, 2014 Transformation Audit.* Cape Town: Institute for Justice and Reconciliation.

———. 2015b. 'Inequality in Democratic South Africa.' In Mangcu, X. (ed.), *The Colour of Our Future: Does Race Matter in Post-apartheid South Africa.* Johannesburg: Wits Press.

———. 2015c. 'Economic Policy in Post-apartheid South Africa.' In De Jager, N. (2015) (ed.), *South African Politics.* Cape Town: Oxford University Press.

———. 2015d. Editorial. *Africa Development,* Special issue 40(3), 1–12.

Gumede, V. 2015e. 'Exploring the Role of Thought Leadership, Thought Liberation and Critical Consciousness for Africa's Development.' *Africa Development,* 40(4).

———. 2015f. *Political Economy of Post-apartheid South Africa.* Dakar: CODESRIA.

Habib, A. 2013. *South Africa's Suspended Revolution: Hopes and Prospects.* Johannesburg: Wits Press.

Hall, R. 2003. 'A Comparative Analysis of Land Reform in South Africa and Zimbabwe.' In Lee, M.C., and Colvard, K. (eds), *Unfinished Business: The Land Crisis in Southern Africa.* Pretoria: AISA Press.

———. 2007. The Impact of Land Restitution and Land Reform on Livelihoods. Programme for Land and Agrarian Studies, University of the Western Cape.

Hamilton, L. 2014. *Are South Africans Free?* London: Bloomsbury.

Hassim, S. 2005. Gender, Welfare and the Developmental State in South Africa. Prepared for the United Nations Research Institute for Social Development (UNRISD) for the Project on Gender and Social Policy. Geneva.

———. 2010. *Social Justice, Care and Developmental Welfare in South Africa: A Capabilities Perspective in Development Dilemmas in Post-Apartheid South Africa.* Pietermaritzburg: UKZN Press.

Hart, G. 2013. *Rethinking the South African Crisis: Nationalism, Populism, Hegemony.* Pietermaritzburg: UKZN Press.

Hebinck, P and Cousins, B. 2013. *In the Shadow of Policy: Everyday Practices in South African Land and Agrarian Reform.* Johannesburg: Wits Press.

Hendricks, F., Ntsebeza, L. and Helliker, K. 2013. *The Promise of Land: Undoing a Century of Dispossession in South Africa.* Auckland Park: Jacana Media.

Herbst, J. and Mills, G. 2015. *How South Africa Works and Must Do Better.* Johannesburg: McMillan.

High Court of South Africa, Transvaal Provincial Division, Case No. 11678/06. Available from: http://www.lrc.org.za.

Hicks, J. 2004. On the Application of Theories on Internal Colonialism to Inuit Societies. Presentation for the Annual Conference of the Canadian Political Science Association. Winnipeg. Available from: www.cpsa-acsp.ca/papers-2004/hicks.pdf. Accessed on March 25, 2015.

Hirsch, A. 2005. *Season of Hope: Economic Reform under Mandela and Mbeki.* Scotsville: UKZN Press.

———. 2013. 'Aspirations to an Elusive Developmental State: The Obstacles to Deep Reform.' In Ngcaweni, B. (ed.), *The Future We Chose: Emerging Perspectives on the Centenary of the ANC.* Pretoria: AISA Press.

Huddle, N. 2007. Land in Zimbabwe, 6579. Available from: http://wiredspace.wits.ac.za.

Hudson, P. 1986. The Freedom Charter and The Theory of National Democratic Revolution. *Transformation,* 1, 638.

Hobsbawm, E. 1962. *The Age of Revolution: Europe: 1789–1848.* New York: Vintage Books.

Howlett, M. and Ramesh, M. 2003. *Studying Public Policy: Policy Cycles and Policy Subsystems.* Oxford: Oxford University Press.

Human Resources for Health South Africa. 2012. HRH Strategy for the Health Sector. University of Witwatersrand.

Human Sciences Research Council. 2004. 'Social Cohesion and Social Justice in South Africa. A Report Prepared for the Department of Arts and Culture.' Pretoria: HSRC Press.

Hussain, M.N., Mlambo, K. and Oshikoya, T. 2009. Global Financial Crisis: An African Perspective. African Development Bank, Tunisia, Tunis Available from: http://www.afdb. org/fileadmin/uploads/afdb/Documents/Publications/00157618-EN-ERP-42.PDF.

IJR. 2010. Transformation Audit. Cape Town: Institute of Justice and Reconciliation.

ILO. 1999. Decent Work: Report of the Director-General, International Labour Conference, 87th Session, Geneva.

———. 2003. Working Out of Poverty, Report of the Director-General, International Labour Conference, 91st Session, Geneva.

International Monetary Fund. 2009. Impact of the Global Financial Crisis on Sub-Saharan Africa. Available from: http://www.imf.org/external/pubs/ft/books/2009/afrglobfin/ ssaglobalfin.pdf.

———. 2010. Sub-Saharan Africa back to High Growth? Regional Economic Outlook: World Economic and Financial Surveys. IMF, Washington DC.

Jaffrelot, C. 2003. For Theory of Nationalism, Working Paper CERI/CNRS.

Jansen, J., and Taylor, N. 2003. 'Educational change in South Africa 1994–2003: Case studies in large-scale education reform.' Country Studies: Education and Management Publication Series, Washington DC: World Bank.

Johnson, C. 1982. *MITI and the Japanese Miracle: The Growth of Industry Policy 1925–1975.* Stanford: Stanford University Press.

———. 1999. 'The Development state: Odyssey of a Concept.' In Woo-Cummings, M. (ed.), *The Developmental State*. Ithaca: Cornell University Press.

Johnson, R.W. 2015. *How long will South Africa Survive the Looming Crisis*. Johannesburg and Cape Town: Jonathan Ball Publishers.

Kane, J. 2001. *The Politics of Moral Capital*. Melbourne: Cambridge University Press.

Karamoko, J. and Jain, H. 2011. Community Protests in South Africa: Trends, Analysis and Explanations. Harvard Law School. Available from: http://www.mlgi.org.za/publications/ publications-by-theme/local-government-insouth-africa/community-protests/Community_Protests_SA.pdf.

Khunou, G. 2013. What Middle Class? The Shifting and Dynamic Nature of Class Position. Available from: http://resep.sun.ac.za/wp-content/uploads/2013/10/Khunou-Main-Article-Black-middle-class-.pdf. Accessed on 27 November 2014.

Klein, N. 2007. *The Shock Doctrine: The Rise of Disaster Capitalism*. Toronto: Alfred Knopf.

Koelbe, T. 2008. 'Market and the economy.' In: Shepherd, N. and Robins, S. (eds.), *New South African Keywords*. Auckland Park: Jacana Media.

Kraak, A. 2008. 'The Education Economy Relationship in South Africa, 2001–2005.' In Kraak, A. and Press, K. (eds), *Human Resource Development Review 2008: Education, Employment and Skills in South Africa*. Cape Town: HSRC Press.

Lapping, B. 1987. *Apartheid: A History*. London: Grafton.

Laishey, R. 1979. 'South Korea: Land Reform – Successes and Failures.' *New Internationalist Magazine*.

Land audit complete: minister. *SAPA and IOL News*. Available from: http://www.iol.co.za/ news/politics/land-audit-complete-minister-1.1473275.

Leftwich, A. 1995. 'Bringing Politics Back In: Towards a Model of a Developmental State.' *Journal of Development Studies*, 31(3): 400–427.

Leibbrandt, M., Woolard, C., and Woolard, I. 2000. 'The Contributions of Income Components to South Africa's Income Inequality: A Decomposable Gini Analysis.' *Journal of African Economics*, 9(1): 79–99.

———. 2007. 'Poverty and Inequality Dynamics in South Africa: Post-apartheid Developments in Light of the Long-Run Legacy.' South African Labour & Development Research Unit, University of Cape Town.

Leibbrandt, M., Woolard, I., and McEwen, H. 2009. 'Employment and Inequality Outcomes in South Africa: What Role for Labour Market and Social Policies?' Southern Africa Labour and Development Research Unit, University of Cape Town. Available from: http://www.oecd.org/els/emp/45282868.pdf. Accessed on February 22, 2013.

Leibbrandt, M., Woolard, I., and de Velliers, L. 2009. Methodology. National Income Dynamics Technical Report, No. 1.SALRDU. Available from: http://www.nids.uct.ac.za/ publications/citations/wave-1. Accessed on February 22, 2013.

Leibbrandt, M., Woolard, I., Finn, A., and Argent, J. 2010. 'Trends in South African Income Distribution and Poverty Since The Fall Of Apartheid'. OECD Social, Employment and Migration Working Paper No. 101. Available from: http://search.oecd.org/officialdocuments/ displaydocumentpdf/?cote=DELSA/ELSA/WD/SEM(2010)1&doclanguage=en. Accessed on February 22, 2013.

Lissoni, A., Soske, J., Erlank, N., Nieftagodien, N and Bashda, O. 2012. *One Hundred Years of the ANC: Debating Liberation Histories Today.* Johannesburg: Wits Press.

Luiz, J. 2002. 'South African State Capacity and the Post-apartheid Economic Reconstruction'. *International Journal of Social Economics,* 29(8): 594–614.

Luthuli, A.J. 1963. *Let my people go.* London: Fontana.

Macias, J., and Massa, I. 2009. "The Global Financial Crisis and Sub-Saharan Africa: The effects of slowing private capital inflows on growth." ODI Working Paper Series, Overseas Development Institute, UK.

Mafeje, A. 2000. 'Africanity: A Combative Ontology.' *CODESRIA Bulletin,* No. 1 and 4: 66–71.

———. 2003. 'The Agrarian Question, Access to Land, and Peasant Responses in sub-Saharan Africa'. UNRISD Programme Papers on Civil Society and Social Movements, Geneva.

Magubane, B.M. 1979. *The Political Economy of Race and Class in South Africa.* New York: Monthly Review Press.

Malcolm, R. 2012. "Not yet *Ubuntu*: A Fanonian Perspective of the Politics of Nation-Building in Post-Liberation South Africa." Speech delivered at the University of Johannesburg, 2 July 2012.

Mamdani, M. 2000. 'A Diminished Truth.' In James, W and Van de Vijver, L. (eds), *After the TRC: Reflections on Truth and Reconciliation in South Africa.* Cape Town: David Phillip.

———. 2013. *Define and Rule: Native as Political Identity.* Johannesburg: Wits Press.

Mandela, N.R. 1994. A Preamble in White Paper on Reconstruction and Development. Available from: http://www.africa.upenn.edu/Govern_Political/RDP_Wh.html. Accessed on November 30, 2014.

Maphai, V. 1993. Prospects for a Democratic South Africa. *International Affairs (Royal Institute of International Affairs),* 69(2): 223–237.

Marais, H. 2010. *South Africa Pushed to the Limit: The Political Economy of Change,* Claremond: UCT Press.

Mathekga, R. 2013. 'State Evolution and Sovereignty; The Case of South Africa.' In Ndletyana, M. and Maimela, D. (eds), *Essays on the Evolution of the Post-Apartheid State: Legacies, Reforms and Prospects.* Johannesburg: Real African Publishers.

Matondi, P.B. 2012. *Zimbabwe's Fast Track Land Reform.* London: Zed Books.

Mayer, M. and Altman, M. 2006. *South Africa's Economic Trajectory: Implications for Skills Development.* Cape Town: HSRC Press.

Mbeki, T. 1978. "The Historic Injustice." Speech delivered at a seminar held in Ottawa, Canada, from February 1922, 1978.

Mbeki, M. 2009. *Architects of Poverty: Why African Capitalism Needs Changing.* Johannesburg: Picador.

Mbembe, A. 2001. *On the Postcolony*, Berkeley: University of California Press.

———. 2012. 'Fifty Years of African Decolonisation.' Chimurenga. 25 December 2010, Available at: http://www.chimurenga.co.za/page-147.html.

McGrath, S. 2004. 'The State of the South African Further Education and Training College Sector.' In McGrath, S., Badroodien, A., Kraak, A., and Unwin, L. (eds), *Shifting Understandings of Skills in South Africa.* Cape Town: HSRC Press.

McGrath, S. and Badroodien, A. 2006. International Influences on Evolution of Skills Development. *International Journal of Educational Development*, 29(5): 483–494.

Meintjies, F. 2013. "The TRC and CODESA failed South Africa: It's Time we Reflected on This." Available from: http://sacsis.org.za/site/article/1783. Accessed on March 21, 2015.

Menocal, R.A. 2004. And if there was no State? Critical reflections on Bates, Polanyi and Evans on the Role of the State in Promoting Development. *Third World Quarterly*, 25(4): 765–777.

Mhone, G. 2004. "Organizational and Institutional Implications of a developmental state." Human Social Research Council paper. HSRC: Pretoria.

Ministry of Higher Education and Training. 2010. Transformation, Social Cohesion and the Elimination of Discrimination in Public Higher Education Institutions. Pretoria: Government Printers.

Ministry of Monitoring and Evaluation. 2012. Development Indicators 2011. The Presidency. Pretoria: Government Printers.

Mkandawire, T. 2001a. 'Thinking about developmental states in Africa.' *Cambridge Journal of Economics*, 24: 289–313.

———. 2001b. "Social Policy in a Development Context. Social Policy and Development Programme." Paper number 7, United Nations Research Institute for Social Development, Geneva.

Mkandawire, T., and Soludo, C. 1999. *Our Continent Our Future: African Perspectives on Structural Adjustment.* Dakar: CODESRIA Press.

Mkokeli, S. 2011. 'Jobless youth a "ticking time bomb" for SA, Vavi warns'. *Business Day*, June 07, 2011.

Mohamed, S. 2010. 'The State of the South African Economy.' In Daniel, J. Naidoo, P., Pillay, D., and Southall, R. (eds), *New South African Review 1: 2010: Development or Decline?* Johannesburg: Wits Press.

Moleke, P. 2005. 'Inequalities in Higher Education and the Structure of the Labour Market.Human Science Research Council Paper Series.' Employment and Economic Research Program. Cape Town: HSRC Press.

———. 2006. *Finding Work: Employment Experiences for South African Graduates.* Cape Town: HSRC Press.

Moyo, S. 2013. 'Zimbabwe's Fast Track Land Reform; Implications for South Africa.' In Hendricks, F., Ntsebeza, L., and Helliker, K. (eds), *The Promise of Land: Undoing a Century of Dispossession in South Africa*, Auckland Park: Jacana Media.

Municipal IQ .2012. Municipal IQ's Updated Municipal Productivity and Hotspots Monitor Results, 28 November 2013. Accessed on 13 October 2014. Available at: http://africacheck.org/wp-content/uploads/2014/03/201312021614519448.pdf.

Munslow, B., and P. Fitzgerald. 1997. 'Search for a development strategy: The RDP and beyond.' In P. Fitzerald, A. McLennan, and B. Munslow, (eds), *Managing sustainable development in South Africa*, Cape Town: Oxford University Press.

National Planning Commission. 2012.The National Development Plan 2030. Ministry of Planning.The Presidency. Pretoria.

National Treasury. 2008. 'Review of the Government Cluster System.' National Treasury, Technical Assistance Unit. Pretoria: Government Printers.

Ndebele, N.S. 2012. "Liberation betrayed by bloodshed." City Press, 26 August.

Ndlentyana, M., Makhalimele, P.O., and Mathekga, R. 2013. *Patronage Politics Divides Us: A Study of Poverty, Patronage and Inequality in South Africa.* Johannesburg: Real African Publishers.

Ndletyana, M., and Maimela, D. 2013. *Essays on the Evolution of the Post-Apartheid State: Legacies, Reforms and Prospects*, Real African Publishers, Johannesburg.

Ndlovu-Gatsheni, S. 2012. Coloniality of Power in Development Studies and the Impact of Global Imperial Designs on Africa. Inaugural Professorial Lecture delivered at the University of South Africa, 16 October 2012.

———. 2013. *Coloniality of Power in Postcolonial Africa: Myths of Decolonization*. Dakar: CODESRIA Press.

NEDLAC. 2009. "Framework for South Africa's Response to the Economic Crisis." National Economic Development and Labour Advisory Committee (NEDLAC), NEDLAC, Johannesburg.

Netshitenzhe, J. 2008. 'The Shift is not Ideological.' In *Mail & Guardian*, October 31–November 6, 23.

———. 2012. 'A Continuing Search for Identity: Carrying the Burdon of History.' In Lissoni, A., Soske, J., Erlank, N., Nieftagodien, N., and Bashda, O. (eds), *One Hundred Years of the ANC: Debating Liberation Histories Today*. Johannesburg: Wits Press.

———. 2013. 'A Pan-African Renaissance in the Next 50 years.' *The Thinker: Journal of Progressive Thought*, 51; 21–23.

———. 2014. 'Role of Capable Developmental State in Addressing the Injustice of Inequality.' Paper presented at the Oxfarm Inequality Symposium, October 29–30, 2014.

Nooyo, D. 2015. *Public Policy-Making in the Mbeki Era*. Centurion: Kwarts Publishers.

OECD (Organization for Economic Co-operation and Development). 2008. *Reviews of National Policies for Education: South Africa*. Available from: http://www.oecd.org/ southafrica/ reviewsofnationalpoliciesforeducation-southafrica.htm Accessed on August 16, 2013.

———. 2010. Development Aid Rose in 2009 and Most Donors will meet 2010 Aid Targets. Available from: http://www.oecd.org/document/11/0,3343,en_2649_34487_44981579_1_1_1_1,00.html.

Oliver, M., and Shapiro, T. 1997. *Black Wealth-White Wealth: A New Perspective on Racial Inequality.* New York and London: Routledge.

Onis, Z. 1991. 'The Logic of the Developmental State.' *Journal of Comparative Studies*, 24(1):109–126.

Othman, P.F. 2001. 'Malaysia.' In Chaudhry, M.G. (ed.) *Agrarian Reforms and Agricultural Productivity.* Asian Productivity Organisation. Available from: http://www.apotokyo.org/ publications/files/agr-10-ar_ap.pdf.

Parliament of the Republic of South Africa. 2013. Overview of Child Mortality in South Africa, Research Unit, March 4, 2013.

———. Our Constitution. Available from: http://www.parliament.gov.za/live/content.php?Category_ID=11. Accessed on November 30, 2014.

Pheko, M. 1994. *The Land is Ours: The Political Legacy of Mangaliso Sobukwe,* New York: Pheko & Associates.

———. "Freedom Charter sold out the dispossessed." *Sowetan Online.* Available from: http://www.sowetanlive.co.za/columnists/2012/02/02/freedom-charter-sold-out-the-dispossessed. Accessed on April 20, 2015.

Pillay, D. 2011. 'The Tripartite Alliance and its Discontents: Contesting the National Democratic Revolution in the Zuma Era.' In Daniel, J. Naidoo, P., Pillay, D., and Southall, R. (eds), *New South African Review 2: New Path, Old Compromises?* Johannesburg: Wits University Press.

Pillay, U. 2011. "Delivery protests National Problem Requires Local, Tailor-made Solutions." *Business Day,* April 1, 2011.

Policy Coordination and Advisory Services in the Presidency. 2008. Towards a Fifteen Year Review, Synthesis Report on Implementation of Government Programmes. Pretoria: Government Communications and Information Systems. Available from: http://www.thepresidency.gov.za/main.asp?include=docs/15year/main.html.

Ramphele, M. 2008. *Laying Ghosts to Rest: Dilemmas of the Transformation in South Africa.* Cape Town: NB Publishers.

Rawls, J. 1999. *A Theory of Justice.* Cambridge, MA: Harvard University Press.

Republic of South Africa. 1996. Constitution, Act 108 of 1996. Pretoria: Government Printers.

———. 2012. National Strategic Plan on HIV, STIs and TB 2012–2016.

Renan, E. 1882. 'What is a Nation?' Conference Faite en Sorbone, March 11, 1882, Oeuvres, Completes.

Reuters. 2009. 'Remittances to Kenya Rise in July from 2008.' Available from: http://www.africagoodnews.com/pan-africa/diaspora/882-remittances-to-kenya-rise-in-july-from-2008.html.

Rodney, W. 1973. *How Europe Underdeveloped Africa.* Dar-Es-Salaam: Bogle-L'Ouverture Publications, London and Tanzanian Publishing House.

Robinson, M. and White, G. (eds). 1998. *The Democratic Developmental State: Political and Institutional Design.* Oxford: Oxford University Press.

Robinson, W. 2004. *A Theory of Global Capitalism: Production, Class, and State in a Transnational World.* Baltimore, MD: John Hopkins University Press.

Sachs, J.D. 2005. 'Investing in Development: A Practical Plan to Achieve the Millennium Development Goals.' UN Millennium Project, 2005, New York.

SACP (South African Communist Party). 1962. 'The Road to South African Freedom.' African Communist, Programme of the South African Communist Party adopted at the Fifth National Conference of the party held inside the Country in 1962. Available from: https://www.marxists.org/history/international/comintern/sections/sacp/1962/road-freedom.htm.

Sayed, Y., Kanjee, A. and Nkomo, M. 2013. *The Search for Quality Education in Post-Apartheid South Africa.* Cape Town: HSRC Press.

Saul, J. 2012. 'Globalisation, Recolonisation and the Paradox of Liberation in Southern Africa.' In Lissoni, A., Soske, J., Erlank, N., Nieftagodien, N. and Bashda, O. (eds), *One Hundred Years of the ANC: Debating Liberation Histories Today.* Johannesburg: Wits Press.

Saul, J., and Bond, P. 2014. *South Africa: The Present as History From Mrs Ples to Mandela and Marikana.* Auckland Park: Jacana Media.

Shivji, I. 2009. *Accumulation in an African Periphery: A Theoretical Framework.* Dar es Salaam: Mkuki na Nyota Publishers.

Schacter, M. 2000. "Public Sector Reform in Developing Countries: Issues, Lessons and Future Directions." Published by the Policy Branch of the Canadian International Development. Ottawa, Canada.

Schick, A. 1998. 'Why most developing countries should not try New Zealand reforms.' *The World Bank Research Observer*, 13(1): 123–131.

Seekings, J. and Nattrass, N. 2005. *Class, Race and Inequality in South Africa.* Connecticut: Yale University Press.

Sen, A. 1999. *Development as Freedom.* New York: Anchor.

———. 2009. *The Idea of Justice.* London: Allen Lane.

Shisana, O. 2011. *National Health Insurance: Green Paper.* Pretoria: HSRC Press.

Sison, A.J.G. 2003. *The Moral Capital of Leaders: Why Virtue Matters. New Horizons in Leadership Studies Series.*UK: Edward Elgar.

Southall, R. 2010. 'South Africa 2010: From Short Term Success to Long Term Decline?' In Daniel, J., Naidoo, P., Pillay, D. and Southall, R. (eds), *New South African Review 1: 2010: Development or Decline?* Johannesburg: Wits University Press.

——— (ed). 2011. *New South African Review 2: New Path, Old Compromises?* Johannesburg: Wits Press.

South African History Online. nd. Dutch East India Company (DEIC)/VOC. Available from: http://www.sahistory.org.za/topic/dutch-east-india-company-deicvoc. Accessed on November 29, 2014.

———. nd. F.W. de Klerk Announces the Release of Nelson Mandela and Unbans Political Organisations. Available from: http://www.sahistory.org.za/dated-event/fw-de-klerk-announces-release-nelson-mandela-and-unbans-political-organisations. Accessed on November 30, 2014.

———. nd. 'The Pan Africanist Congress (PAC).' Available from http://www.sahistory.org.za/topic/pan-africanist-congress-pac. Accessed on April 20, 2015.

———. 2013. Bantu Education Policy. Available from: http://www.sahistory.org.za/topic/bantu-education-policy.

———. 2013. 'Land Dispossession and Segregation in South Africa.' Available from: http://www.sahistory.org.za/topic/timeline-land-dispossession-and-segregation-south-africa-1652-1799.

South African Institute of Race Relations. 2011. Research and Policy Brief: Model C is the Model to Emulate. Available from: http://www.sairr.org.za/sairr-today-1/research-and-policy-brief-model-c-is-the-model-to-emulate-1-february-2011.

———. 2013. 'Racial Transformation'. Johannesburg: SAIRR.

South Africa Overcoming Apartheid Building Democracy. Bantu Education. nd. Available from: http://overcomingapartheid.msu.edu/sidebar.php?id=65-258-2&page=2.

Steward, D. 2015. 'A Country that Belonged to All those who live in It.' Available from: http://www.fwdeklerk.org/index/.php/en/document-liberary/articles. Accessed on February 1, 2015.

Steyn, A. 2009. 'Measuring Student Participation in the Higher Education Sector in South Africa.' Technical Report, University of Stellenbosch.

Stiglitz, J. 2002. *Globalization and its Discontent.* New York: Norton.

———. 2010. *Freefall, America, Free Markets and the Sinking of World Economy.* New York: Norton.

———. 2012. *The Price of Inequality: How Today's Divided Society Endangers Our Future.* New York: Norton.

Stigliz, J., Sen, A. and Fitoussi, J.P. 2010. 'Report by the Commission on the Measurement of Economic Performance and Social Progress." Available from: http://www.stiglitz-sen-fitoussi.fr/documents/rapport_anglais.pdf

Socio-economic Rights Institute. 2013. 'Access to Basic Services.' Available from: http://www.seri-sa.org/index.php/2013-03-07-09-16-20/basic-services.

Swilling, M., Breda J., Van Zyl A., and Khan, F. 2006. 'Economic Policy-making in a Developmental State: Review of the South African Government's Poverty and Development Approaches, 1994–2004.' Economic Policy and Poverty Alleviation Report Series, Research Report 3.

Stalin, J. 1953. 'Marxism and the National Question.' *Works*, Moscow, 2: 300–381.

Statistics South Africa. 2009. 'Quarterly Labour Force Survey.' Pretoria: Government Printers.

———. 2012. *Census 2011.* Pretoria: Government Printers.

———. 2013. Mid-year Population Estimates, May 2013. Pretoria: Government Printers.

——— (various issues). "General Household Surveys." Pretoria: Government Printers.

Tambo, A. 2014. *Oliver Tambo Speaks.* Cape Town: Kwela Books.

Terreblanche, S. 2002. *A History of Inequality in South Africa 1652–2002*, Scottsville and Sandton: UKZN Press and KMM Review and Publishing .

———. 2012. *Lost in Transformation: South Africa's Search for a New Future Since 1986*, Sandton: KMM Review and Publishing.

The Presidency. 2006. Accelerated and Shared Growth Initiative for South Africa. Pretoria: Government Press.

———. 2013. South Africa's Economic Transformation: A Strategy for Broad-Based Black Economic Empowerment. Pretoria. Available from: http://www.info.gov.za/view/ DownloadFileAction?id=70187.

The South African Civil Society Information Service. 2013. 'Prof. Sampie Terreblanche: White South Africans Will Have to Make Some Sacrifices.' Available from: http://sacsis.org.za/site/article/174 9. Accessed on November 23, 2014.

Think Africa Press. 2013. 'South Africa Land Reform Debate and Natives Land Act.' South Africa: Land Reform Debates Heat Up Again, 100 Years after the Natives Land Act, Available from: http://

thinkafricapress.com/south-africa/south-africa-land-reform-debate-natives-land-act.

Thomas, N.H. 2003. Land Reform in Zimbabwe. *Third World Quarterly*, 24 (2): 671712.

Thompson, L. 2000. *A History of South Africa.* Cape Town: Jonathan Ball Publishers.

Tilly, C. 1975. 'Western State Making and Theories of Political Transformation.' In Tilly, C. (ed), *The Formation of National States in Europe.* Princeton: Princeton University Press.

———. 1990. *Coercion, Capital and European States, AD 900-1990.* Oxford: Basil Blackwell.

Tomori, S. 1995. 'Evolving a New Development Paradigm for Africa.' In Onimode, B. and Synge, R. (eds), *Issues in African Development: Essays in Honour of Edebayo Adedeji at 65.* Nigeria: Heinemann.

Turok, B. 2008 . *Wealth Doesn't Trickle Down: The Case for a Developmental State in South Africa.* Cape Town: New Agenda.

UN (United Nations). 2010. 'Africa Economic Outlook.' Available from: http://www.un.org/esa/dsd/resources/res_pdfs/publications/sdt_afri/AEO2010_part1_p76.pdf

UNDP (United Nations Development Programme). 2007. *Human Development Report.* New York: Palgrave Macmillan.

———. 2011. *Human Development Report.* New York: Palgrave Macmillan.

———. 2012. *Millennium Development Goals.* New York: Palgrave Macmillan.

———. 2013. *Human Development Report.*. New York: Palgrave Macmillan.

UN Economic Commission for Africa. 2008. 'Overview of Economic and Social Conditions in Africa.' Meeting of the Committee of Experts of the 2nd Joint Annual Meetings of the African Union Conference of Ministers of Economy and Finance, Addis Ababa, Ethiopia.

———. 2009. 'Economic Report on Africa.' Available from: http://www.uneca.org/eca_resources/Publications/books/era2009.

UN Millennium Project. 2004a. 'An Enhanced Strategy for Reducing Extreme Poverty by the Year 2015.' Interim Report. Task Force on Poverty and Economic Development. New York.

———. 2004b. 'Millennium Development Goals Needs Assessment: Background Chapter to "Ending Africa's Poverty Trap."' Working Chapter. New York. Available from: www.unmillenniumproject.org/html/background chapter.shtm.

———. 2005a. 'Combating AIDS in the Developing World.' New York.

———. 2005b. Coming to Grips with Malaria in the New Millennium, Report of the Task Force on HIV/AIDS, Malaria, TB, and Access to Medicines, Working Group on Malaria. New York.

———. 2005c. 'Environment and Human Well-Being: A Practical Strategy.' Report of the Task Force on Environmental Sustainability. New York.

———. 2005d. 'Halving Hunger: It Can Be Done.' Report of the Task Force on Hunger. New York.

———. 2005e. 'Health, Dignity, and Development: What Will It Take?' Report of the Task Force on Water and Sanitation. New York.

———. 2005f. 'A Home in the City Report of the Task Force on Slum Dwellers. New York.' UN Millennium Project. 2005g. Innovation: Applying Knowledge in Development. Report of the Task Force on Science, Technology, and Innovation. New York.

———. 2005h. 'Investing in Strategies to Reverse the Global Incidence of TB.' Report of the Task Force on HIV/AIDS, Malaria, TB, and Access to Medicines, Working Group on TB. New York.

Valji, N. 2004. 'Race and Reconciliation in post-TRC South Africa.' A Paper Presented at a Conference Entitled Ten Years of Democracy in Southern Africa. Organized by the Southern African Research Centre. Canada: Queens University. Available from: http://www.csvr.org.za/wits/paper/papnv3.htm on 01/11/2010

Visser, N. 1997. 'Post-Coloniality of a Special Type: Theory and its Appropriation in South Africa.' *The Yearbook of English Studies*, 27:79–94.

Wale, K. 2014. 'Reflecting on Reconciliation: Lessons from the Past, Prospects for the Future.' Cape Town: Institute for Justice and Reconciliation.

Wai Yip So, B. 2007. 'Does China Follow the Path of Taiwan's Developmental State Model? The Rise of Hsinchu Science Park and Zhongguancun Science Park', Department of Public Policy and Management. Taiwan: I-Shou University.

Weideman, M. 2004. 'Why Land Reform', Unpublished Doctoral Dissertation. University of the Witwatersrand. Available from: http://wiredspace.wits.ac.za.

Wilkinson, R. and Pickett, K. 2010. *The Spirit Level: Why Greater Equality Makes Societies Stronger.* New York: Bloomsbury Press.

World Bank. 1997. *World Development Report.* Washington: World Bank.

———. 2005a. 'Concept Note: Rethinking Social Policy.' World Bank Conference in Arusha, Tanzania, December 1215, 2005. Avialable from: http://worldbank.org/website/ external/topics.

———. 2005b. *World Development Indicators.* Washington: World Bank.

———. 2006. Global Economic Prospects. Available from: http://www-wds.worldbank.org/external/default/WDSContentServer/IW3P/IB/2005/11/14/000112742_20051114174928/Rendered/PDF/343200GEP02006.pdf.

———. 2009. 'Swimming against the Tide: How Developing Countries Are Coping with the Crisis.' Background Paper Prepared for the G20 Finance Ministers and Central Bank Governors Meeting, Horsham, UK, March 1314.

———. 2010. *Global Monitoring Report: Achieving the MDGs in the Aftermath of the Global Economic Crisis.* Washington: World Bank.

———. 2011. *Global Economics Prospects Report 2011: Navigating String Currents.* Washington: World Bank. Available from: http://siteresources.worldbank.org/INTGEP/Resources/335315-1294842452675/GEPJanuary2011FullReport.pdf.

World Food Programme and the World Bank Group. 2009. 'Rethinking School Feeding: Social Safety Nets, Child Development and the

Education Sector.' Available from: http://www.un.org/en/ga/second/64/socialprotection.pdf.

About the Author

Vusi Gumede is a Professor at the University of South Africa and Director of the Thabo Mbeki African Leadership Institute. Previously, he was an associate professor at the University of Johannesburg. Among other lecturing jobs, he lectured public policy during 2009–2014 at the erstwhile Graduate School of Public and Development Management of the University of Witwatersrand in South Africa. He worked for the South African government in various capacities for about 12 years—he was chief policy analyst, among other things, in The Presidency. Before that, he was a researcher at the National Institute for Economic Policy—he also taught economics at the University of Durban-Westville where he obtained his Masters of Commerce in Economics. He is affiliated with numerous institutions as board or committee member or a fellow. He has also been, among other things, a Distinguished Africanist Scholar with the Institute for African Development at Cornell University and a Yale World Fellow with Yale University, among other fellowships and/or visiting scholarships. He holds postgraduate qualifications in economics and policy studies, including a PhD in economics, obtained in 2003 at the University of KwaZulu-Natal. He is the author of *Political Economy of Post-Apartheid South Africa* (CODESRIA Press), co-editor of *Unite or Perish: Africa Fifty Years After the Founding of the OAU* and of *Regenerating Africa to Bring African Solutions to African Problems* (AISA Press), and he has been guest editor of special issues of *Africa Development* (Vol. 40, No.3, 2015) and *Africa Insight* (Vol. 46, No.1, 2016) and he has authored numerous journal articles, book chapters and essays. He has also written and co-written numerous research reports, edited and co-edited collections of essays and is a member of various editorial boards of journals.

Praise for the Book

"The book is a retrospective analysis of the first two decades of public policy making in post-apartheid South Africa. Its main argument is that the post-independent South African state, through its policies, is failing to uplift the lives of the poor to an acceptable level of humanity. This argument is backed by thorough research that draws on a detailed historical narrative on the political economy of South Africa. The author draws parallels between the post-apartheid and apartheid dispensations' developmental route and he concludes that that they both colluded with global capital to the detriment of the poor. The book is thematically organized in a manner that permits a comprehensive examination of inclusive development in South Africa since 1994. Its innovation is not privileging an Africanist perspective and dealing with the racial inequalities that continue to haunt South Africa while also acknowledging the widely published class analysis of the post-apartheid state.

The author's previous experience as a government bureaucrat offers a rare and unique insider perspective which makes the book stand out. The book raises pertinent issues such as the delicate relationship within the Tripartite Alliance that, in the author's view, impede some of the policy moves that the ANC could have pursued; the violent nature of the post-apartheid state that collude with corporate South Africa to unleash violence on the poor (Marikana massacre is cited as one case in point), the inability to forge a nation despite the progressive Constitution, the ruling class's failure to prioritise the poor in policies, and what the author calls inappropriate theorisation with regard to the conditions and challenges facing South Africa. These are just some of the arguments the author advances in the book and are neatly supported by evidence. This is a highly recommended text for anyone who is concerned about Africa and not just South Africa alone."

—Thandika Mkandawire,
former Director of the United Nations
Research Institute for Social Development
and Chair in African Development at the
London School of Economics (LSE)

* * * * *

"The book is an important contribution to the debates about the future of South Africa, distilling from the first two decades of democracy, particularly from the perspective of developmental state. To what extent have successive post-apartheid administrations in South Africa lived up to the ideal of wanting to be a developmental state in terms of policy conceptualisation and formulation and, importantly, with regard to implementation capacity? The book sets out to answer this question and other relevant questions.

Given the author's broad canvass of theoretical propositions, the author should be congratulated: firstly, for taking up the issue of inclusive development for both theoretical and empirical treatment in the South African situation; and, secondly, boldly proffering strong views on the country's performance in this regard. The result is an important addition to the body of literature on developmental experiences. Critically, the book contains a systematic analysis of South Africa's post-apartheid development trajectory; and seeks to situate this within the context of the post-colonial African experience. Contained in this book are ideas on what further can be done towards sustaining and intensifying the transformation project. This, the author argues, will entail building on the progress that has been made since South Africa attained democracy. But it also demands an honest acknowledgement of weaknesses as well as the impact of factors that were and still are beyond the control of South Africans. Among the latter are issues such as the global environment within which South Africa set out on its transformation journey, the dependence on and influence of global capital, and the trajectory of the global economy during South Africa's 21 years of democracy.

I recommend the book not only to academics, researchers and students, but also to policy-makers in both the public and private sectors. I am also certain that members of the public who want to gain new insights on the trajectories of democratic developmental states and how, as citizens and observers alike, they can exercise agency in influencing South Africa's development trajectory, would gain from this treatise. South Africa's journey to right a historical injustice has just begun. As the country enters the third decade of democracy, it cannot but answer the critical questions about the depth, the speed and the reach of its policies of change. In such a national undertaking, there can be no spectator."

—Joel Netshitenzhe,
Executive Director of the Mapungubwe Institute
for Strategic Reflection (MISTRA)

Index

www.ingramcontent.com/pod-product-compliance
Lightning Source LLC
LaVergne TN
LVHW091527200926
848483LV00002B/321

9781604979299